tear here

Home Safety Checklist

All Rooms:

- ❏ Electrical outlets are covered. Electrical cords are out of reach.
- ❏ Window-covering cords do not have loops and are out of children's reach.
- ❏ Second-floor windows have window guards unless they're used as fire escapes.
- ❏ Stairs have safety gates to prevent falls.
- ❏ Rooms are free of small toys or other objects that young children might swallow.
- ❏ Smoke alarms and carbon monoxide detectors are installed on every level of the home, especially near the bedroom areas.

Nursery:

- ❏ Crib meets current safety standards and has no loose, sharp, or missing hardware.
- ❏ Crib is not near window or window-covering cords.
- ❏ Baby sleeps on her back on a firm mattress without stuffed toys, pillows, quilts, or other soft bedding.
- ❏ Bumper pads are fastened to the crib with snaps or short straps tied to the outside of the crib so the baby can't reach them.
- ❏ Diaper pins, ointment, and other changing essentials are out of children's reach.

Bathroom:

- ❏ Medicine cabinet has child-resistant latch.
- ❏ Toilet has toilet lid latch.
- ❏ Water temperature is no higher than 120°F.
- ❏ Electrical appliances such as curling irons, radios, and hair dryers are stored out of children's reach and not left plugged in.
- ❏ Tub has rubber mat and floor has skid-proof rug to prevent falls.

Bedroom:

- ❏ Furniture is not positioned against windows where a child could climb up and fall out.
- ❏ Perfumes, makeup, hair spray, nail polish remover, and medications are stored out of children's reach.
- ❏ Heavy furniture, especially pieces with drawers or shelves that toddlers might climb, are anchored to the wall.
- ❏ Emergency phone numbers, including for the poison control center, are posted near all phones.

alpha
books

Home Safety Checklist

Living Room/Family Room:

- ❑ Television sits on a stable piece of furniture, not a cart or stand that can be pulled over.
- ❑ The opening to the VCR is blocked so a toddler can't stick his fingers in and get pinched.
- ❑ Tall bookshelves have wall anchors so they can't be pulled down.
- ❑ If you have a fireplace, matches and fireplace tools are not within children's reach.
- ❑ Recliner chairs are left in the closed, upright position, and children are not allowed to play on them.

Kitchen:

- ❑ There are child-resistant latches on the cabinets where you store breakables, sharp utensils, plastic bags, and cleaning supplies.
- ❑ Stove knobs have plastic safety covers. Pots and pans are heated on back burners, and handles are turned to the back of the stove.
- ❑ Highchair has safety straps that are used consistently, and baby is never left alone in it.
- ❑ There are no tablecloths or place mats that a child could pull to cause hot food or drinks to fall on him.

Garage:

- ❑ Chemicals, paints, and other poisonous substances are locked up and kept in the original containers.
- ❑ Tools are kept out of children's reach.
- ❑ The garage door's automatic opener has an auto-reverse feature to prevent it from closing on a child.
- ❑ There are no old freezers, refrigerators, picnic coolers, or other stored items that a child could climb into and be suffocated.

Yard:

- ❑ Playground equipment has soft surfaces underneath, such as rubber mats, mulch, or sand, to cushion falls.
- ❑ Wading pools are used only with supervision and are stored when not in use.
- ❑ Decks, balconies, and porches do not have railings big enough for a small child's head to fit through.
- ❑ Safety gates are used if there are several steps leading from a porch or deck.
- ❑ The yard is kept free of broken glass, nails, or other objects children might fall or step on.

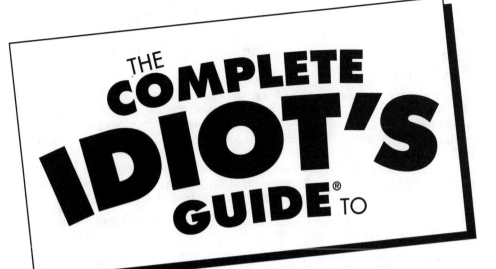

THE COMPLETE IDIOT'S GUIDE® TO

Child Safety

*by Miriam Bachar Settle, Ph.D.,
and Susan Crites Price*

**alpha
books**

Macmillan USA, Inc.
201 West 103rd Street
Indianapolis, IN 46290

A Pearson Education Company

We lovingly dedicate this book to Sarah Beth, to Julie, and to children everywhere.

Alpha Development Team

Publisher
Marie Butler-Knight

Associate Managing Editor
Cari Shaw Fischer

Acquisitions Editors
Randy Ladenheim-Gil
Amy Gordon

Development Editors
Phil Kitchel
Amy Zavatto

Assistant Editor
Georgette Blau

Production Team

Development Editor
Carol Hupping

Production Editors
Christy Wagner
Donna Wright

Copy Editor
Johnna VanHoose Dinse

Cover Designer
Mike Freeland

Photo Editor
Richard H. Fox

Illustrator
Jody P. Schaeffer

Book Designers
Scott Cook and Amy Adams of DesignLab

Indexer
Riofrancos and Company Indexes

Layout/Proofreading
John Etchison
Gloria Schurick

Contents at a Glance

Contents

Part 2: The Most Common Injuries   61

6 Too Hot to Handle: Fire and Burns   63

7 You Put *What* in Your Mouth?: Poison Prevention   75

16 Wheels and Blades: Recreation Safety   175

17 Flex Those Muscles!   185

Part 6: Coping with the Unexpected   281

26 Nannies Need to Know   283

Foreword

Since its founding in 1987, the National SAFE KIDS Campaign has had one over-arching goal: to ensure that all children in America are "safe kids."

As a nation, we are making great strides in keeping children from harm. The unintentional childhood injury death rate has declined more than 30 percent since the Campaign's inception. That's the good news. The bad news is that unintentional injury remains the leading cause of death among children 14 and under.

There's a lot more we can do to prevent injuries. Our government can pass new safety laws and consistently enforce laws already on the books. Companies can develop better safety devices. Most important, we can make sure parents, grandparents, caregivers, and others who raise our children have the knowledge they need to keep them from becoming injured.

Throughout my career in public health, I've seen the tragedies that can result when parents aren't aware of risks their children face. Too often I've heard, "If only we'd known ..."

Information is power. It can save children's lives. We have long needed a book that covered childhood injury prevention in depth, and not just for infants and toddlers but for school-age children as well. These well-qualified authors have written an indispensable tool for families.

Everyone who cares for a child should read this book.

Heather Paul, Ph.D.
Executive Director of the National SAFE KIDS Campaign

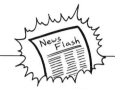

Tales from the Safety Zone

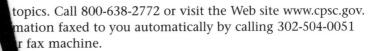

topics. Call 800-638-2772 or visit the Web site www.cpsc.gov.
mation faxed to you automatically by calling 302-504-0051
r fax machine.

mation on the Internet, too. The CPSC, for example, has a
w.cpsc.gov/kids/kids/html. Designed for children ages 8 to
l, interactive, and fun activities about safety issues kids

eep kids safe. Beyond ensuring the safest possible
y can set rules that reinforce what you're teaching at
ol may require kids who ride bikes to school always to

fety education programs. Some teach a specific sub-
afety, but others take a more comprehensive ap-
g many childhood hazards.

h safety, it may be because administrators think they
d safety curriculum can reinforce work in academ-
. (Maybe you can put a bug in their ear!)

f every school curriculum. We like Risk Watch™,
tion Association (NFPA) in collaboration with
rriculum for kids in preschool through eighth
ury to children: fire, burns, motor vehicles, poi-
g, bicycles, falls, firearms, water sports, and
minimum of nine hours per school year. If you
to your school officials, you can get more informa-
at 617-984-7285.

Call the Consumer Product Safety Commission's hotline at 800–638–2772 to find out if a product has been recalled, learn how to return one or arrange repair, obtain information on what to look for when buying products, or report an injury caused by a product. Reporting problems is important since it's often parent complaints that alert the agency to the possible need for a recall.

Tales from the Safety Zone

These stories and bits of information tell what others are doing to help keep kids safe.

Acknowledgements

Many people have had a hand in helping produce this book. Among them, we'd especially like to thank our agent, Nancy Love, for her counsel and patience. We are also grateful to our wonderful development editor, Carol Hupping, who made this a much better book through her thoughtful editing, flexibility, and helpful suggestions.

Others at Macmillan we want to thank include Jessica Faust, who conceived the idea for this book; Randy Ladenheim-Gil, who shepherded it through to publication; and Christy Wagner, the production editor who got our words into print.

We owe much thanks to many experts who provided material or reviewed sections of the book for us. They include: Laura Tosi, M.D.; Dan Ochsenschlager, M.D.; and Evelyn Beockler, R.N.; all of Children's National Medical Center in Washington, D.C.; Rose Ann Soloway, the American Association of Poison Control Centers; Meri-K Appy and Julie Reynolds, National Fire Protection Association; Ellen Schmidt, the Children's Safety Network; Barbara Lee and Chris Hanna, National Children's Center for Rural and Agricultural Health and Safety; William L. Hall, Highway Safety Research Center at the University of North Carolina; Ken Giles, Consumer Product Safety Commission; Randy Swart, Bicycle Helmet Safety Institute; Rhonda Zakocs, University of North Carolina; Emile LeBrun, the HELP Network; Marilyn Adams, Farm Safety 4 Just Kids; Janine Linder, National Safe Place; Cindy Oertel, American Academy of Orthopaedic Surgeons; D'Ann Taflin, National Center for Missing and Exploited Children; and Heather Paul, Genny O'Donnell, and Laura Bos of the National SAFE KIDS Campaign.

We also would like to acknowledge the many fine resources of the American Academy of Pediatrics, particularly its book *Injury Prevention and Control for Today's Youth*, edited by Mark D. Widome, M.D., a tireless leader in the field of childhood injury prevention.

From Miriam:

Children, one's own and others whose lives we share, generate welcome obligations that are among the reasons for writing this book. Encouragement has been received in many forms. In my academic environment at the University of North Carolina, colleagues have expressed pleasure and offered assistance in many ways, nurturing an atmosphere that eased burdens and helped me justify occasional delays in response to their requests. Special appreciation goes to Alan W. Cross, Director, Center for Health Promotion and Disease Prevention, for encouraging me to work on this book. Also, colleagues at the UNC Injury Prevention Research Center expressed strong support for our work and were available as questions arose. Thanks and hugs to my son, Jeff Bachar, who asked perceptive questions and offered significant humorous insights at critical moments. In the wings is my husband Richard, who always believes I will accomplish more than I set out to do. And there to test this book's suggestions is my son, Steve Bachar, with his wife, Sue, and almost-two-year-old Sarah Beth, together experiencing one of life's most pleasurable and rewarding challenges.

From Susan:

Much love and thanks go to my husband, Tom Price, my partner in writing and in life, for reviewing the manuscript and for taking on many other jobs so I could concentrate on this book. I'm also grateful to my 14-year-old daughter, Julie, who humors her overprotective mom. Thanks to Ellen Pinker, who gave me some great ideas, and to Marcela Kogan and Mitchell Bard, authors of other titles in this series, who provided valuable advice. I'm also indebted to the members of my Washington Independent Writer's Group who cheered me on, especially Elise Ford, Heather Taylor, Cheryl Aubin, Amy Aldrich, and Lisa Van Wagner.

Special Thanks to the Technical Reviewer

The Complete Idiot's Guide to Child Safety was reviewed by an expert who double-checked the accuracy of what you'll learn here, to help us ensure that this book provides you with everything you need to know about childhood injury prevention. Special thanks are extended to Dr. Angela Mickalide.

Angela Mickalide, Ph.D., is the program director of the National SAFE KIDS Campaign, the only nationwide program to prevent unintentional injuries among children ages 14 and under. The National SAFE KIDS Campaign has more than 275 state and local coalitions across the nation.

Dr. Mickalide received her Ph.D. at Johns Hopkins University, Baltimore, specializing in public health, psychology, and health education. She is an adjunct associate professor of prevention and community health at the George Washington University School of Public Health and Health Services and an associate in the Department of Psychiatry and Behavioral Sciences at the Johns Hopkins University School of Medicine. Prior to joining SAFE KIDS, she worked at the federal Office of Disease Prevention and Health Promotion, U.S. Public Health Service in Washington, D.C.

Dr. Mickalide has published widely in books and journals on injury prevention, health education, and clinical preventive services. She serves on the editorial boards of Injury Prevention and Health Promotion Practice and served previously on the editorial boards of Patient Education and Counseling, and Health Education and

Behavior. Among her current public health leadership positions are as governing councilor and education board member of the American Public Health Association, and an executive board member of the International Society of Child and Adolescent Injury Prevention.

Trademarks

All terms mentioned in this book that are known to be or are suspected of being trademarks or service marks have been appropriately capitalized. Alpha Books and Macmillan USA, Inc. cannot attest to the accuracy of this information. Use of a term in this book should not be regarded as affecting the validity of any trademark or service mark.

Part 1

Home, Safe Home

Your home is the haven to which you bring your newborn, but it can become a mine-field, too, posing all manner of dangers a child can get into. In this section, you go room by room to spot and eliminate the hazards. By the time your child is a toddler, you can begin to teach him safety lessons, a process that will continue throughout his childhood. Along the way, you'll find shopping tips for all the equipment you'll be buying for your child. You'll learn how to use this equipment—from strollers to highchairs—safely, too. As your child approaches adolescence, we'll help you prepare him for those times when he's home alone.

Chapter 1

Kids Do the Darnedest Things!

In This Chapter

➤ Injury is a child's worst enemy

➤ Why injury rates are dropping

➤ Taking steps to prevent injury

➤ Balancing safety with risk

➤ How to get help

Actress-comedienne Rosanne, speaking on the subject of motherhood, declared: "I figure if the kids are still alive at the end of the day, I've done my job."

Ah yes, some days are like that, aren't they?

Along with the enormous joy children bring to our lives comes off-the-charts anxiety. We love our kids with such a passion that it's no wonder we can end up worrying about everything that affects them.

But a little worry is good if it drives us to take positive actions to keep our kids safe. That's the great thing about injury prevention; it's one thing in life you can do something about!

Injury Prevention 101

Parents who fret about deadly diseases would be better off focusing on the much bigger threat to children—unintentional injury. It is the leading killer of kids.

Each year, one out of four children (from infancy to age 14) will be hurt seriously enough to require medical attention. That's 14 million *preventable* injuries. This book is intended to help you make sure your child doesn't wind up included in that 14 million.

The problem's magnitude is why public health professionals are treating injury as an epidemic and attacking it on many fronts. The good news is that our collective efforts are working. Over the last decade, the unintentional childhood injury death rate has dropped by a remarkable 33 percent.

Tales from the Safety Zone

In a report to the nation in 1998, the National SAFE KIDS Campaign—a leader in the childhood injury prevention field—reported remarkable success against some injuries during the preceding decade. There were 40 percent declines in deaths from bicycle and fire injuries, for example. The pedestrian death rate declined more than 35 percent, and drowning decreased 30 percent. Disappointing, however, were the slow declines in deaths of children under age 1 in motor vehicle crashes. And there was a 4 percent increase in nonfatal injuries to child occupants of motor vehicles. Nonfatal sports-related injuries also have increased. Clearly, there is much work to be done.

The Safety Balancing Act

If scary statistics make you want to wrap your child in a cocoon for the duration of his growing-up years, take heart. There's a lot you can do to make his childhood safer and keep him from becoming a statistic. He needs to be protected yet still be able to explore his world, gradually gain independence, and learn to use his own judgment to avoid danger. You can help him do all of that.

There are four key ingredients in the recipe for keeping kids from injury:

➤ A safe environment

➤ Supervision

➤ Education

➤ Discipline

Creating the Safe Place

Different ages require different prevention strategies. Babies can't protect themselves; we have to do it for them. So our first safety job is to make our homes as hazard-free as possible. A baby crawling near the bottom of the stairs, for example, doesn't understand the danger, and if she crawls up a few steps, doesn't have the skills to stop herself from falling. She needs protective equipment—a baby gate. There's a lot we can do to create a baby-safe environment at home, and the next chapters in this section of the book give you all the specifics.

Being Close at Hand

Unless you turn your home into a padded cell, however, you can't make it 100 percent safe. That's why supervision is essential. Knowing where your child is and what he's up to can head off a lot of disasters. As he grows, the need for supervision gradually lessens, but you'll always be a supervisor to some degree, even when your child is a teenager. (Maybe *especially* when he's a teenager!)

Teaching Safety

As your baby starts crawling and walking, you add the education ingredient. You can start teaching her words such as "hot" if she tries to touch the oven door, for example.

Setting and Enforcing Rules

When kids progress to preschool age (3 to 5), it's time to add discipline. That means setting rules and consistently enforcing the rules set to teach your little one self-control.

A case in point is poison safety. Even if you lock up all the poisons in your home, your child still could encounter something dangerous at a grandparent's or baby-sitter's home. Some cabinets and drawers in your house should be off-limits even when nothing dangerous is stored in them. He needs freedom to explore, but not at the expense of your own needs for order and privacy. If he learns to ask permission before taking something out of a closet, he'll be more likely to do that at others' homes, too.

Kids will be better at abiding by safety rules if parents set a good example. Make it a habit to buckle your seat belt, always wear your bike helmet, and never jaywalk, for example, and, from their earliest ages, explain to your kids why you do certain things. Rules they understand are rules they'll better accept.

A school-age child can learn not only the rules but the reasons for them and the consequences of breaking them. If, for example, she forgets to wear her bike helmet, which protects her head from serious injury, she should know that she won't be allowed to ride her bike for a specified period of time.

Tales from the Safety Zone

September is Baby Safety Month. Here are some things you can do to observe it: Join with friends to enroll in a baby first-aid course; ask your library to set up a display of child safety books and materials; hold a safety shower for a friend who's expecting; or write a letter to the editor of your newspaper about the number of lives that would be saved if all parents buckled their kids up properly in their cars.

Can You Be Too Safe?

Families that become overly protective may end up with children who are so cautious they are reluctant to try new things and unable to cope with the unexpected, but a balanced approach will strengthen your child's courage and his ability to take risks and enjoy adventures—a necessary part of childhood. He can learn to anticipate hazards and handle them, rather than depend on external controls.

Yes, your child needs restrictions, and, yes, you'll need to remind him of them sometimes. But you'll also need to let him gradually take more control over his own safety. Just as he grows taller and increases his vocabulary, he learns safe independence appropriate for his age. That doesn't happen as easily if you just keep saying "no" without explaining the reasons behind safety rules.

Watch Out!

Never underestimate the rapid rate of a baby's physical, mental, and social development. Your child is helpless at birth and may be walking 12 months later. Changes happen in an instant. One day she can't roll over and the next day she can. The trick is to anticipate which new hazards she'll encounter at each stage before she gets to it!

Ages and Stages

With kids, nothing stays the same. Just as your child outgrows her clothes and needs new ones, the dangers she faces change, too. That means you have to stay one step ahead of her, anticipating potential for injury and taking appropriate measures ahead of time.

Sometimes good advice comes from other parents with children a little older than yours. They've already seen what the next developmental stage is like and can help you prepare for it. Other parents also are good sources to turn to for gauging whether you are being too cautious or too lax.

A Little Help from Your Friends

Parents are a big reason for the decline in childhood injuries—they're doing more to educate themselves about the risks and how to prevent them.

They have allies in the battle who help them achieve dramatic results. Who could have imagined that, in just a few years, the rate of sudden infant death syndrome could be cut in half by the simple act of putting babies to sleep on their backs instead of their stomachs? This success flowed from the joint efforts of medical researchers who made the discovery, the doctors who put out the message, the media that spread it wider, and the parents and caregivers who acted on it.

There's lots of good information out there for you and your kids. Take advantage of the safety education opportunities your local police and fire departments or other community groups offer. Many of them sponsor bike fairs, safety exhibits and other fun activities for kids.

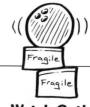

Watch Out!

Never fall for that line "All the other kids are allowed to ...." Before loosening your own restrictions, talk to the parents of your child's friends. You may find that all the other kids *aren't* allowed to. And take into account your own child's maturity and judgment, which may be different than some of her pals'.

The National SAFE KIDS Campaign is one of the leading groups working hard to prevent injuries to children. SAFE KIDS' 275 state and local coalitions are in every state, the District of Columbia and Puerto Rico. Coalitions are made up of a variety of organizations and individuals interested in injury prevention, such as businesses, hospitals, fire and police departments, health departments, schools, and parents. Coalitions have distributed safety equipment, worked to pass and enforce laws, and provided educational programs and materials.

To find out if there is a coalition near you, call 202-662-0600, or check the Web site www.safekids.org, which also contains lots of injury prevention information.

Safety Products Abound

Manufacturers sometimes are allies, also. Many of today's parents didn't grow up with the car seats, bicycle helmets, smoke alarms, and myriad other safety devices that are a basic part of childhood today.

Products posing dangers have been changed, too, in some cases as a result of government mandates and in other cases as manufacturers saw opportunities to increase sales by offering a safer product than competitors. Medicine bottles have child restraint caps. Cigarette lighters are child-resistant. Automobiles have many standard and optional features that reduce injury in the event of a collision.

Tales from the Safety Zone

Builders have joined the child safety crusade. New homes already must meet local building codes, which can dictate everything from the width between the slats on deck railings to anti-scalding devices on faucets. In 1996, a builder in Tennessee went the extra mile. He built a dream house that contained every child safety device imaginable. Features included cabinets with rounded corners, latched appliances, recessed baby gates, lockable storage areas, and electrical outlet covers that snap back in place when a cord is pulled out. Before it went on the market, the house was open for tours to give parents ideas for their own homes. Admission fees were donated to the local children's hospital.

What's Up Doc?

Medical personnel are taking their injury prevention role to heart. When you leave the hospital with your newborn, chances are you'll be asked if you have a car seat for baby's first ride. (Some hospitals even have loaner seats if you don't.) When you take your child for a check-up, your pediatrician may ask him if he always uses his bike helmet, or she might ask you if you have guns in your home and counsel you on proper storage.

Safety Savvy

The American Academy of Pediatrics (AAP) is a leading source of injury prevention information for both doctors and parents. Your pediatrician may have AAP brochures to give you on leading injury areas. You also can get information from the organization's Web site, www.aap.org.

I'm from the Government, and I'm Here to Help You

Many important safety measures—use of child safety seats, smoke alarms, and bike helmets, for example—have been mandated by federal, state, or local governments. Governments also fund and conduct important research that leads to safety standards in products.

The federal government sponsors a wide array of educational programs for parents and children. One way to access them is through the Internet. If you aren't hooked up at home, you may be able to use a computer and modem at your public library.

The Consumer Product Safety Commission's (CPSC) job is protecting the public from unreasonable risk of injury from 15,000 consumer products under its jurisdiction. It's also one of the best resources for parents on child safety topics. Call 800 ˍˍˍˍˍˍˍ www.cpsc.gov. You also can have information faxed ˍˍˍˍˍˍˍ 02-504-0051 from the handset of your fax machin ˍ

Kids can find safety information on ˍˍˍˍˍˍˍ example, has a kid safety Web site at www.cpsc.gov ˍˍˍˍˍ dren ages 8 to 12, the site has educational, interac ˍˍˍˍˍˍˍ ty issues kids encounter every day.

Lessons at School

Schools can do a lot to help keep ˍˍˍˍˍˍˍ afest possible schoolhouse environment, they ˍˍˍˍˍˍˍ you're teaching at home. For example, your schoo ˍˍˍˍˍˍˍ to school always to wear helmets.

Some schools offer their own s ˍˍˍˍˍˍˍ each a specific subject, such as pedestrian or bike ˍˍˍˍˍˍˍ mprehensive approach with a curriculum cov ˍˍˍˍˍˍˍ

If your child's school doesn't ˍˍˍˍˍˍˍ dministrators think they don't have enough time, but ˍˍˍˍˍˍˍ nforce work in academics such as reading compreh ˍˍˍˍˍˍˍ g in their ear!)

We believe safety should be ˍˍˍˍˍˍˍ n. We like Risk Watch™, produced by the National ˍˍˍˍˍ) in collaboration with other national safety exper ˍˍˍˍˍˍˍ eschool through eighth grade covers the leading c ˍˍˍˍˍˍˍ urns, motor vehicles, poisoning, choking, suffocati ˍˍˍˍˍˍˍ arms, water sports, and pedestrian injuries. The le ˍˍˍˍˍˍˍ hours per school year. If you want to suggest this curriculum ˍˍˍˍˍˍˍ ou can get more information from NFPA at 617-984-7285.

The Least You Need to Know

➤ Unintentional injury, the leading killer of kids, is preventable.

➤ Kids need a safe environment, supervision, education, and consistently enforced rules.

➤ Safety measures must be regularly updated as your child matures physically and mentally.

➤ Parents should be models of good safety behavior.

➤ All schools should offer some kind of safety education.

Caution: Household Danger Zones Ahead

In This Chapter

➤ Conducting your own room-to-room safety survey

➤ Choosing and installing safety devices

➤ Getting into the safety habit

➤ Updating safety measures as your child grows

If you're about to have a new baby, you're probably looking at your home sweet home in a whole new way. The rooms and furnishings are undoubtedly set up for the convenience of adults. But a new pint-sized member of the family means rethinking everything—from where you put things to what safety gadgets you'll need.

Some new parents are so overwhelmed by the task they hire a professional. A whole new industry has sprung up—professional "child-proofers" or "baby-proofers," as they call themselves, who will come to your home, conduct room-by-room inspections and recommend solutions for the hazards they find—all for a price, of course.

But, if you follow the steps in this chapter, you can be your own professional. We're going to take you on a room-by-room tour so you can create a "kid-safe environment" and give yourself some peace of mind.

We're not going to call it child-proofing, however, because there's really no such thing—unless you mean a business establishment with "No One Under 18" signs! Anyone who's been around a tyke just learning to crawl or walk knows that, no matter how diligent you are, you can't anticipate every single thing a child might get into. Instead, we'll help you make your home as safe as possible and combine that with the lessons you can teach your kids about avoiding risks.

Nursery Nights—and Days

If you're bringing home a newborn, start your safety survey in the nursery. Your child—and you—will be spending a lot of time here.

Cribs

Ideally, the crib is a place for blissful sleep. Well okay, we'll admit that the crib's not always a blissful place, especially when your baby won't go to sleep. But at least it should be comfortable and safe.

Unfortunately, however, cribs can be very dangerous. In the United States about 50 babies a year suffocate or strangle in cribs. This especially happens in used ones that aren't in good repair or may have been made with older, unsafe designs. It's best to buy a crib with a certification seal showing that it meets national safety standards. If you have a used one, there are ways to make sure it's safe. (For details, see Chapter 3, "The Well-Equipped Parent.")

Make sure the crib is not so near a window that, when your baby learns to stand, she could fall through it. To protect her from strangulation, keep the cords from blinds or curtains out of her reach or retrofit the cords with safety tassels. (For more on preventing strangulation, see Chapter 9, "Why Is Junior Turning Blue?: Airway Obstruction.")

Watch Out!

Never put your baby to sleep on her stomach. Babies who sleep on their backs have a much lower incidence of sudden infant death syndrome (SIDS). Between 1992 and 1998, the SIDS death rate plummeted by nearly 50 percent, thanks to a public education campaign by the American Academy of Pediatrics and other groups. Just remember the slogan—"Back to Sleep."

Also be careful what you put in the crib with the baby. Those soft, fluffy pillows and quilts may look adorable, but they aren't safe. Babies have suffocated when they fell asleep face-down on soft bedding. Blankets or quilts aren't necessary if you dress your baby in layers, including a blanket sleeper on cold nights. Put your baby to sleep on a firm crib mattress and save the money that you'd otherwise spend on fancy bedding.

Leave stuffed toys out of the crib, too. They can be a suffocation hazard for infants. Older babies plotting a crib escape can turn large stuffed animals into great step stools.

Bumper pads of cloth or vinyl are a good way to protect your baby from hitting against the side of the crib, but make sure you fasten the pad with snaps or straps tied on the outside of the crib so the baby can't reach them. To prevent strangulation, cut the ties so they are no longer than seven inches. Remove the bumper pad when the baby is able to stand up so it won't become a launching pad for climbing out.

Get in the habit of always putting up the side of the crib as soon as you put the baby in. If you turn your back for a second, she could fall out.

Changing Tables

Babies, even little ones, have incredible energy and love to move about, especially, so it seems, when their diaper's being changed. Falls are most likely to happen when you're reaching for a fresh diaper or searching for a clean outfit. That's why the best changing tables are those that come with straps to secure baby. Even when strapped, a squirmy baby can fall, so don't leave her unattended. Also, keep diaper pins, ointment, and other changing essentials in your reach but out of baby's.

You don't really need a changing table at all. It's just one more thing that takes up space and costs money, and it will outlive its usefulness pretty fast. You can easily improvise with a changing pad on the floor for diaper changes. You can also use the crib by lowering the side and spreading a waterproof pad on top of the mattress. Just make sure you gather up the wipes, diaper, and clothes before you put the side down so you can keep your hand on the baby while you change her. If you have to leave for even a moment, put the side up first.

Tales from the Safety Zone

The Consumer Product Safety Commission has mounted a national campaign to promote "baby safety" showers for new and expectant mothers. They've been organized by community groups nationwide. Mothers receive written materials and participate in games and activities centered on a 12-point safety checklist. If you're planning a shower for a friend, consider making it a safety shower, or at least put some safety gifts on the wish list. These could include home safety devices, a first-aid book, and a gift certificate for a baby first-aid class. Details on games and activities are available from the CPSC Web site or Fax-on-Demand service (see Appendix A, "More Helpful Resources").

Gadget Guide

Did you know that young children can drown in just an inch of water? Toddlers' large heads make them top heavy; if they fall into a toilet, they may not be able to get out. The safest course is to install a toilet lid latch. If you use a diaper pail to soak cloth diapers, make sure it's latched, too.

Beware the Bathroom

Just think about what's behind that bathroom door! We don't know exactly what's in *your* bathroom, but we bet there's enough potential trouble there to warrant a door latch that will keep your toddler from wandering in on his own. Install a latch or hook well above his reach. If the door can be locked from the inside, you might want to disable the lock so he can't lock himself in.

There should definitely be a child-resistant latch on the medicine cabinet. You'd be surprised at how early curious kids are able to climb onto a toilet or use a stool to explore the mysteries that lie behind the mirror!

Babies can drown in a small amount of water in a tub, five-gallon bucket, or diaper pail. (Courtesy of the Consumer Product Safety Commission)

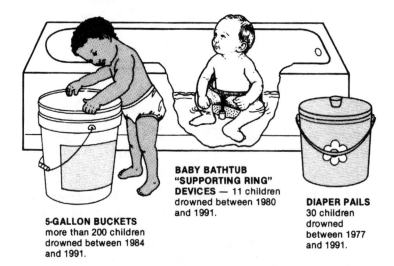

5-GALLON BUCKETS
more than 200 children drowned between 1984 and 1991.

BABY BATHTUB "SUPPORTING RING" DEVICES — 11 children drowned between 1980 and 1991.

DIAPER PAILS
30 children drowned between 1977 and 1991.

Rub a Dub Dub

Once your infant outgrows his baby bathtub, you can use the regular tub with a rubber mat in the bottom. Skid-proof rugs on the floor are a good idea, too.

Always test the water with your entire hand before putting your baby in the tub, and set your water heater thermostat no higher than 120°F. Use a meat or candy thermometer to test the temperature in a glass of hot water from your tap. If it's too hot, turn the thermostat down, wait 24 hours, and test the water again. Repeat this process until you reach the 120°F mark. You'll be rewarded for your efforts with a safer water temperature and slightly lower utility bills. (For more information on preventing scaldings, see Chapter 6, "Too Hot to Handle: Fire and Burns.")

Live in an apartment and can't control the water temperature? Then select faucets and shower heads with anti-scald technologies. If the water temperature becomes too hot, a valve in the device expands and stems the flow of water. Don't bother buying the color-changing temperature indicators. These gadgets, which come in cute designs, go in the tub and change color if the water gets too hot. Your hand works just as well.

You also can buy cushioning devices that fit over the tub faucets and spout so exuberant bathers don't hurt themselves by banging their heads.

Watch Out!

Baby bath seats, like the ones with rubber suction cups, can give you a false sense of security. Your wiggly baby can slip out of one of them and drown in the time it takes you to answer a ringing phone. Keep your hand on your baby whenever he's in the tub; don't expect an older child to be a reliable substitute for you. Babies need adult supervision in the bathtub.

Electrical Appliances

Everybody knows that electricity and water are a deadly mix. Keep electrical gadgets like curling irons, radios, and hair dryers out of reach of little hands in the bathroom. If these appliances are on and slip into the tub, they can cause electrocution, and curling irons can burn small children. Just imagine what can happen if an adult plugs the iron into a bathroom outlet and then walks away while it heats up. It's awfully tempting to a toddler who wants to mimic the big folks.

To be extra safe, just don't use these electrical appliances in the bathroom. Wherever you use your curling iron, make sure it's out of your child's reach, hot or otherwise, because kids learn quickly how to plug things in.

Bedroom Basics

Windows, especially when they're above the first floor, should be shielded. Screens are not strong enough to prevent even a small child from falling through. (See Chapter 8, "Kids Don't Bounce: Preventing Falls," for hardware solutions for window fall prevention.) Position furniture so your junior mountain climber who scales it can't fall through a window.

Dressers, with their handy drawers, make tempting jungle gyms for fearless climbers and can topple over on a child. One solution is to anchor the dresser to the wall using small, L-shaped brackets from the hardware store. There are other types of anchors made just for this purpose; some use straps that mount to the wall and to the back of a piece of furniture. Check for them in juvenile products stores or catalogs.

Watch Out!

Don't put your baby to sleep alone in your bed. Babies can suffocate or strangle in bedding or by becoming wedged between the bed and the wall, or the frame and the mattress. Waterbeds are particularly dangerous. Tempted to let your infant share your bed? Be aware that a few babies have died when parents rolled over onto them, especially during sound sleep induced by alcohol or sedatives. Weigh whether the advantages of the family bed outweigh the safety risks.

Gadget Guide

Smoke alarms have saved countless lives. It's best to have them on every floor and especially near the bedrooms. (See Chapter 6 for details on buying and installing them.) We also strongly urge you to install carbon monoxide detectors to alert you to this colorless, odorless—and deadly—gas. (Information on using CO detectors is in Chapter 7, "You Put *What* in Your Mouth?: Poison Prevention.")

You probably already know to keep cleaning supplies and other poisonous liquids out of children's reach, but did you know some of these might be lurking in your bedroom? Perfumes and cosmetics are harmful to kids, but they seem more benign than, say, bleach or floor cleaner, so parents sometimes leave them where kids have easy access. Medicines, deodorant, hair spray, nail polish remover, and contraceptive creams are among items commonly found in bedrooms that shouldn't get into little hands.

Living It Up in the Living Room/Family Room

As benign as this room looks, there are things to watch out for here, too.

The TV

Television doesn't just addle a kid's brain. Believe it or not, it's also a frequent cause of injuries treated in emergency rooms. The scenario is simple enough: a toddler reaches up to a TV sitting on a cart, stand, or flimsy table and pulls it over on himself. Your best bet is to put the television on a low, stable piece of furniture, as far back against a wall as possible.

The VCR's tape insertion slot is an enticing little compartment that kids love to stick things into. A child's fingers can be pinched in the slot (not to mention what foreign objects do to your VCR!). Block the opening with a device made for this purpose, or keep the VCR in a cabinet that can be closed.

Furniture and Fireplaces

A breakable, glass-topped coffee table is not a good idea in a home with young children for obvious reasons. Kids also have been known to pull over tall furniture, especially bookcases. Furniture is even more dangerous if it sits partially on a rug, or the floor is uneven. Anchor unstable furniture to the wall (for tips on how to do this, see the "Bedroom Basics" section, earlier).

Fireplaces pose numerous hazards. Tongs and other tools can crush fingers or injure eyes. Keep these and fireplace matches out of children's reach. Never leave a young child alone in the room if there is a fire or hot coals in the fireplace, or if the fireplace doors are still hot. Even an unused fireplace is a hazard if a child crawls around it and breathes in the soot. Use a screen even if you have fireplace doors because they can become very hot. And teach your child to stay away from the fireplace.

Safety Savvy

Unless you live in a one-story house with no steps anywhere, you'll need gates to keep your child from becoming Humpty Dumpty. You'll also need barriers for decks, balconies, and other elevated sites. (See Chapter 8 for details.)

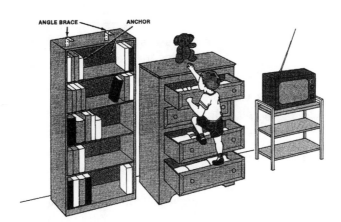

ANGLE BRACE   ANCHOR

Young children can be killed when furniture tips over.
(Courtesy of the Consumer Product Safety Commission)

Hazards Found in Any Room

These potential hazards are not unique to the living room; they're found in other rooms as well:

➤ Electrical outlets

➤ Electrical cords

➤ Cords from blinds or drapes

➤ Small objects that can be swallowed

Gadget Guide

Clever entrepreneurs have come up with various cushioning devices to soften sharp edges on coffee tables, cabinets, and raised hearths. You might be able to get them locally at a hardware or baby furniture store, or you can order the devices through the catalogs listed at the end of this chapter.

Safety Savvy

To get a baby's-eye view of your house, get down on your hands and knees and crawl around. From there you can see a nail sticking out of the baseboard, a small object that rolled under the couch, or a lamp cord that your baby could pull on. You'll be surprised how many hazards you'll find—and thus be able to eliminate.

To a small child, the holes in an electrical outlet are tempting places to stick things. The result can be severe shock and electrical burns. Don't take chances: put child-resistant covers on all unused outlets. There are several types on the market, but it's best not to use the little plastic plugs with two prongs and a base that were popular a few years ago. It's been found that kids can sometimes pull them out and try to swallow them, posing a choking hazard.

Wall-mounted lights are safer than table lamps with cords that a crawling baby can pull over. There's also a risk of serious mouth burns if a child chews on an electrical cord. Try taping the cords to your baseboards or running them under furniture so they're out of reach as much as possible, but don't put the cords under rugs or nail them to a floor or wall because you could be creating a fire hazard. Unplug extension cords when not in use, and reduce the slack in cords being used by coiling the excess and securing it with a rubber band or string.

Keep window blind and drapery cords out of reach by wrapping them around a high hook. They're a strangulation hazard.

Crawlers and toddlers love to examine things with their mouths. Keep your floors free of small objects such as coins, paper clips, beads, or anything that a curious child might pick up and swallow. After you vacuum, carefully examine your floors for objects such as straight pins that the vacuum cleaner might have missed.

Chef's Little Helper

The kitchen area is full of knives, scissors, small appliances, breakables such as dishes and glasses, hot things such as ovens and toasters, and several intriguing little cupboard doors to tantalize a curious tot.

Just where do you begin? For starters, put child-resistant latches on the cabinets where you store breakables, sharp utensils, and cleaning supplies, and use high cabinet shelves instead of under-the-sink storage. We also recommend plastic safety covers on stove knobs so a child can't turn them.

It's best to keep very young children from playing in the kitchen while you cook. If there isn't a safe play area nearby, put your little one in a playpen in the kitchen. When cooking, turn the handles of pots to the back of the stove and use the rear burners instead of those in the front whenever possible. Put appliances with cords to the back of the counter and don't leave knives or hot beverages near the edge. Get rid of table-cloths and placemats that your baby could pull on and cause food or hot beverages to fall on her.

Gadget Guide

The kitchen is a good place to keep a fire extinguisher. It can stop a small fire from becoming a big one. For tips on using one, see Chapter 6.

Some parents mount their microwave ovens above the counters to save space and keep them out of reach of children. That's best for young children, but when your child is old enough to use it, you should move it to a lower spot so the child won't be lifting hot foods above his head. (For information on kids using microwave ovens, see Chapter 5, "What Was That Noise?: Kids Home Alone.")

When you load the dishwasher, put sharp utensils in with the handles up, and never leave the dishwasher standing open. We know of a child who tripped on an open dishwasher door, fell on the silverware basket and was poked in the nose with a fork, causing an injury serious enough to warrant emergency room treatment.

Garages and Basements

Tools and chemicals pose the biggest problems here. Also, kids have been known to crawl into clothes dryers and empty freezers and refrigerators. Keep chemicals, paint, and other poisonous substances locked up. Kids inevitably will put tools to purposes other than those for which they're intended, so store them out of reach.

Watch Out!

Don't overlook the outside of your house when conducting your safety survey. The yard, the deck, and any playground equipment need special attention, as do backyard pools, hot tubs, and other outdoor structures. These areas are covered in detail in Chapters 14, "Life's a Playground," and 15, "On the Waterfront."

If you've got an automatic garage-door opener, be sure that it has an auto-reverse feature so that it reverses itself when it touches something on the way down; this way the door won't close on your child.

We've just skimmed the surface of potential hazards when a young child is alone in a basement or garage. If in doubt about how thoroughly you can get rid of hazards, or if it just isn't practical to do it all, then play it safe and put a lock on the door to keep little ones out in the first place.

Safety Savvy

As your baby progresses to new stages—crawling, then walking, then running, then figuring out ingenious ways to open things—you'll discover new hazards you didn't think about when he was a babe in arms. It's best to anticipate what he'll do before he's able to do it. This is where a friend with an older child can be very helpful. She can spot things you might not think of because she's already been through these stages.

Gadget Guide

Want to shop for child safety products from the comfort of home? Here are two catalog companies specializing in these items: *Perfectly Safe* (800-837-5437), and *Safe Beginnings* (800-598-8911).

Home Sweet Office

With so many parents working at home these days, it's inevitable that kids are going to get early lessons in office equipment. At the minimum, kids may mess up your papers or spill juice on your keyboard. At worst, they can get seriously hurt on a file cabinet's sharp corner or by swallowing paper clips or push pins. Be especially vigilant about the myriad cords that run from office equipment and phones. (You can buy a flexible plastic cable to cover all those cords, and also special covers for power strips containing multiple plugs.)

Kids want to be where you are, but, if you're trying to concentrate on work, you may not really be "there" with them. Set aside a special spot in your office, maybe a playpen for babies and a little table and chair with crayons and paper, so your child can "work" in the office with you, yet stay out of trouble.

Getting More Help

When you make your tour of your home, take along the tear-out card in the front of the book to use as a checklist. And keep it handy because you'll need to take the tour again as your child grows.

If you still feel you're too busy to take on the job of going over your house, there's still the option of hiring help. These professionals typically sell safety products and usually will install them for you. Some charge an inspection fee, but others just rely on the profits from the product sales.

To find one, check the Yellow Pages under such headings as "baby-proofing," "child-proofing," "baby," or "safety." Before using a professional, inquire about fees, and ask for references from other parents in your area. Some of them work with day care centers and may provide a center director as a reference as well.

The Least You Need to Know

➤ Take a safety tour of your home to uncover the hidden hazards to your baby or young child.

➤ Even if you've been thorough in eliminating safety hazards, supervision of young children is still important.

➤ To uncover hazards you might have missed, get down on the floor at child's-eye level and crawl around.

➤ Enlist a more experienced parent to help you spot trouble your child might get into.

➤ Safety issues change as your child changes, so be vigilant about regularly checking your house for potential hazards.

The Well-Equipped Parent

In This Chapter

➤ Choosing the right products

➤ Using equipment correctly and safely

➤ Products to avoid

➤ Keeping up with recalls

➤ Reporting safety problems with products

One reason it costs so much to have kids is all the paraphernalia you have to buy! Whether you go top-of-the-line, or save money by shopping at consignment stores and yard sales, consider safety before price or looks. Safety is particularly critical when you look for such key items as the baby's crib and car seat. (You'll find an entire chapter later in the book, Chapter 11, "Use Some [Car] Restraint," on choosing and properly using car seats.)

Baby product manufacturers know how to read demographics. They've seen the rise in spending on the babies of well-off Boomers, and they've responded with a dizzying array of new products boasting increased convenience, durability, and safety. It's no wonder that you can get bogged down in decisions about what to buy!

In this chapter, we'll help you shop for everything from cribs to high chairs, with an emphasis on the safety aspects.

Lullaby and Goodnight

Hand-me-down clothes may be okay but second-hand cribs often aren't. More infants die every year in crib mishaps than with any other nursery product. Cribs made before the federal government issued mandatory safety standards in 1973 will likely be unsafe. Additional voluntary standards were adopted by manufacturers in 1992, so it's best to use one made after that time. When you shop, look for a crib with a JPMA certification seal.

Safety Savvy

The Juvenile Products Manufacturers Association (JPMA), representing 95 percent of its industry, has a voluntary certification program to help parents select safe products. JPMA standards were developed jointly with the American Society for Testing and Materials, the Consumer Product Safety Commission (CPSC), and others. Look for the JPMA seal on products you are considering, or check the list at JPMA's Web site, www.JPMA.org.

The CPSC says a safe crib has:

➤ No missing, loose, broken, or improperly installed screws, brackets, or other hardware on the crib or mattress support.

➤ No more than 2⅜ inches between crib slats so that a baby's body cannot fit through.

➤ A firm, snug-fitting mattress so a baby can't get trapped between the mattress and the side of the crib.

➤ No corner posts higher than $\frac{1}{16}$ inch above the end panels (unless they are more than 16 inches tall for a canopy), so a baby can't catch clothing and strangle.

➤ No cutout areas on the headboard or footboard, so a baby's head can't get trapped.

➤ A mattress support that doesn't easily pull apart from the corner posts so a baby can't get trapped between mattress and crib.

➤ No splinters or rough edges.

When you buy a crib, it comes with those ominous words: "Some Assembly Required." Follow the instruction manual carefully, and make sure the hardware is tightened properly and that there are no sharp edges. After you start using it, check the crib periodically to make sure nothing has come loose.

Crib Toys

Your newborn may enjoy mobiles attached to the crib or the baby gyms that stretch across it, but these items should be removed as soon as your child is old enough to push up on his hands and knees—usually around five months. At that stage, these toys pose a choking or strangulation hazard because a baby can reach high enough to pull them into the crib.

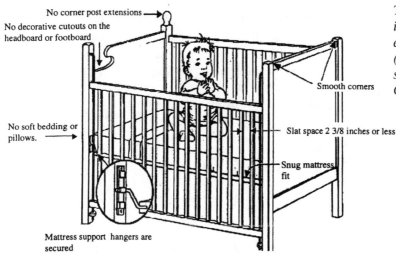

No corner post extensions

No decorative cutouts on the headboard or footboard

No soft bedding or pillows.

Smooth corners

Slat space 2 3/8 inches or less

Snug mattress fit

Mattress support hangers are secured

This crib safety guide illustrates the important elements of crib safety. (Courtesy of the Consumer Product Safety Commission)

Bassinets

Since bassinets take up little space, some parents use these for their newborns, especially if the baby is to sleep in the parents' room initially. As with cribs, make sure the mattress is firm and fits snugly to avoid a risk of suffocation. Also, make sure the folded legs lock into place so the bassinet won't collapse. Some babies have been hurt when siblings tried to lift them out of their bassinets. For that reason, we don't recommend using them if there are other young children in the house.

Move your baby to a crib when he reaches the weight limit set by the manufacturer (which can vary depending on the model) or when he starts to turn over.

Watch Out!

Don't skimp on quality when you buy crib sheets. When the Good Housekeeping Institute tested two dozen sheets, the majority shrank and fit poorly after five machine washings. Sheets that don't fit snugly on the crib mattress could pop off the corners and get twisted around baby, increasing the risk of strangulation.

Doubling Up: Bunk Beds

Many toddlers and older kids love bunk beds and so do their parents, who see them as real space savers. If you're thinking about getting them, be aware that some deaths and injuries have occurred because children got their heads caught between the bed frame and guard rails on the top bunk. For this reason, the CPSC says the gap should be no more than 3½ inches. A few children, most under age 1, have died when they became trapped between the bed and the wall. That's why a guardrail next to the wall is recommended on both top and bottom bunks.

Here are other bunk-bed safety tips:

➤ The CPSC says children under age 6 should not be allowed on the top bunk.

➤ Mattresses and foundations should not rest only on bed frames; they need support from wooden slats, metal straps, or sturdy wires.

➤ Kids should use the ladder to get on and to leave the top bunk—no jumping or rough-housing in the beds!

Attach additional boards to the bunk bed to close up any space more than 3½ inches between the lower edge of the guardrails and the upper edge of the bed frame to prevent possible entrapment and strangulation. (Courtesy of the Consumer Product Safety Commission)

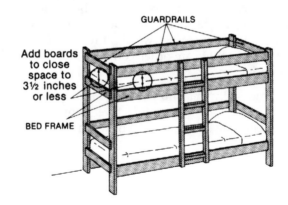

GUARDRAILS

Add boards to close space to 3½ inches or less

BED FRAME

Don't Fence Me In

Playpens—sometimes called play yards by people who think the former raises the specter of baby as prisoner—can be very handy for parents. A playpen offers a safe place to confine a baby, in the kitchen while you're cooking dinner or in the home office while you're working, for example. (Lucky you if your baby plays happily in one and doesn't start to howl the instant she's put in!)

The typical playpen has mesh sides and a wooden floor that bends in the middle for folding. The mesh should have a small weave, less than ¼ inch, so fingers or buttons can't get caught. On wooden models, the space between slats should be no wider than 2⅜ inches. It is crucial that playpens be set up properly with sides locked into place.

Watch Out!

Even though the typical use of a playpen is to confine the baby while you're busy, don't leave him alone there. Keep him in your sight, and never leave the side down on the playpen even when the baby isn't in it. Whether he's inside or out, your baby could crawl or roll into the pocket that forms when the side is down and suffocate.

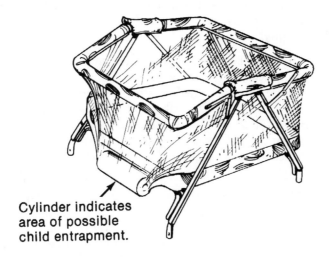

Always keep your baby in your sight, even in his playpen.
(Courtesy of the Consumer Product Safety Commission)

Cylinder indicates area of possible child entrapment.

Since babies like to chew, regularly inspect the vinyl or fabric rail covering in case there are tears or loose pieces that your little teether could break off and choke on.

Playpens are not recommended for babies who weigh more than 30 pounds or who are taller than 34 inches. When it appears your child may be able to climb out, it's time to give up the playpen. Don't put in boxes or other items that a shorter baby could stand on to make an escape.

Watch Out!

Never use a string to hang an object on a playpen, crib, or portable crib. Your baby could strangle.

Safety Savvy

Quite a few playpen models have been recalled for a variety of hazards. Before you accept a hand-me-down, call the CPSC hotline at 800-638-2772 or check the Web site at www.cpsc.org to see if that model is on the recall list. It's wise to double-check even on one you bought new, in case you missed a recall announcement.

Portable Cribs

For babies on the go, portable cribs are becoming increasingly popular. They are lightweight and fold up in a carrying case for travel. Some parents also use them as a substitute for a playpen.

As with a playpen, take care to set up the portable crib properly, locking the sides in place so they won't collapse, and never leaving the sides down. Don't add padding beyond the mattress that comes with it. Stop using it when your child is able to climb out, usually around 30 inches or 30 pounds.

Walkers

We do not recommend using walkers because of the thousands of injuries they cause. (For you neophytes, a walker is a contraption on a wide base in which a baby can stand or sit and push himself around.) Walkers once were a very popular item of baby equipment, but some safety experts—including the American Academy of Pediatrics—have recommended that they be banned.

The typical injury happens when a child scoots the walker near steps and goes down, walker and all. These injuries occur even when a parent is in the room supervising, because babies can move in them faster than you might think. Some babies have been burned when they bumped into hot liquids such as coffee or touched hot surfaces such as oven doors.

New walker models have bases wider than a standard 36-inch doorway. Others, sometimes called activity centers, have no wheels—babies can stand and swivel in them but not move across the floor. The former still don't prevent a child from getting through larger openings, and the latter could frustrate babies who want to get somewhere.

Please Be Seated

There are all manner of seats made for babies to help them reach the dining table or just to make it easier to carry them around. Here's a rundown on the safety aspects of baby seats.

Highchairs

The key to safe use of a highchair is to get one with both a waist strap and a strap that runs between the legs—and then to always use both of them.

Falls from highchairs often happen when a child stands and topples out. Others slide out under the tray, and some kids have strangled on the waist strap or when their heads were trapped between the tray and the seat.

Gadget Guide

It once was thought that walkers help babies learn to walk. On the contrary, studies show excessive use can actually delay walking by preventing certain muscles from developing as quickly as they would if the baby were allowed to crawl and walk on her own.

Tales from the Safety Zone

Illinois parents Linda Ginzel and Boaz Keysar turned their family tragedy into a potential lifesaver for other parents. The couple's 17-month-old son died in 1998 when his portable crib collapsed while he was at his day care provider's home. Mixed with the parents' grief was their outrage that the crib had been recalled five years previously, but the announcements had not reached many of the parents and child care providers using them. The couple has founded Kids in Danger, a nonprofit organization that educates parents about recalls. Visit their Web site at www.kidsindanger.org.

When you buy a highchair, try the straps to make sure they're easy to use so you won't be tempted to skip using them. Ideally, you should be able to operate the tray with one hand since you'll usually be holding the baby with the other. Choose a highchair with a wide base so it's less likely to tip over.

Safety Savvy

Always fill in and mail back the registration cards that come with your baby's equipment. These records allow companies to notify you in the event of a recall. You can skip the questions that are asked strictly for marketing purposes if you don't feel like helping the manufacturers pitch you more products.

Watch Out!

Restaurant booster seats may not have any straps and may tip over if your child squirms. It's better to take your own so you'll know it's safe. Seat your child away from the path of the servers who might bump into her while carrying trays of hot food or dirty dishes. Don't let toddlers out of their seats to wander around on their own.

Here's some advice for using highchairs safely:

➤ Don't let your child climb in unassisted.

➤ Place it far enough from the table, wall, or other hard surface so your child can't push it over while seated in it.

➤ Don't leave your baby unattended in the highchair.

➤ If you have a model that folds, double-check that the locking mechanism is fully engaged before you put your baby in.

Portable Hook-On Chairs and Booster Seats

Hook-on chairs are handy for those occasions when a highchair isn't available, such as in a restaurant or at Grandma's house. Remember the rule to always strap your child in.

When you buy a hook-on chair, make sure it has a strong clamp to attach to the table and has both waist and crotch straps. Only use the seat on a sturdy table that won't tip over from the weight of the baby. These seats are not for use on glass top or center pedestal tables or on the table's extension leaf. Don't put a regular chair under the hook-on seat, because your child could use it to push up, and stop using the hook-on chair when your child reaches the maximum weight limit set by the manufacturer.

A booster seat is used primarily by kids who have outgrown their highchairs. It is placed on a dining chair to boost up a small child to a convenient height at the table. The safest ones have two straps—one to anchor the booster to the chair and a waist strap to hold the child in place.

Infant Carriers

Since ancient times, parents have strapped their babies onto their bodies and carried them while they went about their daily business. Today's more modern versions come in a variety of styles and sizes.

There are two basic kinds: soft carriers, which are worn on the front or back, and framed carriers, which look like backpacks. Soft ones tend to be for small infants and have supports for the head as well as the body.

The CPSC warns that framed carriers shouldn't be used until a baby is four or five months old, so her neck is able to withstand the jolts from the parent's stride.

When you buy a carrier, try it on with the baby in it and check for:

> ➤ Enough depth to support the baby's back.

> ➤ Leg openings big enough to avoid chafing the baby's skin but small enough that the baby won't slip out.

> ➤ Sturdy construction and materials, and heavy-duty fasteners, again to prevent falls.

> ➤ Padded covering over the metal part (if any) nearest the baby's face for bump protection.

Two other tips when using a carrier:

> ➤ When you fold a framed carrier, make sure the baby's fingers are clear of the frame joints.

> ➤ If you lean over, bend from the knees, not from the waist, to prevent the baby from falling out through the top of the carrier (this seems obvious, but parents have occasionally forgotten this law of gravity!)

> ➤ Don't drink hot beverages while carrying your baby on your front (it's not really worth the risk, is it?).

Watch Out!

Some framed carriers have a folding base that opens and keeps the carrier upright on a surface to help you put it on. Don't leave your baby sitting in the framed carrier—he could topple over.

Infant Carrier Seats

For babies who can't sit up on their own, the infant seat is a wonderfully handy item. It gives your baby a comfortable place to recline while you tote her around or place her somewhere. Some babies nap in them, too, especially in the models that can be rocked.

Injuries and some deaths have resulted from use of these seats, largely due to lack of parental supervision. Some infants have become tangled in the restraining straps while others have fallen out because they weren't strapped in or because the seat was placed on a soft surface, such as a bed, and it toppled over. A few babies have been injured when parents dropped the seat.

When shopping for a seat, choose one with easy-to-use straps and a base or rear support wider than the seat itself. A non-skid surface on the bottom helps prevent the possibility of the baby's movement causing the seat to scoot off a kitchen counter or other smooth surface.

Here are some tips for safe use:

➤ Always fasten your baby in with the straps.

➤ Don't place the seat on a soft surface such as a bed or couch.

➤ Stay within arm's reach of the baby when her seat is on an elevated surface such as a table or countertop.

➤ Follow the manufacturer's age and weight limits.

Swings

Many a parent has been able to get through a meal thanks to a baby swing. The rhythmic motion, produced either by a wind-up or battery-powered mechanism, can lull a fussy infant into contentment and give you a needed break (one parent we know dubbed it the Neglect-o-Matic!). The downsides are that swings take up a lot of space because of their wide bases, and babies outgrow them fairly quickly.

Once again, remember these two safety rules: Always use the straps and don't leave the baby unattended. Also, it's important to stop using a swing once the baby reaches the weight limit established by the manufacturer. Be vigilant if you have other children. Small siblings may be attracted to the swing mechanism and a few have been known to get their heads caught between the swinging seat and the frame.

Strollers on the Move

It's hard to imagine any parent living without a stroller. For infants, the most popular models are a combination carriage/stroller with backs that recline. Shopping for one is tricky because the choices are endless! From a safety standpoint, considerations include whether:

➤ The brake is easy to operate and works effectively.

➤ The seat and crotch belts are connected, fit snugly around your child, and are easily fastened.

➤ There is a barrier or covering to enclose the opening between the handrest and the seat when the stroller's backrest is reclined.

The last feature is recommended because some babies have died when left sleeping in strollers. In the upright position, babies' legs extend through the leg openings, but from a sleeping position, they may scoot feet first toward the front and fall through a leg hole where their heads become entangled. The other rule here is not to leave your baby unattended in the stroller.

Never leave a child unattended in a stroller. Babies have been known to slip through a leg hole and strangle.
(Courtesy of the Consumer Product Safety Commission)

Other safety tips:

➤ To avoid pinching or smashing your baby's fingers, keep him away from the stroller when you are folding it.

➤ Don't put soft pillows or blankets in a stroller or carriage; they pose a suffocation hazard.

➤ Don't let your kids play with the stroller unattended.

Safety Devices

In Chapter 2, "Caution: Household Danger Zones Ahead," you read how to go about protecting your child from home hazards. Every year brings new, often ingenious safety products to help you, but sometimes safety devices can become hazards themselves.

One classic example is the baby gate. The once-popular accordion-style gates with V-shaped openings at the top and bottom and large diamond-shaped openings between the slats caused the deaths of a few children whose heads became trapped

Watch Out!

Pressure gates sometimes can be pushed out by a strong child, so they should not be used to prevent falls from the top of a stairway. Also, install them with the pressure bar on the side away from the child. Some kids have used this bar as a toe-hold to climb over the gate.

Safety Savvy

If a product is recalled after you've bought it, you may not be aware of the problem. To receive notices of product recalls, sign up on the CPSC Web site at www.cpsc.org, or call the hotline at 800-638-2772, and ask to be placed on the mailing list. Share the announcements with your child-care provider.

when they tried to crawl through. These gates have not been manufactured since 1985, but used ones still turn up at yard sales or are handed down in families.

Choosing a Safe Baby Gate

Gates are for use at the top and bottom of stairs to prevent falls or in doorways to keep babies confined to one area. Safe, modern gates typically have a straight top edge and rigid bars or mesh screens. There are two main types: mounted gates and pressure gates.

Mounted gates are secured to the doorframe or walls. They have locks that parents can open but young children typically cannot, so the gate can be swung open and closed. The safest kind opens toward you rather than out over the stairs.

A pressure gate is held in place across an opening by a pressure mechanism and can be installed and moved quickly and easily.

For more information on buying and using baby gates, see Chapter 8, "Kids Don't Bounce: Preventing Falls."

Toy Chests

We include toy chests here because they need an important safety device: a support that holds the hinged lid open. Otherwise, the lid could fall on your child's head or neck. A few children have died in toy chests because they climbed in to hide or sleep and then suffocated. Ideally, your toy chest should have ventilation holes on the front or sides or a gap between the lid and chest sides to allow for ventilation.

If you are using a chest that wasn't designed for storing toys, either remove the lid or install a lid support device that you can buy in hardware stores. Add vent holes by pounding in and then retracting a large nail. Don't buy a chest that latches, because your child could become trapped inside.

An easy and safe alternative to using a toy chest is to store toys on low shelves or in plastic baskets or bins.

The Least You Need to Know

➤ To be on the safe side, look for the Juvenile Products Manufacturers Association certification seal when you shop for children's products.

➤ Check with the Consumer Product Safety Commission to find out if products you are using have been recalled.

➤ Follow manufacturers' instructions, and don't take chances—always use safety devices such as restraint straps.

➤ Most infant seats cannot be used for car seats.

➤ No matter how safe the product, there is no substitute for careful supervision.

Chapter 4

Home for the Holidays: Winter and Summer

In This Chapter

➤ Decorating safely for the winter holidays

➤ Shopping for toys

➤ Having a happier Halloween

➤ Cautions about Fourth of July fireworks

➤ Safe fun in the summertime

Holidays and other special times of the year pose their own potential dangers to children. No one wants such traditionally happy days to be marred by mishaps, and the chances of that happening can be reduced by using the safety tips in this chapter. Let the good times roll!

Christmas Cautions and Other Holiday Tales

Whatever you celebrate—Christmas, Hanukkah, Kwanzaa—your winter holiday festivities will probably include some decorations. It's easy to get focused on the beauty and overlook the hazards. The National Fire Protection Association, a nonprofit safety group, says candles, for example, cause an average of 6,700 home fires a year, and Christmas trees cause another 600 blazes annually. Here's how to decorate safely.

Gadget Guide

A safer alternative to flame candles are artificial candles that either plug into an outlet or run on batteries.

Candle, Candle, Burning Bright

If you use candles for your holiday celebrations, put them in non-tip holders before lighting them, and then place them out of reach of children and away from curtains, Christmas trees, or other flammables. Don't forget to put all candles out before you go to bed.

Don't leave children unattended in a room with burning candles. If your family lights a menorah, keep it well out of reach of young children while it's burning. Be sure to keep matches and lighters out of reach, too.

Lights

Many families would find holidays dull without decorative lights. Holiday lights can be safe as well as festive if you:

➤ Use lights and extension cords that carry the label of an independent testing laboratory such as UL (Underwriters Laboratories).

➤ Inspect your lighted decorations each year for exposed or frayed wires, loose connections, and broken sockets.

➤ Keep cords out of small children's reach.

➤ Don't run cords under carpets.

➤ Don't overload extension cords.

Safety Savvy

We cannot stress enough the importance of having working smoke alarms installed in your home and practicing an escape plan in case of fire. For details, see Chapter 6, "Too Hot to Handle: Fire and Burns."

➤ Make sure your outdoor lights are labeled specifically for outdoor use. Indoor lights shouldn't be used outside.

➤ Don't leave outdoor lights up for long periods after the holidays are over; they can become damaged by harsh weather. (And your neighbors will think you're weird, too!)

Christmas Trees

If you buy a fresh tree (not an artificial one), look for one that is still soft and supple. Needles that are brittle and fall off when you brush over them means the tree is already drying out, and is a fire hazard. When you bring the tree home, cut off a small slice from the bottom of the trunk, and put the tree into water immediately. Check the water level daily, and keep the container full. If you use evergreen garlands to decorate your home, mist them using a spray bottle of water to keep them moist.

Here are some more Christmas tree basics:

➤ Use a wide, sturdy stand or tether your tree from a hook in the ceiling so the tree can't fall over.

➤ Don't put the tree close to heat sources such as fireplaces, radiators, or furnace registers.

➤ Pine needles can be swallowed or breathed in by a baby or toddler. Sweep them up often.

➤ When you decorate the tree, keep lights, tinsel, breakable ornaments, and ornaments with small parts off the lower branches where they can be grabbed by a young child.

➤ Don't leave the lights on when you're not at home or when you'll be out of the room for an extended period.

➤ If you buy an artificial tree, make sure it's labeled "fire retardant."

The Myth of the Deadly Poinsettia

Poinsettias have gotten a bad rap—they aren't deadly to children. They can, however, cause mouth irritation if kids chew or swallow them. Eating mistletoe or holly berries can cause nausea, vomiting, or diarrhea. Keep these plants out of reach, and watch for berries that fall onto the floor.

Tales from the Safety Zone

The Pittsburgh Poison Control Center surveyed 68 such centers nationwide to see how deadly holiday plants could be. Reporting on the study, *USA Today* said no child died from chewing or eating leaves or berries from poinsettias, holly, and mistletoe. Even illnesses were rare. Effects ranged from skin irritations to upset stomachs.

Teach your kids never to eat anything without checking with you first. For more information on plants that are especially hazardous, see Chapter 7, "You Put *What* in Your Mouth?: Poison Prevention."

Holiday Cookies

What, you say, could be wrong with cookies? It's not the cookies themselves that are dangerous. Just don't let young children get hold of the raw ingredients that go into those cookies. A swig of flavoring such as vanilla or almond extract can be harmful due to the high alcohol content. Don't let kids eat dough with raw eggs, either, because of the risk of salmonella.

Fake Snow

It's best not to use artificial snow and sprays around young children. These substances can cause irritation to lungs, eyes, and nose.

Gift Wrap

Discard wrappings after gifts are opened. Ribbons can choke or strangle a small child. Teethers might be tempted to put shiny foil and colored wrapping paper in their mouths, and they may contain lead.

Balloons

Balloons kill more kids than any plaything except bicycles and other riding toys, according to the *Journal of the American Medical Association*. This doesn't mean you can't include them in party decorations; just exercise caution.

Federal law requires that balloons carry labels warning that they pose an asphyxiation hazard to children under the age of 8. The risk is approximately twice as high for kids 3 years of age and older as for those younger. Supervise your kids when they blow up balloons and dispose of the pieces right away when one bursts, especially if you have a baby or toddler who might put a stray piece in his mouth.

Party Hardy—but Carefully

Kids like a good party as much as adults. If they're invited along with you, by all means take them, but supervise them closely. Here are some things to watch out for:

➤ Keep an eye out for bowls of peanuts, hard candies, or popcorn. These can choke a young child. So can toothpicks in party food.

➤ Young kids have been known to sip left-over alcoholic drinks. As little as one or two ounces can slow a small child's breathing and lead to unconsciousness.

➤ People you visit may not be as conscious as you are about small items that can choke children under age 3. Be especially alert in homes with older children who may have toys with small parts.

To Grandma's House We Go

If you'll be traveling over the holidays to visit relatives, remember that their homes probably won't have gone through the same hazard reduction process that yours has. And you can hardly expect others to turn their houses upside-down and invest in child-safety devices for your occasional visit.

Supervision is critical to keeping your kids out of trouble. The good thing is that there will be more adults around to do that. Just make sure someone takes the lead. Kids have been hurt because each adult thought someone else was watching the baby.

Safety Savvy

If you're the one hosting the get-together and your guest list includes children, forget lighted candles or a fire in the fireplace. They may add atmosphere, but you'll be worrying all night about small kids getting jostled in a crowd of big people and possibly getting burned.

Safety Savvy

On a holiday trip, take along a bottle of syrup of ipecac (sold at pharmacies without a prescription), and find the number for the local poison control center when you reach your destination just in case you need it. Do not administer the syrup of ipecac unless instructed to do so by the poison center, as its use is only appropriate in some cases.

Watch Out!

Find out if your relatives use patches that dispense medications through the skin. If a patch is discarded in a waste basket where a toddler can find and chew it, there could be enough medicine left in it to be dangerous.

Watch Out!

Let the labels on toys be your guide. They take into account not only a child's cognitive skills but his ability to handle the toy safely as well. When the label says, "Not recommended for children under 3," it's not because the manufacturer thinks the item might be too tough for your 30-month-old to figure out but because the toy is small (or has small parts) and poses a choking hazard.

Be especially cautious about medications in the homes of older relatives and friends. The Consumer Product Safety Commission (CPSC) reports that approximately 20 percent of children who are poisoned by pharmaceuticals ingested a grandparent's medicine.

Seniors often get their prescriptions in bottles that don't have child-resistant caps. Medicines for such ailments as high blood pressure, heart trouble, and diabetes can be dangerous to kids even in very small doses. Child-*resistant* bottles are not child*proof,* so make sure all medicines are stored out of reach, including those that may be in Grandma's purse. The same advice applies when grandparents or friends visit you.

For advice on safe car and airplane travel, see Chapters 11, "Use Some (Car) Restraint," and 22, "Travels with My Children."

Toy Shopping

Gift-giving is half the fun of the holidays, but it can be a big challenge when you hit the stores and are confronted with some of the 2.6 billion toys and games sold in the United States each year!

There are three key rules when it comes to toy safety:

➤ Buy toys that are appropriate for your child's age.

➤ Make sure the toys are used properly.

➤ Supervise the kids—and join in the play sometimes.

If you've got older children of your own, they probably have toys that pose choking and other dangers for a younger sibling. Store such toys separately; don't leave them accessible to little ones.

Here are some other toy safety tips:

➤ Don't give babies toys with strings or cords longer than seven inches (because of the strangulation danger) or stuffed animals with button eyes that can come off and be swallowed.

➤ Check seams of stuffed toys regularly to make sure the insides aren't falling out. Some kids will eat anything!

➤ Loud toys can damage a child's sensitive hearing. Hold a noisy toy next to your ear so you can judge if it's too loud for your little one.

➤ Discard plastic wrappings immediately because they can suffocate a young child.

➤ Avoid toys that shoot darts and other projectiles that can hurt eyes.

➤ Look for non-toxic art supplies.

➤ Toys with a heating element—powered either with a battery or electrical plug—are not appropriate for children under age 8.

➤ Children under 8 should not have toys with sharp edges or sharp parts.

➤ Chemistry sets are best for children 12 or older, and even then they require some adult supervision.

Gadget Guide

Batteries are not only toxic, but the small ones are a choking hazard as well. Don't allow children to change batteries, and check battery-operated toys regularly in case wires have become loose or exposed.

Halloween Scares

When you think of Halloween safety hazards, contaminated candy may be the first thing that comes to mind. Of course you should check everything that comes home in that treat bag, but pedestrian injuries, burns, and falls may be more likely to occur.

Street Smarts

A Centers for Disease Control and Prevention study says children 14 and under are four times more likely to be hit by a car on Halloween than on any other night of the year. It's understandable. Kids who would normally be more careful get distracted by their friends or excited by the trick-or-treating. Careless street crossing coupled with drivers' more limited vision at night can make for a deadly mix.

Safety Savvy

Just as you wouldn't give your child a battery-run toy without providing batteries, you shouldn't give him recreation equipment such as a bicycle or in-line skates without the proper safety equipment. Wrap up a helmet, knee pads, or whatever is called for as a separate present. It could be the most valuable gift you give him.

Gadget Guide

Help drivers see your little one. Put reflective tape or stickers on kids' costumes, shoes, or treat bags. You also can have them carry flashlights. That not only helps them be seen but see better, too, so they're less likely to trip and fall.

Gadget Guide

A safer alternative to candles is to use flashlights in pumpkins. They can even be used at parties instead of candles for spooky lighting effects.

In general, children under the age of 10 should be accompanied by an adult or a responsible older sibling on their Halloween rounds. For older kids, you'll have to decide how mature they are and how safe your neighborhood is before deciding when it's okay to let them go without an adult. In any event, they shouldn't go off on their own, but always with a friend or friends.

Don't wait until the big night, when their attention span is short, to remind them not to dart into the street between parked cars, not to cross mid-block, and to look left, right, and left again before crossing at a corner. For a review of pedestrian safety skills, see Chapter 12, "Where the Sidewalk Ends: Pedestrian Safety."

Here are other Halloween trick-or-treat tips from the National SAFE KIDS Campaign:

➤ If your kids are going out without an adult, set a time for them to return home.

➤ Make sure they have change so they can call you from a pay phone if they have a problem.

➤ Restrict their visits to homes with porch or other outside lights illuminated.

➤ Instruct the kids to travel only in familiar areas and along a pre-established route.

➤ Tell them never to enter a home or an apartment building unless accompanied by an adult you approve.

Fires

Halloween costumes can catch fire. It sometimes happens when children trip into jack-o'-lanterns or luminaries. Candles used as decorations at Halloween parties are a hazard, too, especially when put too close to crepe paper or in a place where they are knocked over easily.

If you use a candle in your jack-o'-lantern, place it away from where children will be walking. Remind your kids to steer clear of jack-o'-lanterns that may not be as strategically placed at neighbors' homes.

The National Fire Protection Association suggests these additional tips:

➤ Purchase only those costumes, wigs, and props labeled "flame resistant" or "flame retardant."

➤ When creating a costume, avoid highly flammable fabrics and accessories.

➤ Don't make costumes with billowing or long trailing features.

➤ Be sure your child knows the "stop, drop, and roll" technique if his clothing catches fire (see the accompanying Safety Savvy).

Safety Savvy

Teach your kids the phrase "stop, drop, and roll." Then have them pretend to put out the flames by stopping immediately, dropping to the ground, covering their faces with their hands (so their faces won't be burned and smoke won't go into their lungs), and rolling over and over to put out the fire.

Candy Is Dandy, But ...

Although the incidents of contaminated candy have been few, it's best to be on the safe side. Have your child bring home the candy for inspection before eating it. Check that the wrappers are intact. If he's been given fruit, check the skin for punctures, then wash it well and cut it open before he eats it.

Tales from the Safety Zone

Trick-or-treating remains a popular tradition despite stories of pins and razors in Halloween candy. But what about kids with conditions such as diabetes or food allergies, for whom treats are dangerous? They still want the fun of showing off their costumes and going house to house with their friends. We know a dad with a diabetic son who pays him a nickel for each piece of candy he collects. Some of his close neighbors who know of the boy's condition give him stickers or small toys instead of sweets. A mother with a daughter who has severe food allergies goes to her neighbors prior to Halloween night and distributes safe treats that they can give her child.

Falls

Costumes that drag the ground can trip kids up. Masks contribute to falls, too, because they limit how much a child can see, especially in the dark. Young kids often balk at wearing masks anyway, so consider face-paint as a safer alternative. If your child insists on a mask, cut the eye holes large for better visibility.

Additional tips for a really Happy Halloween:

➤ Secure hats so they don't slip over your children's eyes.

➤ If your children carry props such as swords or knives, make sure they're made of flexible material so they won't cause injury during a fall.

➤ Warn your kids not to cut across yards, which can conceal hazards in the dark such as clotheslines or lawn ornaments.

➤ Adult shoes may look cute with a kids' costume, but they also can cause a tumble. Stick to shoes that fit, preferably with non-skid soles.

Fourth of July Fun

One of the best parts of July 4th celebrations is the fireworks. The safest way to enjoy them is watching at a community celebration where professionals set off the display.

Do-it-yourself displays in the backyard are dangerous. Of the thousands of fireworks-related injuries suffered by Americans each year, more than half are to children. The 10-to-14 age group suffer more injuries more than any other, according to the National SAFE KIDS Campaign. Sparklers, which many people consider the safest kind of fireworks, are most frequently associated with injuries to children 4 and under.

The National SAFE KIDS Campaign offers these recommendations for backyard fireworks for families who insist on doing it themselves:

➤ Only adults should handle fireworks. Tell your kids to leave if their friends use them without an adult to supervise.

➤ Read labels and follow directions.

➤ Have spectators stand out of range before lighting them, and light them on a smooth, flat surface away from the house, dry leaves, or flammable liquids.

➤ Never light them indoors.

➤ Never try to re-ignite fireworks that malfunction.

➤ Keep a bucket of water handy.

Watch Out!

A few states have banned all types of consumer fireworks because of the numerous eye, finger, and hand injuries they've caused, but a majority of states allow certain types. Some local jurisdictions have their own regulations, so make sure you know what the rules are where you live before you purchase fireworks. Never use homemade fireworks.

Tales from the Safety Zone

Although states make individual decisions on what consumer fireworks they permit, the Consumer Product Safety Commission has banned from all public sale several kinds of large fireworks, as well as mail-order kits for making them at home. CPSC also set a federal standard in 1997 to eliminate the tip-over danger in large multiple-tube fireworks; manufacturers now must use a safer base design.

From Memorial Day to Labor Day

When the last school bell rings and the kids pour out for summer vacation, the only thought on their minds is having fun. You can encourage them to have *safe* fun. Here are some items to put on your checklist to review before summer starts.

Fun in the Sun

Stock up on sunscreen because that's one of the most important protective products for babies and older children alike. Remember that sun exposure in childhood and adolescence contributes to skin cancer, and sunburns make children mighty uncomfortable. In general, children's skin is thinner and therefore more sensitive than an adult's. For information on what types of sunscreen to use, see Chapter 23, "The Great Outdoors."

Playgrounds

Your young kids probably will spend a lot of happy summer hours either on your backyard play equipment or at public playgrounds. As soon as the weather turns warm, check out your swing set or climbing frame and surface for any needed maintenance. Watch for the same thing in your local park, and notify park officials if you spot any unsafe conditions. See Chapter 14, "Life's a Playground," for details on playground safety.

Water Fun

Don't put off signing up your kids for swimming lessons. Even if your child has had lessons, strict supervision is a must. If you take the kids boating, make sure they wear personal floatation devices (and all adults, too). For more information on water safety, see Chapter 15, "On the Waterfront."

Biking, Skateboarding, In-Line Skating

As soon as a child takes to wheels, he enters into a thrilling—and risky—dimension. Helmets are essential. For in-line skating, other safety gear is recommended as well. See Chapter 16, "Wheels and Blades: Recreation Safety," for all the scoop.

Safety Savvy

How old should a youngster be to mow the lawn? The American Academy of Pediatrics recommends children be at least 12 to use a walk-behind power mower and 14 for a ride-on. Even then, consider how responsible your child is and whether she's likely to follow safety rules. Also think about the yard's terrain and if there are steep slopes requiring extra strength.

Gadget Guide

If you've got a small yard, consider using a manual push mower instead of a power mower. It's safer, quieter, less polluting, and provides more exercise.

Lawn Mowers

Cutting the grass is an essential summer activity. Every year, approximately 10,000 kids ages 14 and under are injured by power mowers, either the walk-behind kind or ride-ons. Both the users of mowers and kids who are just in the vicinity can be hurt.

Injuries include eye lacerations from flying stones, and deep cuts or loss of fingers and toes from the blades. Parents can't hear over the sound of the engine, so they don't always realize when kids come too close. Some children have been hurt when they fell from a parent's lap while on a riding mower. Kids should never be lawn mower passengers!

Here are some lawn mower safety tips from the American Academy of Pediatrics:

➤ Buy a power mower that has a "dead man" control so the mower stops if you let go of the handle.

➤ Before mowing, pick up or rake away small objects such as rocks or toys, which could become flying objects.

➤ When you mow, keep children out of the area to protect them from flying objects. Keep them away from the gas can or electric cord as well.

➤ Wear sturdy shoes—not sandals, sneakers, or bare feet—when mowing, and also wear sunglasses, glasses, or goggles.

➤ Only an adult should change the blade setting or dislodge debris and only when the mower is off.

The Least You Need to Know

➤ Prevent fires by decorating safely for winter holidays.

➤ When buying toys, follow ages recommended on the labels.

➤ Keep Halloween happy with simple costumes, treat bag inspections, and pedestrian safety rules.

➤ Families should attend organized fireworks events rather than light their own.

➤ Inspect play equipment before summer vacation arrives.

➤ Sunscreen is a must for young, sensitive skin.

➤ Bikes, skates, and skateboards are "serious" playthings that call for proper care and safety accessories.

➤ When handling lawn mowers, use eye protection and good common sense.

Bump!

Chapter 5

What Was That Noise?: Kids Home Alone

In This Chapter

➤ How old is old enough?

➤ Preparing your child for self-care

➤ Setting house rules

➤ Supervising from a distance

➤ Enlisting help from other adults

➤ Monitoring how it's going

Eventually, every parent has to face the question: Is my child old enough to be left "home alone"? Any one who's seen the movie by that name has an exaggerated picture of what kids can get into when there's no adult around. The movie parents accidentally leave behind their 8-year-old son when they depart for a trip—and he spends his time gorging on junk food, watching videos, and fending off two very persistent would-be burglars.

Of course the movie is fiction, but being home alone can mean bad news if you haven't thought through this decision carefully and then prepared your child for it. The up side is that kids who care for themselves successfully gain confidence and independence.

In most families, the subject comes up gradually. First, you leave your child for a few minutes to go next door. Then maybe your absence stretches to an hour while you run a couple of errands. But when can you safely go out on Saturday night without having to hire a baby-sitter?

The questions keep getting harder. An evening is one thing, but if you work outside the home you eventually face the big one: When can I regularly leave my child home alone before or after school? As with many other child-rearing dilemmas, the answer is: It depends. In this chapter, we'll help you decide when your child is ready to be home alone and what steps to take to ensure his safety when he is.

Ready or Not

Let's start with a benchmark used by many child development experts: Kids usually aren't mature enough to stay home unsupervised for long periods of time until the age of 11 or 12. This is not an iron-clad rule. Some 10-year-olds are very mature and some 15-year-olds aren't. The heart of the matter is how well your child will handle the responsibilities of caring for himself and staying safe. If there's a fire, for example, will he leave the house immediately, or will he run around inside trying to save the cat? Would he panic if he sliced his finger on a kitchen knife or eyed a stranger on the front porch?

Another issue is how long the child will be on his own. Some children are quite content to be alone for a couple of hours, but become lonely during longer stretches. Will it be dark when you arrive home during the winter, and will that make him—or you—nervous?

Self-Care Readiness Quiz

Answer Yes or No to the Following	
1. Will your child follow the rules you set?	_____
2. Does he usually use good judgment?	_____
3. Has he handled himself well when left for brief periods of time in the past?	_____
4. Is he able to manage simple chores such as taking phone messages or fixing himself a snack?	_____
5. Does he have the self-discipline to complete his homework without adult supervision?	_____
6. Does he follow directions well?	_____
7. Is he good at problem-solving or does he leave that up to you?	_____
8. Does he cope well when unexpected situations arise?	_____
9. Is he expressing interest in staying home alone after school?	_____

If you answered "yes" to most of these questions, that's a good indication your child would be responsible and mature enough to stay home alone. But, your child's maturity isn't the only consideration. You also have to decide whether your neighborhood is safe. It's not just a question of crime statistics, but whether there are any close neighbors at home during the day that your child could turn to if he needed help.

Finally, how do you feel about it? If you're going to worry so much or feel so guilty that you have trouble remaining productive at work, it's probably better to postpone self-care for a while.

Caring for Siblings

It's alarming how many kids ages 10, 11, or even younger are caring not only for themselves but also for younger siblings. A child who stays by himself may not yet be ready for the additional responsibility of caring for others. It's one thing to get himself out if there's a fire, but quite another to help a little sister escape, too.

Watch Out!

Some communities have laws governing how old a child must be if left home alone. Sometimes, the age limits differ depending on whether the child is alone in daytime or at night. Some laws cover the minimum age a child must be to be left in charge of other children. Contact your local law enforcement agency or child welfare department to see whether your community has such laws.

Even if your older child occasionally baby-sits for you, he may resent the burden of supervising a sibling every day after school, especially if it limits his after-school activities. Don't put your child in that position. Wait until the younger sibling is old enough to care for herself before letting them stay home alone together.

Self-Care Boot Camp

If you've decided to go forward with self-care, you'll need to give your child some basic training. Take a tour of your house together. Make sure your child can lock and unlock the doors and windows. If he's allowed to operate certain appliances, make sure he knows how. The same goes for adjusting the temperature on the thermostat.

Put a first-aid kit in a handy location such as the kitchen and teach him some basics: how to stop bleeding from a cut and deal with a minor burn, for example. The kitchen also is a good place to keep a flashlight, batteries, and battery-powered radio in case there is a power outage due to a storm. Tell him not to light candles. Teach him where to go if the storm becomes severe: maybe it's the basement or on the ground floor under a piece of sturdy furniture.

Make sure your child knows how to call 911. Post your work numbers and those of neighbors he could call for help. Write your home address and phone number on the list, too, so he won't forget them in a moment of panic. Make sure he always has

Gadget Guide

A keypad door lock eliminates the hassle of keeping track of keys. Then the only question is whether your child can remember which numbers to push!

Safety Savvy

The start of self-care is a good time to do another home safety survey. Check each room and your yard for hazards you might not have noticed before—anything from frayed appliance cords and loose area rugs to broken glass in the back storm door. It's bad enough when a child gets hurt, but worse when he has to cope with an injury alone.

change so he can call you from a pay phone in a pinch, such as if he's locked out and can't find a neighbor.

Leave a spare set of keys with more than one neighbor in case he loses his. Don't hide one outside your house—burglars know all the places to look! And don't put your name or address on your child's key or key chain. This makes it easier for a person who finds it to break into your home. Have him wear the key on a chain around his neck or on a chain threaded through his belt loop. Tell him to keep it hidden under his shirt or in his pants pocket.

Fires: How to Get out Alive

Go over what your child should do in case of a fire. Have a fire drill and practice different escape routes. If you live in a house with a second story, it's a good idea to have a rope ladder in case a fire should block the stairway. If you live in an apartment building, remind your child that in case of fire he should exit by the stairs and not in the elevator.

Stress that if there's a fire, he should leave the house immediately, and go to a neighbor to call for help. The same rule applies if he smells gas. Unless a fire is very minor, such as in a pot on the stove that can easily be smothered with a lid, your child should not try to put it out himself.

Cooking food left unattended is a major cause of house fires. For that reason you might be wise to prohibit your child from using the stove, at least initially. Since microwaves do not have open flames and they shut off automatically, this is a somewhat safer cooking alternative as long as your child has been well trained in its proper use, especially the rule about not putting metal utensils in it.

Space heaters are another high-risk appliance and should not be used by children in self-care.

Teach him to stop, drop, and roll on the ground to put out the flames if his clothes should catch on fire. If rooms are smoky, he should crawl on his hands and knees to escape. If he's behind a closed door, he should feel it to see if it's hot before opening it. For more tips on getting out during a fire, see Chapter 6, "Too Hot to Handle: Fire and Burns."

Caution in the Kitchen

A session on kitchen safety is a must for kids who will be making their own snacks and who might eventually progress to starting dinner before you get home. Here are some of the things your child should know:

Gadget Guide

Fire extinguishers can be difficult for a child to use and any delay during a fire could be dangerous. Teach him to leave the house instead of playing firefighter. Kitchens can be replaced; kids can't.

➤ Keep handles on pots on the stove turned to the inside.

➤ Avoid wearing loose clothing—especially big sleeves—around the stove.

➤ Use a wooden spoon to stir hot foods instead of a metal one which can become hot.

➤ Point knife blades down and away from you, never toward your fingers.

➤ When using a vegetable peeler, scrape away from the body.

➤ To take something out of the oven, use oven mitts or pot holders to pull the rack out first, and then lift the dish.

➤ To avoid falls, clean up spills on the floor immediately.

➤ Concentrate when you cook. Don't get distracted while cutting with a knife or wander off to watch TV when something is cooking on the stove.

If your child will be using a microwave oven, it's safest if the oven is placed no higher than his eye level. Ovens installed higher, such as above the stove top, make it easy for kids to spill hot foods on themselves when they are lifting from overhead. Also, remind your child to be careful when removing dish covers or opening popcorn popped in bags because hot steam can escape and burn him. Tell him to use oven mitts and open hot dishes away from his face.

Gadget Guide

A sharp knife actually is safer than a dull one, which might cause your child to struggle harder when he's cutting something. A safer alternative is kitchen scissors, which work for soft cutting jobs—everything from pizza to canned tomatoes. Don't let your child use sharp knives when you aren't home unless he has had a lot of experience using them safely.

Avoiding Strangers

It's probably a common occurrence for strangers to phone your house or knock on your door. Usually none of them means any harm, but a child home alone cannot take chances.

While she's in the house, your child should keep the doors and windows locked. It's a good idea to

Gadget Guide

A peephole in the front door lets your child see who is outside without having to unlock the door. If you don't have a peephole (and there's not a curtained window near the front door that serves the same purpose) consider installing one.

Safety Savvy

If you don't already own a dog, now might be the time to think about getting one. Some kids in self-care like the company of a pet, and dogs also provide an extra measure of protection against intruders.

keep ground floor curtains closed, too, so strangers can't peer inside. If someone knocks, your child should find out who it is and only open the door if it's someone she knows.

If a stranger comes to the door, your child should not let that person in under any circumstances. Some kids have trouble following this rule because they're tempted to trust their instincts instead.

For example, if a delivery person says he has a package for the child's father and she must sign for it, she might think that's safe, but it's safer to tell the stranger that her dad can't come to the door right now and to come back later. If a stranger says she needs to use the phone because there's been an accident, a child's natural inclination is to be helpful. Instead, she should summon a neighbor by phone, or place a 911 call for the stranger instead of letting her inside.

Tell your child that if she doesn't recognize the person at the door, she has the option of simply not answering it or talking through the door.

Don't schedule deliveries or repair people to come to your home when you aren't there. It's too much responsibility for a child, and it means they have to break the rule about not letting in strangers.

Phone calls are tricky, too. Some kids feel they are lying when they say "My parents can't come to the phone right now" when the parents aren't at home. Assure them that the statement is literally true. They can offer to take a message and tell the caller that the parents will return the call soon. They also shouldn't give out personal information on the phone, such as their names. Some children avoid the problem of answering calls from strangers by screening callers with an answering machine or with a caller ID feature on the phone.

If the unthinkable happens, and your child hears someone trying to break into your home, she should escape out another door and run for help. If escape isn't possible, the next option is for her to lock herself in a room, preferably with a phone, and dial 911. If possible, she should stay on the phone until help arrives; if not, she should still leave the phone off the hook after calling 911 because the emergency operator may be able to trace the call and send police to the right address.

Since situations involving strangers are many and varied, it's a good idea to do some role-playing with your child. Practice phone calls in which you try to get information from her and she learns how to respond. Do the same with visitors at the door. Your child will be more confident if she has practiced what to say.

If your child walks home from school, she also should be well versed in avoiding stranger danger on the street. For more information on this and other aspects of personal safety, see Chapter 25, "It's My Body: Personal Safety."

The House Rules

Work with your child to draw up a list of your family's house rules. For example, you might decide that she:

➤ Must call you to check in as soon as she arrives home.

➤ Can use the microwave but not the stove. (Pans left on a burner can catch fire if she wanders off and forgets.)

➤ Has to do her homework before she can watch TV.

➤ Can't get on the Internet so you can keep the phone line open to check in periodically.

➤ Must have your permission before she goes to play at a friend's house.

➤ May not have friends visit when she's home alone.

Kids react better to rules if they understand what's behind them, so explain why each rule is important. Review the list periodically; some of the rules may change over time as you see that your child is handling herself responsibly and safely.

Watch Out!

Caution your child that, if she sees a door or window ajar when she comes home, she must not enter the house because an intruder could be inside. Instead, she should go to a neighbor's house and call the police. She also should be alert to strange people or vehicles parked near your home and tell you or another trusted adult if she sees something suspicious.

Safety Savvy

We recommend putting the rules in the form of a contract that you and your child both sign. Post it on the refrigerator (that's the first place he'll head when he comes home!) as a reminder.

Supervising from a Distance

Out of sight, out of mind is not the image you want to project to your home-aloner. You still need to be in touch by phone, and if you can't be, it's important to arrange for a stand-in.

Gadget Guide

Your child will have more peace of mind if you carry a cellular phone or beeper so she can reach you easily. You might also want to install a second home phone line or get call waiting in case your child frequently ties up the line chatting with friends when you're trying to check in.

Safety Savvy

Some Boys and Girls Clubs, Scout troops, and recreation centers teach kids home alone safety. Check if any organizations in your community offer self-care classes and encourage your child to enroll. It's often more fun to learn alongside other kids.

There should be a daily check-in call from your child when she gets home, for two reasons. First, it gives the child incentive to come home promptly. Second, it lets her know you care even when you aren't with her.

If you aren't going to be near a phone during the after-school hours, perhaps you could arrange for a colleague, a relative or a neighbor to take your child's check-in call and be available if she needs to call back later to ask a question or get help.

Keep Adults in the Picture

Even if you can't be there, your child doesn't have to be home alone every day. Especially if the hours between her arrival and yours are long, find some situations where she will be around other adults—at least for some of the time.

Look at after-school activities—sports or art classes, for example—to occupy her some afternoons each week. For ideas, check your child's school, the YMCA/YWCA, or community recreation center. If transportation is a problem, see if you can trade car-pooling with a parent who's available in the afternoon in exchange for some service you could offer evenings or weekends.

Just as you arranged play dates when your child was younger, you can schedule some now in the homes of her friends where there is an adult present. Reciprocate by including those kids in your family's activities on weekends.

Maybe you could find an at-home mother in the neighborhood who'd pay for your child to entertain her younger kids once or twice a week while she's busy with household chores. Or look in your neighborhood for a senior citizen who'd enjoy a child's company.

Arrange for your child to stop by on her way home from school, have a snack and visit the neighbor. She can feel happy about doing a good deed and not even realize she's getting something out of it, too.

There might be some volunteer work she could do, too. Maybe she could spend one afternoon helping the staff at her former after-school child-care program, or she might enjoy shelving books for the school librarian.

Tales from the Safety Zone

Some communities have telephone services that link volunteers with home-alone kids who want someone to talk to or need help with homework. The Girl Scouts started a program that matches elderly or homebound adults with home-alone Scouts to keep each other company. The adults will alert a Scout's parents if she fails to make her scheduled call.

Keep Monitoring the Situation

It's a good idea to start self-care gradually. Let your child come home after school one or two afternoons a week to begin with to help both you and her assess her readiness. Even after she starts self-care on a regular basis, continue to monitor the situation. Talk to her about how it's going so you can see if she's having second thoughts or has particular concerns.

Let close friends in the neighborhood know your child is regularly going to be home alone and tell them what rules you've set. If you have decided not to let your child have guests when you're not home, for example, your friends can alert you if they notice that the rules are being broken.

If your child shows responsibility and practices good safety habits, you can gradually extend more freedoms to her.

Tales from the Safety Zone

Many years before the movie *Home Alone*, Dr. Seuss took up the subject in perhaps his most famous book, *The Cat in the Hat*. In case you need a refresher, two bored kids, home alone on a rainy day, let the cat come inside against the warnings of their pet goldfish. The cat dazzles the kids with his bag of tricks but also creates all manner of chaos. Just as Mom is about to return, the cat puts everything right and disappears, leaving the kids with that age-old dilemma: Should we tell Mom what happened? For an interesting dinner table conversation, ask your kids what they would have done in that situation.

The Least You Need to Know

➤ Carefully assess your child's maturity as well as the safety of your neighborhood before allowing self-care.

➤ Teach your child how to handle emergencies, as well as strangers on the phone and at the door.

➤ Keep in touch with your child regularly by phone.

➤ Have a back-up plan if your child can't reach you.

➤ Check your house for hazards and provide safety equipment such as a first-aid kit.

Part 2

The Most Common Injuries

Some of the most frequent causes of serious harm to children are fires, poisoning, falls, choking/suffocation, and firearms. There's a chapter in this part on each of these subjects to help you understand the ways kids encounter these dangers and how they might react, depending on their stage of development. We give you information on the latest prevention measures and safety devices as well as what lessons to teach your children.

Chapter 6

Too Hot to Handle: Fire and Burns

In This Chapter

➤ Fire risks change as children grow

➤ Choosing and using smoke alarms

➤ Devising an escape plan

➤ Teaching kids to respect fire

➤ Preventing home fires

Most of us learned as children the Smokey Bear mantra that "Only you can prevent forest fires." Of course, it's not just forest fires we've got to prevent, and now as adults we've got to protect our children from becoming fire victims.

Although there's been a dramatic decline in the fire death rate in the last decade, fires and burns remain the third leading cause of unintentional injury deaths among kids in the United States. According to the National SAFE KIDS Campaign, each year, more than 800 children ages 14 and under are killed in residential fires, and 60 percent of them are 4 and under. The youngest kids are the least able to understand the danger— and the least able to react to it.

Because children's skin is thinner, it will burn at lower temperatures than an adult's, and children's faster metabolic rates make them less able to withstand the effects of smoke. (It's estimated that up to three fourths of fire-related deaths are from smoke inhalation.)

Burns aren't caused only by fire. Kids who come in contact with hot objects, hot liquids, steam, or electricity can suffer serious burns, too.

There is much we can do to eliminate fire and burn hazards. Should a fire occur, we must be prepared to get our families out of a burning home without injury. Finally, we need to teach these lessons to our children throughout their growing-up years.

Tales from the Safety Zone

The National SAFE KIDS Campaign is one of the groups working hard to prevent burns and other injuries to children. The group's 275 state and local coalitions are in every state, the District of Columbia, and Puerto Rico. Each coalition is comprised of organizations and individuals who work to prevent injuries to children, such as hospitals, fire and police departments, health departments, government officials, schools, and parents. Coalitions have distributed smoke alarms, worked to pass laws requiring them, and provided educational programs and materials. To find out if there is a coalition near you, call 202-662-0600 or check the Web site www.safekids.org, which also contains lots of injury-prevention information.

Safety Savvy

In an emergency, a pre-schooler could be frightened by a firefighter dressed in heavy equipment. Take your child and her friends on a tour of your local fire station so they learn what firefighters look like up close and how they help people.

Ages and Stages

Fire safety education can begin early. As soon as your baby is mobile you can start teaching her the words "hot" and "no," while at the same time moving her away from a potential burn hazard. Use that special tone of voice that says "I really mean it." Long before your child can talk, she'll understand what you are saying.

Here are the burn-related dangers to watch for as your children grow:

➤ Somewhere between 4 and 7 months, most babies start to grasp objects and learn to crawl. Things that had been out of reach in the first three months, such as electrical outlets, appliance cords, and hot oven doors, now become objects kids want to explore.

➤ At about 9 months, most babies can pull themselves up, and soon they can stand on their own. Then they can pull a cup of hot coffee onto their heads if it's left on the edge of a table.

➤ Around 12 to 15 months, they start walking, and their speed and skill at getting into things takes another leap. They may drink a hot liquid or open the oven. A 1- to 2-year-old toddler playing with matches is capable of starting a house fire.

Safety Savvy

Each developmental milestone is a signal to you that it's time to update your home safety inspection and eliminate any new safety hazards.

➤ Pre-schoolers, ages 3 to 5, like to imitate adults. They may want to try using a curling iron, the barbecue grill, or the toaster oven.

➤ Older children find fire fascinating, which can lead to dangerous experimentation with matches, lighters, fireworks, or candles.

Smoke Alarms—Gotta Have 'Em!

Your chances of dying in a fire are cut in half if you have a working smoke alarm.

The majority of states require smoke alarms to be used in both new and existing homes, and more than 90 percent of homes have at least one. The early warnings these devices provide are a big reason why the nation's fire fatality rate has been dropping.

Unfortunately, many homes have alarms that aren't in working order, and the danger here is clear: Approximately 90 percent of child fire deaths occur in homes without working smoke alarms.

Some homes don't have enough smoke alarms or don't have them located properly. Smoke alarms should be on every level of your home and near the bedrooms—they have to be close enough to wake you in case a fire breaks out during the night. They should be installed on the ceiling or on the wall 6 to 12 inches below the ceiling.

If you have an alarm that gives frequent nuisance alarms—such as in the kitchen when you burn the toast or in the bathroom where steam can set it off—don't simply disconnect it. First, clean it according to the manufacturer's recommendations. If it still goes off, move it to a nearby location.

Smoke Alarm Maintenance

Batteries should be changed annually or when a chirping noise indicates the battery power is low. Test your alarms monthly.

Tales from the Safety Zone

Some smoke detector history, courtesy of the National SAFE KIDS Campaign: In the 1920s, a merchant marine pumped air from below the ship's deck into a glass box. If the box turned dark, he knew there was a fire. Today's technology is based on a concept developed in the 1930s by a Swiss doctor who discovered that electricity can't pass through smokey air. His system set off an alarm when the air in a special chamber became smokey. Today's alarms activate when smoke breaks an electrical current or beam of light.

The National Fire Protection Association recommends an alarm be replaced after 10 years even if the monthly tests indicate it is still working. Over that many years, smoke alarms lose sensitivity and eventually fail. A national study found that when they fail, they do so suddenly. Since alarms can be purchased for as little as $8, this is a small price to pay to make sure your alarm will save your life.

Smoke alarms should be kept clean. Accumulated dust, cobwebs, or insects can reduce the alarm's sensitivity. Vacuum them occasionally or follow the manufacturer's cleaning instructions.

Gadget Guide

Along with smoke alarms, every home should have carbon monoxide detectors to alert family members to this odorless, deadly gas that is emitted by poorly maintained furnaces and other fuel-burning appliances. See Chapter 7, "You Put *What* in Your Mouth?: Poison Prevention," for detailed information.

What to Buy

There are two types of alarms: ionization and photoelectric. Ionization alarms are quicker at sensing flaming fires that have little smoke, and photoelectric ones are faster at detecting smoke from a smoldering fire such as one that starts slowly in upholstery. Either type provides adequate protection for homes. To be extra safe, some people buy both kinds or a combination unit. Whatever you buy, it should meet the standards of an independent testing laboratory such as Underwriters Laboratories (UL) and carry that label.

There also are differences in how alarms are powered. Most alarms are battery-operated, but some new homes have alarms that are hardwired into the electrical system. The hardwired ones can also be interconnected so that, if an alarm goes off in one part of the home, the others will sound, too. The national fire alarm code, the recognized industry standard, calls for hardwired and interconnected smoke alarms in newly constructed homes. Hardwired alarms should have battery back-up power so an electrical outage won't render them inoperable.

Tales from the Safety Zone

The tragic story of a Maryland family underscores the importance of having battery back-ups for hardwired smoke alarms and the danger of candles. A storm caused a power outage in their upper middle-class neighborhood. To compensate for the lack of lights, the family lit candles. One candle was inadvertently left burning after the family went to sleep. When the candle started a fire, the smoke alarms didn't work. Two children died.

Fire Extinguishers

It's smart to have fire extinguishers in areas where a fire is most likely to start, such as the kitchen, but it's not enough to just have them handy. You've also got to know how and when to use them properly. They should only be used on small, self-contained fires, such as in a trash can, and only when you've got a clear exit in case the fire spreads fast. The decision about whether to use an extinguisher is complicated and must be made immediately. For these reasons, children should be taught to leave fire extinguisher use to grownups. Teach them to always leave the house if there's a fire of any kind or size and then call for help at a neighbor's house.

The Great Escape

Fire can spread in an instant, so seconds count in getting out of the house safely. Having a good escape plan and rehearsing it saves lives. This is especially crucial for young children who, without advance preparation, may instinctively hide under a bed or in a closet if they haven't been trained to leave the house.

Have a plan to get out of each room of the house and have a back-up plan in case the fire blocks your exit path. Discuss the plans with your children so they understand the importance of escaping the house.

Watch Out!

It's best not to use a fire extinguisher on a grease fire on the stove. Instead, cover the pan with a large lid and turn off the burner. Never throw water on a grease or electrical fire.

Upper-floor bedrooms should have escape ladders. Show older children how to attach them, and tell them to back out of the window to climb down, but don't actually practice this during a drill because of the risk of falling.

Don't just draw your escape plan on paper. Have fire drills like in school. By actually going through the motions, you'll discover whether your child is capable of opening all the windows and doors and thoroughly understands the route.

Gadget Guide

The Home Fire Sprinkler Coalition urges homeowners to install indoor sprinkler systems, especially in new homes. A few communities already mandate sprinklers in new-home construction. They can add 1 to 2 percent to the home's cost but provide excellent protection to people and property in the event of a fire. But you still need smoke alarms, too.

Pick a spot outside your home where family members will gather after escaping a fire. That way everyone can be accounted for quickly. Practice in both daytime and at night since many fires occur while people are sleeping.

Remember to update your escape plan periodically. When your child is old enough to open doors and get out on his own, your family plan will be different than when he was a baby and had to be carried out by a parent. Kids need to practice so they'll remember in an emergency.

Other lessons to teach your children:

➤ Feel a door with the back of your hand before opening it. If it's hot, leave by another route.

➤ Smoke rises, so crawl on hands and knees to get under it.

➤ Never go back into a burning building. Call the fire department from a neighbor's home.

Another important lesson for kids is stop, drop, and roll. Have them practice putting out pretend flames on their clothing by stopping immediately, dropping to the ground, covering their faces with their hands (so the face won't be burned and smoke won't go into the lungs), and rolling over and over to put out the fire.

Playing with Fire

It's normal for children to be interested in fire. They associate it with pleasurable experiences—candles on their birthday cake or the warmth of a fireplace, for example. Kids may be curious enough to light a fire themselves, and that's why teaching them to respect fire is so important. Playing with fire is the leading cause of fire deaths in young children. Most of these fires are started by kids younger than 6.

Conveying the Message

First, model good behavior, and don't treat fire casually. Parents who wouldn't think of leaving a loaded gun on the coffee table might not give a second thought to leaving decorative fireplace matches on the hearth, but they're just as deadly.

Talk to kids about what fires can do, both the positives and the negatives. Explain, for example, that the charcoal grill is a helpful tool but it is only to be used by parents because fire is hard to control.

Get the child's agreement that he'll tell an adult if he finds matches or lighters.

If Your Child Sets a Fire

Some children play with fire because they are curious and don't realize the risks. Take fire play seriously. Talk with your child calmly but firmly about the dangers: He could hurt his friends, his toys, his pets, himself.

If the behavior continues, it may be that something is troubling him and he's using the fires to attract attention. Get professional counseling to help you sort out the problem and stop this potentially deadly behavior.

Stopping Fires Before They Start

In Chapter 2, "Caution: Household Danger Zones Ahead," you found ways to identify and eliminate potential fire and burn hazards around your house. Now let's turn to the other common causes of home fires.

Watch Out!

Never let your kids use fireworks. On 364 days a year, we teach kids not to play with fire. Why make an exception on the Fourth of July? Even sparklers, considered benign by many parents, burn as high as 1,200°F. They catch clothes on fire, lacerate eyes, and send many children to the hospital each year.

Watch Out!

December through February are the peak months for home fires. The holidays are an especially risky time—candles, Christmas trees, and decorative lights all can be hazards. See Chapter 4, "Home for the Holidays: Winter and Summer," for details on special cautions to prevent holiday fires.

Baby, It's Cold Outside

When the temperature falls outside, the heat comes on inside. Most of the fires caused by central heating, fireplaces, wood stoves, and supplemental heaters are due to human error and are easily prevented.

Safety Savvy

The Consumer Product Safety Commission offers safety information for operating home heating equipment. To request publications, call the hotline at 800-638-2772, or check www.cpsc.gov. You also can call CPSC's fax-on-demand service, 301-504-0051, from the handset of a fax machine to receive materials immediately.

Here are a few key safety rules:

➤ Keep space heaters at least three feet from furniture, drapes, bedding, or anything else that will burn. Don't leave them turned on when you aren't in the room or are sleeping. Supervise kids and pets around space heaters.

➤ Have heating systems, chimneys, flues, and wood stoves inspected annually and cleaned if necessary. Regular cleaning of chimneys is especially important because it removes creosote build-up that can cause chimney fires.

➤ Put a screen around your fireplace so sparks can't fly out and ignite the carpet.

➤ Carefully follow the manufacturer's instructions on using a wood-burning stove. Use an approved floor protector that extends 18 inches beyond the stove on all sides.

Stand by Your Pan

Cooking is a leading cause of home fires. Keep a close eye on foods cooking on the burners. Don't leave the stove if you are frying something in grease. For foods baking in the oven, set the timer and check on them every half-hour or so.

Don't store things over your stove that could catch on fire, such as pot holders or plastic utensils. Don't put cookies or candy above the stove, either, so your child isn't tempted to climb up to get it. Keep young children out of the kitchen when you cook.

Watch Out!

Don't pile newspapers, oily rags, clothes, or other flammables near your furnace, water heater, or space heaters.

If you're sterilizing baby bottle nipples, be especially careful not to leave a pan of nipples boiling in water for so long that the water evaporates and the rubber ignites. It's happened many times. Play it safe and set a timer to remind you to turn off the stove.

Cigarettes, Cigars, and Pipes

Smoking materials are the leading cause of fire-related deaths. Many of these fire deaths result from smoking in bed.

Because kids are harmed by second-hand smoke and can be burned by cigarettes and the fires they cause, it's best to keep your children away from those who smoke. Hire only a non-smoker as a baby-sitter, for example.

If you're reluctant to ask visitors in your home to refrain from smoking, provide deep ash trays, and douse the butts before tossing them into a trash bin. Never let anyone smoke while holding your baby, and make sure lighters or matches aren't left in a purse or somewhere else a child could find them.

Tales from the Safety Zone

In 1994, the Consumer Product Safety Commission required that disposable and novelty cigarette lighters be child-resistant. Since then, the numbers of children hurt or killed from playing with fire has dropped significantly. It's important to remember, though, that child-*resistant* doesn't mean child*proof*. Don't leave lighters where children can try their skills at over-riding the safety feature!

Electricity

An electric current can be mighty powerful. Just because you can't see it or smell it doesn't mean it's not dangerous. Some words to the wise:

➤ Keep cords out of reach, and cover outlets. A child who chews an electrical cord might be permanently disfigured from burns that can result.

➤ Some fires start when outlets are overloaded or when electric cords are frayed or cracked. Don't run cords under rugs or heavy furniture; they can get damaged this way.

➤ Get in the habit of unplugging appliances that heat up—coffee maker, toaster, iron, hairdryer, etc.—when they are not in use.

Watch Out!

Vacuum cleaners pose a unique risk. Tots have suffered friction burns when their hands or feet got caught in the beater bar. When you leave a room, unplug the vacuum so that it can do no harm should a curious youngster tip it over and try to turn it on.

Tales from the Safety Zone

You get what you pay for, says *The Washington Post* in a report on a Virginia woman who bought a cheap outlet multiplier at a store where everything costs a dollar. Deep discount stores typically sell overstock, discontinued items, and cheap imports. Electrical items, such as extension cords, are too important to skimp on. The plug the Virginia woman bought to turn a single outlet into three blew up in her hand. The same thing happened with a night light from the same store. Before you buy any electrical product, make sure it has a UL safety label, model number, manufacturer's name, and the capacity. If you have a malfunction, report it to the CPSC hotline, 800-638-2772.

Fuels

Keep flammable liquids, such as gasoline, kerosene, and paint thinner, away from heat and flames. Gasoline is the most dangerous of these and should be used only outdoors. If you store gasoline, keep it in a sealed, approved safety container. Flammable liquids are best stored in a shed or detached garage and, of course, out of the reach of children.

Gadget Guide

Some homeowners install security bars to protect them from intruders without realizing the bars can trap them inside during a fire. There are bars with quick-release devices to eliminate this problem. For a free information packet, call the National Fire Protection Association (NFPA) at 617-984-7826.

Clothing

Loose-fitting clothing can be a fire hazard if children brush against a flame, such as a match or stove burner. Girls in billowing nightgowns or kids who sleep in oversized cotton T-shirts have air pockets between the fabric and their bodies that can fuel a flame once it catches on the clothing.

It's best to choose either tight-fitting sleepwear or garments that have been chemically treated to resist burning. Note that polyester doesn't need to be chemically treated because it is inherently flame-resistant.

Getting Into Hot Water

Because of their thin skin, children exposed to hot tap water at 140°F for only three seconds will sustain third-degree burns and require hospitalization and skin grafts.

Keep your water temperature no higher than 120°F. (See Chapter 2 for details on how to set the temperature of your water heater.) When filling the tub for your baby's bath, turn the cold water on first and then add the hot water to it. Test the water with your whole hand before putting the baby in.

Other common sources of scalds include hot liquids left within a child's reach, especially cups with hot drinks. Don't carry your baby while you're also carrying hot coffee.

When cooking, turn pot handles toward the back of the stove, and use the rear burners as much as possible. Food and liquids warmed in the microwave heat unevenly. Mix them thoroughly and test before feeding your baby.

For information on first aid for burns, see Chapter 27, "First Aid to the Rescue!"

Tales from the Safety Zone

School safety education is spotty. Some schools teach only one or two topics, such as being a safe pedestrian or bike rider. We believe safety should be a part of every school curriculum, and we like Risk Watch™, a curriculum for kids in preschool through eighth grade, produced by the National Fire Protection Association and Lowes' Home Safety Council in collaboration with national safety experts. It covers the leading causes of injury to children: fire and burns, motor vehicles, poisoning, choking/suffocation/strangling, bicycles, pedestrians, falls, firearms, and water safety. The lessons take a minimum of nine hours per school year. If you want to suggest this curriculum to your school officials, you can get more information from NFPA at 617-984-7285.

The Least You Need to Know

➤ Talk to your kids about the dangers of fire and how to prevent them.

➤ You can cut your chances of dying in a fire nearly in half if you have working smoke alarms in your home.

➤ Draw up an escape plan that your family practices regularly.

➤ Have heating systems, fireplaces, and wood stoves inspected annually and cleaned when necessary.

➤ Lock up matches and cigarette lighters.

➤ Set your tap water temperature to no more than 120°F.

Chapter 7

You Put *What* in Your Mouth?: Poison Prevention

In This Chapter

➤ Using the poison control center

➤ Hazards of medicines, plants, and household products

➤ The silent killer: carbon monoxide

➤ Lead in your child's environment

➤ The dangers of inhalant abuse

When they enter the world, babies spend most of their time eating and sleeping. They learn from day one that eating—well, drinking—is pleasurable. Little wonder that as they grow they can't resist the urge to taste everything in sight. When they start crawling, and then walking, their access to household products, medicines, plants, dirt, and thousands of other things increases exponentially.

The tendency to put things in their mouths, coupled with the fact that their small bodies have less tolerance to harmful chemicals than adults, means they are at high risk of eating something toxic.

Each year, poison centers handle more than 1.2 million cases of unintentional poisoning of children ages 12 and under. Kids ages 5 and under account for nearly 90 percent of those cases, according to the American Association of Poison Control Centers (AAPCC). With children this young, the primary defense against poisoning is limiting kids' access to dangerous substances.

As children get older, they learn what to avoid, but you must continue to teach about poison risks throughout childhood. Long after kids have learned not to drink cleaning products, for example, some start to experiment with inhalants or pharmaceuticals, which can be just as toxic.

Tales from the Safety Zone

The National SAFE KIDS Campaign reports the good news that the poisoning death rate in children is declining. It dropped 28 percent between 1987 and 1997. One reason is the growing use of child-resistant packaging for medicines. Another is greater parent awareness of how to prevent poisoning. Perhaps most important is the nation's network of poison control centers, whose staffs provide parents with immediate help, which averts tragedies.

Some Basic Prevention Steps

Better safe than sorry:

➤ Keep medicines, cleaning supplies, paints, and other hazardous substances in cabinets with child-resistant locks.

➤ Buy products in child-resistant packaging, but remember that they aren't child-proof, so they still must be stored away safely.

➤ Store products in their original containers. That way, if your child ingests something, you'll be able to identify the product.

➤ Don't store inedible products in food containers. Kids may not know the difference.

➤ Teach your child not to put things in her mouth without first asking an adult if it's okay.

Watch Out!

If your child is unconscious, having seizures, not breathing properly, or has other serious symptoms, call 911 to summon an ambulance. If you have the poison container, take it with you to the hospital so the contents can be identified.

Poison Control Centers to the Rescue

Most cases of poison ingestion are treatable, but quick action is required. That's why every part of the country now has 24-hour-a-day phone access to one of the country's 75 poison control centers.

Poison centers are staffed by doctors, nurses, and pharmacists, and most problems can be handled over the phone. Center staff will instruct you about what to do, and they'll keep in touch with you by phone to be sure everything is okay. If they advise you to take your child to the hospital, they'll call ahead and let the doctors and nurses know you are coming and what treatment is needed.

Don't hesitate to phone the nearest poison center if you have the slightest doubt about the safety of something your child has ingested. Along with their expertise, the poison center staffs have access to extensive databases that can quickly provide information on thousands of substances. The staff would rather you call to be safe than be sorry.

When you call about a suspected poisoning, the staff will need to know your child's age and weight, the substance involved (including brand name, so bring the container to the phone) and how much you think your child might have consumed.

Poison centers don't handle poisonings only from things kids and adults swallow. They deal with all the ways the body can be exposed to harmful substances: skin and eye irritants, inhaled fumes, and animal and insect bites.

What If It's Not an Emergency?

Don't feel you have to wait until you have an emergency to call. Poison center directors say they'd rather get a hundred calls asking what precautions to take than one call about a youngster who's ill.

Let's say you are having your house treated for termites, or you're hiring a lawn care company.
It's wise to get the names of the products the companies propose to use, and call the poison control center to see what precautions to take so that your family and your pets don't risk any dangerous exposure.

Gadget Guide

Every home should have syrup of ipecac (and, if your local poison center recommends it, activated charcoal). Ipecac is available in drug stores without prescription for about $2. Never use it unless you are instructed to do so by a doctor or your poison control center because it induces vomiting, which is not safe in every type of poisoning case. Check the expiration date and replace it when necessary.

Safety Savvy

If you've already been through one poisoning incident with your child, be extra vigilant. A child who has swallowed something harmful once is likely to try it again within a year, according to the American Academy of Pediatrics.

Gadget Guide

Ask your poison center if it provides stickers with its telephone number that you can put on your phones. That way you won't have to waste time checking the phone book in an emergency. Or make your own stickers. Refer to the front page of emergency numbers in your phone book for the center nearest you.

Another thing the center's staff can provide is regionally specific information. A generic list of poisonous plants might not include certain ones that grow only in your part of the country. The poison center can give you a localized list.

Help Them Help Others

Funding for many poison control centers is very unstable. Sources of money may include hospitals, local government, foundations, and individual donations. There were approximately 100 centers in the early 1990s, but that number has dropped to 75 due to lack of funds. This places more burdens on the ones that are left as they broaden their geographic coverage to pick up nearby communities where a center has closed.

Congress has considered, but not passed, legislation to establish a national 800 number for contacting a poison control center and provide a stable base of funding.

Call your center to find out what kind of help it needs. You might be asked to send a donation, volunteer in community education, or write a letter urging government support. If you write a letter, point out that every dollar spent on poison control centers saves the country $7 in medical costs from unnecessary emergency room visits. More important, the centers save lives.

Safety Savvy

The AAPCC Web site offers useful poison-prevention information for parents. Check out www.aapcc.org.

Medicines

Medicines account for a large portion of child poisonings, and over-the-counter drugs can be just as harmful as prescription drugs. Kids are attracted to medicines because they like to imitate adult behavior. They may confuse pills with candy, or think bottles of brightly colored liquid contain fruit juice.

Medicines among the most dangerous to children are pain relievers, cold and cough remedies, iron supplements (such as prenatal vitamins), and drugs commonly taken by older adults for heart problems, diabetes, arthritis, and high blood pressure.

When you dispose of medicine that has expired, be sure to place it in a waste bin to which your child won't have access. Liquids or pills also can be flushed down the toilet. Patches worn to dispense medicine through the skin should not be tossed in a wastebasket where small kids might explore. Some children have been known to wear or chew used patches, and there could be enough medicine left to be harmful.

Be careful when you give your child his own medicine. If you misread the label and give him two tablespoons rather than two teaspoons, he's had three times more than the proper dose. Co-ordinate with your spouse or baby-sitter so you don't duplicate his doses.

Watch Out!

Children's chewable vitamins resemble candy, but they shouldn't be confused with sweets. If your child takes them, give him one and store the bottle locked and out of sight. This is especially important with vitamins containing iron, which can be very harmful to children in large enough quantities.

Tales from the Safety Zone

The Consumer Product Safety Commission (CPSC) says several hundred children's lives have been saved since requirements for child-resistant packaging took effect in the 1970s. Unfortunately, the bottles were hard for some adults to open, especially older people who have arthritis or lack strength, and as a result, some request non-safety caps for their prescriptions or leave the top off. CPSC now requires that caps be easier for older adults to use. New cap designs take less strength but more mental ability to open so, theoretically, a small child can't figure out how to do it. It's still possible, however, so keep medicines out of reach.

Plants and Wild Mushrooms

Plants not only can make your child sick, they also can cause choking if he chews off pieces of leaves. It's best to keep indoor plants out of reach and to supervise your child carefully when he's outside. Diffenbachia (also called dumbcane) and philodendron are two common houseplants that cause mouth pain and swelling if chewed. Children are especially attracted to flowers and berries. Keep them away from azaleas, rhododendron, oleander, and holly. When they are old enough, teach them how to handle and care for plants, not eat them. (See Chapter 4, "Home for the Holidays: Winter and Summer," for more information on holiday plants.)

Safety Savvy

Learn the names of the plants in and around your home. If you ever have to call the poison center because your child ate a leaf, you'll need to be able to identify it as something more specific than "a green houseplant."

Much more dangerous are many wild mushrooms. These can pop up overnight, especially if there has been a lot of rainfall. Some can be fatal even in small amounts. Don't let your child play around them, and don't serve your children mushrooms you collect yourself unless they have been identified by an expert.

Other Poisons Around Your House

Cleaning supplies are dangerous, especially drain cleaners, which can cause chemical burns. Some other high-hazard substances are nail polish remover, paint thinner, gasoline, kerosene, antifreeze, and windshield washer solution.

Tales from the Safety Zone

Did you ever call late afternoon "the arsenic hour"? By that you probably meant that it's the time of day when kids get tired and cranky and parents are so exhausted they're ready to do themselves in. The staffs of poison control centers have a different interpretation. Late afternoon is their peak time for calls because kids get into things while parents are distracted cooking dinner, helping an older child with homework, or coping with other demands.

Pesticides and lawn chemicals can be toxic to humans. Don't use products that require you to leave powder or pellets in the areas where your child plays. Follow the instructions carefully.

When you buy art supplies for your child's use, make sure the label states that the product complies with federal regulations for art materials used in homes with children. The label will say: "Conforms to ASTM D-4236." If you have art supplies in the home for adult use, keep them stored in a locked cabinet.

Alcohol

Some people are surprised to learn that small amounts of alcohol can be deadly to children. It's why mouthwash, perfume, almond and vanilla extracts, and other products with high alcohol content can be dangerous. Even one or two ounces can slow down a small child's breathing and heart rate.

Kids like to imitate grown-ups and won't know that a grown-up's drink could be poison to them. When you entertain, make sure you empty any glasses or bottles standing around that contain leftovers of alcoholic drinks.

Watch Out!

Kids have actually died from eating cigarette butts. Keep ashtrays clean. Better still, don't allow smoking around your child.

The Silent Killer: Carbon Monoxide

Carbon monoxide (CO) is a colorless, odorless gas produced by incomplete burning of fuel. Victims suffer flu-like symptoms including headache, nausea, vomiting, and sleepiness. In a short time they can become unconscious and then die. Babies and small children are more vulnerable because of their higher metabolic rates; they use more oxygen faster than adults so they breathe in more of the CO gas.

CO Detectors

Leading safety groups and the CPSC agree: Every home should have at least one carbon monoxide detector. It's best to have one on each floor. Be sure one is placed on the ceiling or high on the wall near your bedrooms.

Preventing CO Emissions at Home

Detectors are your last line of defense. To prevent carbon monoxide from invading your home in the first place, make sure your furnace, water heater, dryer, stove, and other fuel-burning appliances are properly maintained. The CPSC recommends having a qualified service technician inspect your home heating system annually. Chimneys and flues should be checked for blockages and leaks.

Gadget Guide

Battery-powered or plug-in CO alarms can be purchased for between $35 and $80. Buy one that meets the latest Underwriters Laboratories (UL) Standard 2034–1998. These provide a greater margin of safety and fewer false alarms than older detectors. Follow the manufacturer's instructions for installation. Also note the product's life expectancy so you can replace it when the time comes.

Watch Out!

Call for an inspector if your pilot light or burner flame is yellow-orange instead of blue, if your furnace runs all the time, if your hot water supply is decreasing, if rust or stains appear on vents or chimneys, or if there is soot on your appliances. Any of these could be signs of carbon monoxide emission.

Safety Savvy

After you buy a CO alarm, call your fire department's non-emergency number and ask what number you should call if your alarm goes off. Post that number on your list of emergency numbers by your phone in case it's ever needed.

Don't leave your car engine running in the garage, especially if your garage is attached to the house. Entire families have been wiped out when someone left the motor on and fumes seeped through the home's walls.

Some newer appliances turn off automatically if there is a malfunction. Don't try to operate an appliance that keeps shutting off; call a repairman.

Some carbon monoxide poisonings occur during power outages when families turn to alternative heat sources, such as gas stoves or even charcoal grills. This should never be done; it is extremely dangerous. If you use a portable generator to provide electricity during an outage, keep it outside so the exhaust remains out there.

Got Symptoms?

If your family experiences symptoms of carbon monoxide poisoning, get into fresh air and seek medical help. Even if your own symptoms are mild, your baby could be suffering more severe effects and need prompt medical attention.

Food Poisoning

You don't usually think of food as being harmful, but people *can* die of food poisoning. Elderly adults and children are particularly vulnerable. Symptoms may include nausea, vomiting, or diarrhea. You may notice this right away or not until a day or two after your child has eaten contaminated food.

These tips for preventing food poisoning come from the American Association of Poison Control Centers:

➤ Thaw frozen poultry in the refrigerator, not at room temperature.

➤ Dispose of perishable food that has been left sitting at room temperature for more than two hours.

➤ Don't use canned goods if the cans are bulging or cracked.

➤ Cook meat, eggs, and seafood thoroughly.

➤ Carefully rinse fruits and vegetables that are to be eaten raw.

➤ Outdoors, keep foods in an ice chest away from direct sunlight until you are ready to serve.

For more on food safety, see Chapter 23, "The Great Outdoors."

Get the Lead Out

You may not think there's much you can do to protect your child from pollution in soil, air, and water, but in the case of one childhood nemesis—lead poisoning—you can do quite a lot.

Although lead is found in soil, water, and air, the main culprit is lead-based paint. Small children, who put everything in their mouths, ingest it through paint flakes or dust that accumulates wherever paint is disturbed, such as near window frames and doors.

Gadget Guide

Don't use cardboard or plastic CO detectors that indicate the presence of high CO levels by changing color. They aren't very reliable, and they don't emit a sound to alert you.

Children with lead poisoning may have no symptoms, or their symptoms may mimic other illnesses such as the flu. But the effects can be devastating:

➤ Mental retardation or learning disabilities

➤ Shorter attention span or hyperactivity

➤ Growth problems

➤ Anemia or kidney problems

Although some parents think it's a problem only in dilapidated housing, lead-based paint can be found in the majority of homes built before 1978. Homes undergoing renovation may have extremely high levels because of all the paint dust that's generated.

Testing Your Child

Although routine screening for elevated lead levels is not necessary for all children, the Centers for Disease Control and Prevention recommends it for kids at risk. This includes children who live or visit often in a house or child-care facility built before 1950, or if the home was built before 1978 and has been renovated recently. Also test your child if a sibling or playmate has high levels because chances are they've been exposed to the same source.

Gadget Guide

You can buy do-it-yourself lead testing kits, but the Consumer Product Safety Commission says laboratory testing is considered more reliable. Costs range from $20 to $50 for lab testing.

Safety Savvy

State and local health departments and housing authorities can direct you to testing labs and contractors who can remove lead-based paint safely. If you are hiring a contractor, ask about his qualifications, experience with lead-based paint removal, and his plans to follow the guidelines established by the U.S. Department of Housing and Urban Development. Also, be sure to check his references.

Safety Savvy

The EPA Web site—www.epa.gov—lists professionals who have passed EPA's qualifying exam for radon mitigation services. You'll also find information there for homeowners who want to do the work themselves. Asbestos, another environmental hazard in some homes, also is covered on the site. (For more information on asbestos, see Chapter 20, "School Days.")

Testing Your Home

If your home was built before 1978, it's wise to have it tested for lead-based paint if you are planning to renovate or if the paint is deteriorating. Remedies include covering lead paints with sealants or hiring a professional abatement company to remove it. Don't attempt removal yourself. Some states only allow certified professionals to remove lead-based paint.

In the meantime, wipe sills, frames, and doorways regularly with a wet cloth to remove lead dust and flakes. Mop the floors frequently, too. Wipe children's hands and faces before meals (a good idea under all circumstances!) and wash their pacifiers and toys often.

Other sources of lead paint:

➤ Tap water from pipes lined or soldered with lead

➤ Vinyl mini-blinds made outside the United States before July 1996

➤ Antique furniture and old painted toys

➤ Food stored in certain pottery dishes, especially those made in countries without lead regulations

➤ Hobby materials such as stained glass, fishing weights, and buckshot

Detecting Radon in Your Home

Radon is a leading cause of lung cancer, and all homes should be tested for it.

Radon is a colorless, radioactive gas that comes from decay of uranium in the ground. Although high levels are found in certain parts of the country, small amounts exist in soil and ground water throughout the United States. It can seep into houses through cracks in the basement wall and other openings. Even if your neighbor's home doesn't have it, yours could.

Testing is easy and inexpensive. Buy a kit at a hardware store; make sure it's certified by the Environmental Protection Agency (EPA). If the test shows your house has elevated levels of radon, you can hire a professional to correct the problem or you can tackle it yourself. The typical fix is to seal cracks in floors and walls.

Sniffing Glue and Other Toxic Substances

Inhalants are commonly found in homes—glue, nail polish remover, typewriter correction fluid, felt-tip markers, butane lighter fluid, oven cleaners, hair spray, and furniture polish are just a few. As with other kinds of drug abuse, kids use inhalants for the stimulation or "high." Because these substances aren't illegal, they're easy and cheap for kids to obtain and simple to hide at home or at school.

The number of children who abuse inhalants has doubled in the last decade. The risk is enormous because the effects of inhaling toxic chemicals are so unpredictable. A child who tries a certain amount and appears okay could use the same amount another time and get very sick or even die. Some kids have died the very first time they've sniffed an inhalant; their parents never even had the chance to notice warning signs.

Watch Out!

New paint, wallpaper, synthetic carpet, and some types of new furniture can produce harmful chemical fumes. If you are going to redecorate the nursery, try to do it several weeks before the expected birth date. As soon as the work is completed, ventilate the nursery by opening windows or using the air conditioning for a few days. Consider using environmentally friendly paints that don't emit as many fumes.

The American Academy of Pediatrics (AAP) says it takes the body at least two weeks to rid itself of these toxic chemicals through the urine and through exhaling, which is why an inhalant user's breath often has a chemical smell.

Here are other signs the AAP says to look for:

➤ A chemical smell, paint, or stains on clothing or the child's body

➤ Spots or sores around the mouth

➤ A drunk, dazed, or glassy-eyed look

➤ Nausea, loss of appetite

➤ Anxiety, excitability, irritability

To prevent your kids from trying inhalants, educate them in how harmful these products are. Kids who don't die from inhaling can still suffer hearing loss, short-term memory loss, muscle spasms, and permanent brain damage.

Encourage your child to get involved in activities such as clubs or sports. Keeping kids busy in wholesome activities reduces the chance that boredom will lead to drug experimentation. Help build your child's self-esteem by encouraging him to set goals, and praise him when he achieves them. Self-confident children are less likely to turn to drugs as a way to feel good about themselves. Self-confidence in their decision-making also equips kids to resist peer pressure.

The Least You Need to Know

➤ Lock up medicines, cleaning supplies, and toiletries.

➤ Carefully supervise young children when you're outdoors or visiting homes where dangerous substances might be accessible.

➤ Call the poison control center if you suspect your child has ingested something hazardous.

➤ Equip your home with carbon monoxide alarms.

➤ Teach younger kids to ask for your okay before eating things, and teach older ones about the dangers of inhalants and drug abuse.

Kids Don't Bounce: Preventing Falls

Chapter 8

In This Chapter

➤ Preventing falls from windows

➤ Blocking stairs with gates

➤ Shopping cart cautions

➤ Kids who climb

➤ Safe play on playgrounds

One of the first thoughts many parents have when handed their squirming newborn for the first time is: "Gosh, I hope I don't drop this baby!"

Seldom does that happen, but, gravity being what it is, kids are going to fall down plenty on their own. Kids usually bounce back just fine from such tumbles. It's the spills from high off the ground and onto hard surfaces that are most likely to cause serious injuries, especially to the head.

Falls are the primary reason children visit emergency rooms. Kids 10 and under are at greatest risk because their curiosity, combined with their still-developing motor skills, can lead them into danger.

With infants, the greatest risks are falls from furniture, stairs, and baby walkers. Toddlers fall from windows more often, and older children tend to be injured in falls from playground equipment. Reducing some of these injuries is easy; preventing others requires more complicated measures, but nearly all injuries from falls are preventable. Here's how.

At the Window

Plunges from windows are more likely to kill or severely injure a child than other kinds of falls. Even a first-floor window can be a considerable distance from the ground. A window open only five inches is wide enough for a typical 9-year-old to fall through.

One thing you can do is keep windows closed and locked when young children are around. Unfortunately, this isn't practical if you want fresh air in your home. (Never rely on window screens to keep kids from falling out. They aren't strong enough—they're designed only to keep bugs from coming in.)

Safety Savvy

Children who fall from windows are more likely to be male, under age 3, and playing unsupervised. Not surprisingly, 70 percent of fatal falls from windows happen during spring and summer, because that's when windows are more likely to be open.

A better option is to open only those windows high enough to be out of your child's reach. A double-hung window can be opened from the top, for example. And make sure you don't position beds, chairs, or other furniture close enough to windows so your child could use them to reach the window ledge.

Installing window guards is a good idea, especially on windows above the first story. These are available at most hardware stores. One caution, though: If you put them on windows to be used as exits in case of fire, the guards should have a quick-release device adults can open easily from inside.

As is the case with other causes of injuries, window falls can be prevented if children are carefully supervised.

Window guards can help prevent falls. (Courtesy of the Consumer Product Safety Commission)

- Open windows from the top, not the bottom.

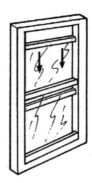

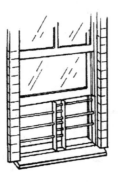

- If local fire codes permit window guards, install these metal bars in the lower half of the window to prevent falls. In New York City, for example, the Health Department requires the use of window guards in multi-family housing.

Tales from the Safety Zone

Laws, coupled with education, can go a long way toward preventing injuries such as falls. A good example is New York City's "Kids Can't Fly" campaign. The city cut its high rate of window-fall fatalities by a whopping 35 percent in two years by mandating the installation of window guards on all windows not designated as emergency exits in apartments where children under age 10 live, providing guards to low-income families, and launching an education campaign. Other cities now require landlords to install window guards, too.

Upstairs, Downstairs

As soon as kids learn to crawl, they'll likely try climbing the stairs. That's why baby gates are an important piece of safety equipment. Gates not only prevent falls, they also are good for confining kids in safe areas. Some parents use one when they cook to keep their toddlers out of the kitchen, for example.

In Chapter 3, "The Well-Equipped Parent," we discussed the different kinds of gates, including mounted gates that are secured to the door frame or walls, and gates with a pressure mechanism that allows them to be installed and removed easily. Pressure gates aren't as strong so they should be used only at the bottom of a stairway or in a doorway where a toddler who manages to push it out won't fall a great distance.

Installing a Mounted Gate

Measure the opening you need to fill before you go shopping. Look for a gate that doesn't have openings big enough to give your child a foothold that could tempt him to climb it. Also look for a gate with a smooth top edge. You don't want protrusions that could catch on a child's clothing and cause him to strangle.

Safety Savvy

Building codes in some communities have regulations mandating that window guards must be able to be removed or opened quickly to allow for emergency escapes or rescues. Your fire department should have information on what's required in your area.

Watch Out!

Baby walkers cause more injuries than any other nursery product. Often the injury is caused when a child in a walker falls down stairs. Don't use a walker! (See Chapter 3.)

Safety Savvy

If you have stairs leading to a basement or attic, it's best to keep the door locked using a bolt placed high up. This not only prevents falls but keeps your child away from other hazards he might encounter in these areas.

When you install a gate, never leave more than an inch or two of clearance between the gate and the floor. And don't leave large objects, such as toys, near the gate. They can become stepping stones that your child uses to climb over.

Follow the installation directions carefully. If you have a gate that mounts with hardware into the wall, be sure to look for a wood stud; the gate will not hold strongly if its hardware is only screwed into plasterboard.

Using Gates

Manufacturers typically label gates as being for use with children up to 24 months old. After that, a child starts to become big enough to climb over. By that time, your child probably will have learned to navigate the stairs safely on his own. It's okay to continue using gates as a reminder to children of the potential hazard, but, after age 2, don't rely on the gates to stop a child determined to get over them.

No gate is foolproof for a child of any age. Don't leave young children on their own without supervision. As soon as they're old enough, teach your kids to hold the handrail when going up or down stairs. Also remind them not to run or play on the stairs.

Manufacturers recognize that you may have an opening much wider than the typical baby gate—between the living and dining areas for example—and have responded with a variety of gates that expand to several feet in width. These are good for separating kids from certain rooms or areas of your house to make supervision easier.

Gates should not have openings where children can get their heads caught. (Courtesy of the Consumer Product Safety Commission)

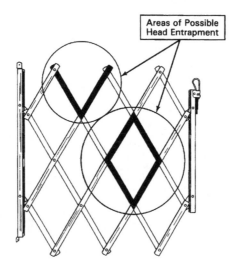

Areas of Possible Head Entrapment

On the Edge

Balconies, decks, and porches are places kids will want to play. Two problems with these are their height—which makes a tumble from them very dangerous—and the openings between railings that can trap a child's head.

If you have railing spaces wider than 3 inches, you should cover them. You can buy clear, rigid plastic or mesh shields designed specifically for this purpose indoors or out. These are especially helpful if you have a split-level home with a railing across a high floor. Fix any broken rails right away, and make sure there are no protruding parts.

Gadget Guide

The once-popular accordion gates, with V-shaped openings at the top and bottom and large diamond-shaped openings between the slats, have not been manufactured since 1985 because a few children died when their heads became trapped as they tried to crawl through. Don't use these gates.

Swings and Things

Backyard and public playgrounds provide hours of happy play, good exercise, and motor skills development. All this can be done safely if the equipment—and the surface below—are designed with safety in mind and if kids are taught playground safety rules.

Falls account for 90 percent of the most severe injuries related to playground equipment, according to the National SAFE KIDS Campaign. These tend to be fractures and head injuries.

Playground safety is such a big issue that we've devoted an entire chapter to the subject later in this book. Here are just some basic tips to prevent injuries from playground falls:

➤ Make sure that the surface underneath equipment is soft. Packed dirt and even grass make for hard landings. The safest surfaces are made of at least 12 inches of wood mulch or chips, pea gravel, fine sand, or cushioning mats.

➤ Have kids wear rubber-soled shoes and keep their laces tied so that they'll be less likely to fall. Wearing sandals or going barefoot is not safe.

➤ Clean up broken glass and other sharp objects you see on the ground.

Watch Out!

Don't let kids play on high porches or balconies without supervision. Never let them play on stairs or fire escapes.

Gadget Guide

So many children have been seriously injured in falls from trampolines that doctors recommend no child use one without adult supervision. We believe this argues against having one in the backyard. It's too hard to make sure your kids are supervised every time they use it. It's better to confine trampoline use to gymnastics classes where supervisors are on hand to direct the activities.

➤ Always supervise young children at playgrounds. It's especially important to make sure they use the equipment that's right for their ages and that they don't push, shove, or use equipment inappropriately.

Shopping Carts

Many parents are surprised to learn that falls from shopping carts are a leading cause of kids' visits to the emergency room. And the problem is growing. The number of children ages 5 and under injured in shopping cart incidents has increased 30 percent since 1985, according to the National SAFE KIDS Campaign.

Carts are top heavy because they have a narrow wheel base and a high center of gravity. When a cart is loaded and also has a child in the seat, it's easy for it to tip over if the child stands up.

Some kids have gotten hurt by climbing on a cart and it falls; by pulling carts over on themselves by climbing on the outside of them; and by running into a cart or getting their fingers or toes pinched in the wheels or the folding seat. Falls are the most common injury and pose the biggest risk because kids can sustain concussions and even skull fractures.

To prevent falls from carts:

➤ Always strap your child into the seat.
➤ Don't let your child ride in the large part of the cart where you place the groceries.
➤ Never let your child stand up in the cart.
➤ Stay close to the cart when your child is in it.

If broken or missing belts is a chronic problem at a store where you shop, point this out to the manager. He or she should be happy to rectify the situation, given the potential legal liability.

Tales from the Safety Zone

Bottle bills don't just clean the environment, they protect kids. A study by Susan Baker, co-director of The Johns Hopkins Injury Prevention Center, found that in one community that passed a bill requiring deposits on beverage bottles, the local pediatric emergency department recorded a 70 percent decline in kids treated for lacerations from broken glass encountered out of doors.

Your child should ride in the seat section of the cart with the safety strap fastened.
(Courtesy of the Consumer Product Safety Commission)

Moving Stairs

Shopping trips also can expose kids to escalators, which are very dangerous places for children to fall. That's why you should hold your child's hand at all times.

You also should teach your child these basic rules of elevator safety:

➤ Always hold the hand rail.

➤ Stand upright; never lean on the side or sit on the stairs.

Gadget Guide

The vast majority of kids who fall from shopping cart seats are unrestrained. This usually happens when the cart isn't equipped with a seat belt or because the belt is broken. To avoid this problem, bring your own safety belt. These can be purchased through catalogs and stores where you buy baby equipment. You also can buy padded seats with straps for extra comfort.

➤ Stay clear of moving parts; keep hands, feet and clothing clear of the side panels.

➤ At the end of the ride, pick up your feet and step over the combplate; never drag your feet across it.

➤ Never run or play on the escalator.

➤ Don't walk down the "up" escalator or vice versa.

Watch Out!

One cause of injury on escalators is clothing. Drawstrings, scarves, or shoe laces can become entangled in the machinery and pull a child into the moving parts. Check your child for any dangling items before you board.

Gadget Guide

If your child is in a stroller, don't drive it onto the escalator. The stroller wheels could pivot and jam just as you reach the end of your ride, causing your baby to fall out and creating a pile-up for people behind you. Opt for an elevator instead. If that's not possible, fold the stroller and carry your child while you are on the escalator.

Slip Sliding Away

Learning to walk (and then run) is tough enough on little kids without obstacles underfoot that might cause their feet to slide out from under them. Here are some simple prevention steps.

Help your kids keep their toys picked up. When they get old enough, make this one of their regular chores. Minimize your own clutter, too. A laundry basket left at the top of the stairs, for example, is a fall waiting to happen.

If you have area rugs, they should have non-slip padding underneath to keep them from sliding. You can buy an inexpensive material designed for this purpose and cut it to size. On small rugs, some people use heavy-duty, double-stick tape (it may leave a mark on the floor, though, so do it only where the rug will be more or less permanently in place).

Stairways with bare hardwood are much less slippery if they are covered with a carpet runner. Put non-skid treads on your painted porch steps, and don't forget to put non-skid decals or a rubber mat in your bathtub.

Kids can hit their heads if they fall against furniture or hearths with hard corners. All manner of cushioning devices are on the market to soften sharp edges. Check for them in the stores or catalogs where you buy other safety devices.

Mt. Everest or Bust

The story of Humpty Dumpty is lost on some kids. They just love to climb up high. Little daredevils who have no fear of falling are fascinated by their new motor skills and want to keep trying them out. Any young child may try some climbing, that's why we advised you in Chapter 2, "Caution: Household Danger Zones Ahead," to secure tall furniture to walls and to put child latches on drawers that could be used as ladder rungs.

Still, some kids will climb repeatedly even if they've fallen before, and they will need close supervision. If you have a child like this, you might sign him up for a toddler gymnastics class or take him to a playground with safe climbing equipment where he can satisfy his mountain-climbing urges.

Buckling Up for Safety

Falls by infants and babies can be prevented if you're diligent about using safety straps. High-chairs, infant carrying seats, swings, changing tables, and strollers all come with straps, for ex-ample, yet every emergency room doctor has treated countless kids who fell because the care-givers just turned their backs for a minute before they'd gotten around to fastening those straps. Make buckling up a habit.

Make sure older kids use protective gear, too. Most wouldn't think of playing football or hockey without a helmet, but many of those same kids resist strapping on gear when they are engaged in other recreation. A fall from a bike can result in serious, sometimes fatal, head injuries for anyone not wearing a bike helmet. The same goes for a fall during in-line skating, skateboarding, and other fast-moving activities. See Chapters 13, "A Ticket to Ride: Safe Biking," and 16, "Wheels and Blades: Recreation Safety," for details on protective gear for these sports and more.

Watch Out!

Keep driveways and sidewalks well shoveled during times of snow and ice. Spread rock salt to melt ice, or spread sand to improve traction—for your own benefit as well as your children.

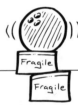

Watch Out!

Store portable ladders where they won't tempt children who like to climb.

Gadget Guide

Be sure to use the side railings on bunk beds, and make sure your child uses the ladder to get in and out of the top bunk instead of climbing up from the end. See Chapter 3 for details on safe rail-ings.

The Least You Need to Know

➤ Install guards on windows not designated as fire exits (unless you use a guard with a quick-release device).

➤ Don't use a baby walker.

➤ Block stairways with gates.

➤ Use the safety straps in shopping carts and on baby equipment.

➤ Check for soft surfaces (and no glass or sharp objects) under playground equipment.

➤ Require your child to wear a helmet for biking, in-line skating, and other sports.

Chapter 9

Why Is Junior Turning Blue?: Airway Obstruction

> ### In This Chapter
>
> ➤ The biggest hazards
>
> ➤ Foods that young children shouldn't eat
>
> ➤ Toys kids could possibly choke on
>
> ➤ Preventing strangulation
>
> ➤ First aid for airway obstruction

Exploring the world is a child's job. While he's still just an infant, he'll discover his fingers—and check them out by putting them in his mouth. His hand is the first of many objects he'll want to size up with his tongue. As he progresses to crawling and walking, he'll make other interesting discoveries. Help encourage his explorations by keeping his space clear of small objects, cords, and other objects that could keep him—and you—from breathing easy.

Ages, Stages, and Definitions

Airway obstruction is the leading cause of unintentional, injury-related death among children under age 1, and 80 percent of all airway obstruction fatalities occur in children younger than age 5.

Several terms are associated with airway obstruction, but they all refer to a lack of life-sustaining oxygen getting to the lungs. This is what the terms mean:

➤ *Suffocation*, also called asphyxiation, occurs when something prevents oxygen from getting to or through a child's mouth and nose.

➤ *Choking* occurs when a small object, such as a piece of food, blocks a child's internal airway.

➤ *Aspiration* happens when a child inhales and causes an object to be sucked into his windpipe or lungs.

➤ *Strangulation* occurs when something becomes wrapped around a child's neck and interferes with breathing.

Young children, especially those under 3, have small upper airways. It doesn't take much to block the trachea, also called the windpipe, which carries air to the lungs. These young children also haven't become adept at chewing, and they love to stick everything, edible or not, in their mouths.

Infants are at special risk because they can't lift their heads and can easily suffocate in soft bedding. An infant doesn't have the strength to pull his head out if it gets caught somewhere such as between the side of a crib and a loose-fitting mattress.

All rather gruesome news, for sure, but fortunately all of these injuries are preventable.

Suffocation

A baby can suffocate if something covers his mouth and nose, thus preventing breathing. Plastic bags and soft bedding are the main culprits. A portion of the deaths that have been attributed to sudden infant death syndrome (SIDS) in the past are now thought to really have been cases of suffocation on soft bedding.

Forget Pillows and Blankets

Babies need a firm mattress for sleeping. That's all. If the nursery is too cool, they should be dressed in pajama sleepers. They don't need—and shouldn't have—pillows, quilts, blankets, stuffed toys, or anything else in their cribs that could interfere with breathing. Remember that an infant can't easily lift his head or roll over if something covers his face.

For this reason, young babies should not be put to sleep alone in an adult bed. Sleeping with an adult can be dangerous, too. A few babies have died when sleeping with parents who rolled over on them. This is more likely to happen if the parent is sleep-deprived from taking care of the new baby or has taken medications or alcohol.

Around the age of 4 to 7 months, the danger of suffocating while sleeping lessens because that's when most infants begin to roll over on their own.

Tales from the Safety Zone

Putting infants to sleep without covers may seem like an over-reaction to some parents, but federal regulators say getting rid of blankets, quilts, and comforters could save the lives of 900 babies a year! Recent studies have concluded that nearly one third of the babies whose deaths are attributed to sudden infant death syndrome (SIDS) were sleeping with blankets that were believed to be a contributing factor. The Consumer Product Safety Commission is urging stores to change displays so they no longer show off baby quilts and comforters in cribs.

Plastic Bags

On average, 20 kids die each year from suffocation by plastic bags. The bags used by dry-cleaners are especially hazardous because the thin plastic can easily conform to a small child's face and create an air-tight barrier. Garbage bags also have caused deaths when kids climbed into them or babies rolled onto them while sleeping. Teach your child not to play with these bags. Dispose of them in a receptacle in a cabinet fitted with a child-resistant lock.

Watch Out!

Many lives have been saved since the word went out that infants should sleep on their backs. Remember the slogan "back to bed"—and make sure your caregiver knows it, too.

Getting out of Tight Places

You used to hear more often about kids who'd find an abandoned refrigerator, climb in to play, then get trapped and suffocate. Today's household refrigerators have latches that can easily be opened from the inside, but some old freezers and refrigerators are still around and are potentially lethal.

Clothes dryers have a tight-fitting gasket and enough insulation that a child trapped inside can run out of air. Large picnic coolers and ice boxes in campers have also caused suffocation. Teach your child not to climb into these items. Explain that with the door closed, there's not enough air for him to breathe, and that he probably wouldn't be heard if he called for help.

If you have an old, unused freezer or refrigerator in your basement, remove the door. Many communities require this before these appliances can be discarded. It's a simple process that can be done with a screw driver. An alternative is to fasten the door with a chain and padlock.

Car Trunks

Car trunks can be attractive—and deadly—hiding places for children at play. Trunks are especially dangerous when it's hot outside because a child can die from the heat in a matter of minutes.

Car makers are addressing this problem. General Motors was the first to offer a dealer-installed retrofit kit with a lighted escape handle so the trunk can be opened from the inside. The retrofit includes a modified trunk latch with a lever that an adult has to reset in order for the trunk lid to close. The kit costs $50. Other carmakers have started offering similar fixes for older cars.

In cars now being built, manufacturers are employing a variety of trunk release technologies. General Motors, for example, uses an infrared system with heat and motion detectors that pop the trunk open if the car is in park and a person is inside. This kind of passive system means a child doesn't have to do anything in order to open the trunk and escape. There also is a manual handle inside.

General Motors' experiments with trunk releases found that passive systems are best because many young children won't understand they can open the trunk with a release handle. It's best to keep the car inaccessible by keeping your keys out of children's reach and teaching them never to get into the trunk.

Choking

There are countless things a baby or small child could choke on in your house, and a baby will put anything in his mouth. That's why keeping small objects out of reach is so important.

Among the major choking hazards are coins, paper clips, buttons, beads, pen caps, little toys, and small, disc-shaped batteries. But the most common cause of choking is the one thing children are supposed to put in their mouths—food.

Watch What They Eat

Imagine eating only with your gums. That's all the equipment babies have. It takes a long time for toddlers' teeth to emerge, and the molars, so important for grinding, are the last to make an appearance. Too often, kids swallow foods whole rather than chew them up, even when they have some teeth. The foods you give them have to be soft and cut up in small pieces.

If your baby tends to stuff too much in her mouth at once, give her only a little bit of food at a time until she learns to go slow.

The top choking hazards among foods are:

➤ Nuts

➤ Hot dogs

➤ Grapes

➤ Hard candy

➤ Popcorn

➤ Raisins

➤ Raw carrots

➤ Spoonfuls of peanut butter

➤ Chunks of meat

Gadget Guide

A food processor or blender is a useful appliance for chopping up food for babies and toddlers.

The American Academy of Pediatrics says children younger than 4 years should not be given these foods or any other food that is firm and round unless it is completely chopped up. Fruits should be peeled and seeds carefully removed. Seeds can be inhaled and may lead to lung infections. Don't give kids under 5 sunflower or pumpkin seeds to eat.

Lollipops pose multiple threats. First, they are hard candy and should therefore be reserved for older children. Second, even an older child can be injured by a lollipop's rigid stick if he falls with one in his mouth. A safer alternative is the kind of pop that has a pliable loop in place of a stick.

Peanuts cause choking injuries among children more often than any other food. (Peanuts can also be life threatening for the growing number of children who are allergic to them.) Grapes and hotdogs pose serious hazards because their skins can easily cover a small child's windpipe. Don't give them to children under 4, and cut them up in small pieces for older ones.

Never let any child (or adult for that matter) eat peanut butter by the spoonful. Even adults have died from a glob of peanut butter that stuck on their windpipe. Instead, it should be spread in a thin layer on a cracker or small piece of bread that can be easily swallowed.

Watch Out!

Be careful what your kids eat in the car. Even older kids who normally can eat hard candy safely could choke if the car bounces on a pothole, forcing the candy into the throat. If you don't want to risk having to stop your car on the interstate and administer first aid, let your kids eat only soft foods while travelling in the car.

Pieces of crusty bread or bagels can turn gummy in the mouth and get stuck over the trachea. These should be not be given to babies.

You need to be cautious about *how* your child eats as well as *what* she eats. Keep her in her highchair during meals. Don't let her run around and play while she's eating. Discourage laughing or horse-play while her mouth is full, because she could inhale a piece of food.

Remember that kids can choke on any food. Always supervise yours when she's eating.

Watch the Balloons

Balloons are one of the leading causes of asphyxiation in children. Part of the trouble is that these toys are designed to be put in the mouth, at least when they're being inflated. It's understandable, then, that a small child might put one in his mouth, swallow or breath in, and get it caught in his windpipe.

Watch Out!

The string attached to a balloon is a safety risk, too. If it's tied to a stroller or playpen, for example, a toddler could get the string around her neck and strangle. Cut it so it's no longer than seven inches.

Packages of balloons are required by law to carry a warning label saying that they are hazardous to children under age 8. The risk is twice as great for kids 3 and under.

If your child is given a balloon that's already blown up, there's a chance that it will burst, and the pieces will end up in his—or a younger sibling's—mouth. Don't leave a young child alone to play with a balloon, and pick up the pieces right away if the balloon bursts or deflates.

Mylar balloons are safer than the common latex balloons because they won't break into small pieces. If you must use latex balloons, store them out of children's reach and don't allow kids younger than 8 to inflate them.

Toys Can Choke Kids, Too

Kids can also choke on small toys such as balls, marbles, and game pieces. Give your older kids a safe storage area for their toys, and make sure they keep their belongings stowed away from younger siblings.

Tales from the Safety Zone

The Child Safety Protection Act of 1994 made an important advance in protecting children from choking on toys. Under this law, warning labels must appear on packaging for small balls, balloons, and marbles as well as games or toys with small parts that are intended for use by children ages 3 to 6. Small toys that may pose a choking, aspiration, or ingestion hazard are banned if they are for use by children younger than age 3. The Consumer Product Safety Commission enforces the regulations and also works with toy manufacturers to make toys safe.

Always follow the recommended age on a toy label. These ages do not reflect whether a child is developmentally advanced enough to use it but whether it poses a safety hazard to younger children.

Sometimes a toy or item of baby equipment that seems safe when it's first manufactured is later found to pose a choking hazard. In those cases, the CPSC notifies consumers and the media about recalls. You can get these notices automatically by signing up on the agency's Web site at www.cpsc.org. To report products that pose a choking hazard, call CPSC's hotline at 800-638-2772.

Don't give kids under age 3 dolls or stuffed toys with eyes, noses, or ribbons that might come off. Also, check toys regularly to make sure they are still in good condition. Sometimes parts break off. Repair or discard any toys that are broken.

Safety Savvy

Fast-food chains displayed their marketing genius by creating meals especially for children. Kids love getting a toy with their food, but be sure to tell the clerk when you order if your child is younger than 3. If that week's toy isn't suitable for younger children, the chains typically stock substitutes that are.

Wraps and Labels

Be sure to discard the packaging, including gift wrap, or ribbons—especially plastic wrap—on a new toy you give your child. Plastic labels or decals on toys and juvenile products are a choking hazard, too. Peel them off. Don't remove permanent paper warning labels, however.

Rattles and Teethers

In 1978, the U.S. government issued rules that require rattles to be large enough so that they can't lodge in a baby's throat. They also have to be sturdily made so they won't break into pieces

Gadget Guide

For \$1 or \$2, you can buy a small parts tester at a juvenile products store. If an object is small enough to fit through the tube, it's too small for children under age 3, according to the federal standard: $1^1/4$ inches by $1^1/4$ inches by $2^1/4$ inches.

that can be inhaled or swallowed. Sometimes these items are recalled because they pose a hazard, but not always. Don't take chances: Inspect them regularly.

Take rattles, teethers, and squeeze toys out of the crib or playpen when your baby is sleeping, and don't buy rattles or squeeze toys with ball-shaped ends.

Gulp!

If your child puts a small object in her mouth and it disappears, call your pediatrician. The item could be lodged in the esophagus or it could have gone into the digestive tract.

Most foreign bodies that are swallowed will pass through the digestive tract without doing damage, so your doctor may suggest letting nature take its course. In some cases, however, your doctor may recommend an X-ray to determine exactly where the object has gone, and the foreign body may have to be removed. Often this can be done with an endoscope that can be passed down the esophagus. Surgery is necessary only in rare cases when the object is stuck firmly or is large or sharp.

Watch Out!

Sometimes novelty rattles are used as cake decorations or on gifts and floral arrangements. These may be too small to meet safety requirements. These aren't intended for use by babies and should be discarded.

Tales from the Safety Zone

Kids don't put small objects only in their mouths or noses. Sometimes things go in the ears. You'd be astounded at what pediatricians have seen in ear canals—everything from ball bearings to Lego blocks—and not just in younger kids. Thirteen-year-olds have been known to do some pretty silly things, too. If something gets stuck, don't try to remove it yourself. You could force it in even farther. Take your child to the doctor.

Strangulation

The first rule for preventing strangulation is never tie a pacifier, teether, or necklace around a baby's neck. The cord can catch on crib posts, toys, and pieces of furniture, among other things, and strangle a small child. Never tie one to the crib or playpen either. Remove bibs or other clothing tied around your baby's neck before putting him in the crib or playpen.

Pacifiers

Before government regulations were issued in 1977, pacifiers posed a serious choking hazard. The rules eliminated much of the problem by requiring pacifiers to be strong enough so that the parts don't separate and to have shields large enough to prevent baby getting the whole pacifier in his mouth.

Pacifiers can deteriorate with age, exposure to food, and sunlight, however, so check them regularly for wear. It's best to replace them every few months.

Furniture and Juvenile Products

A baby can be strangled by anything he can get his head caught in. Common offenders are cribs, bunk beds, and playpens. Others that have proven dangerous on occasion are highchairs, baby carriers, strollers, and baby swings. To refresh your memory, go back to Chapter 3, "The Well-Equipped Parent," for advice on how to use these products properly to minimize the risk.

One item of furniture you might not think about as dangerous is the recliner chair. Yet several children have died or suffered severe brain damage when their heads got caught in the folding mechanism. The CPSC says the typical victim was between 1 and 5 years old and had been left unsupervised. The child climbed onto the leg rest while the chair was in the reclining position, and his weight made the leg rest fold down. The child's head then got caught in the opening between the foot rest and the seat.

Safety Savvy

The chair industry has adopted voluntary guidelines for recliners that limit the size of the opening between the leg rest and the seat (and that require a warning label). If you shop for a new recliner, look for one that meets the voluntary guidelines. If you have an old recliner, don't leave it open.

Ties That Bind

Cords for window blinds and draperies left dangling are accidents waiting to happen when there are children under age 5 around. The youngest become victims of strangulation most often when their cribs are placed near windows with cords. Kids ages 2 to 4 are most likely to become entangled when they climb onto furniture to look out a window where a cord is hanging loose.

Here are some possible safety fixes:

➤ With a cord that is a loop, cut it in two pieces above the tassel and add a separate tassel at the end of each cord.

➤ Install a cleat a few inches below the top of the shade that you can wrap the cord around.

➤ Use a clamp or clothes pin to keep the cord gathered and out of reach.

➤ For drapery cords, install a tie-down device (see the following illustration).

(Courtesy of the Consumer Product Safety Commission)

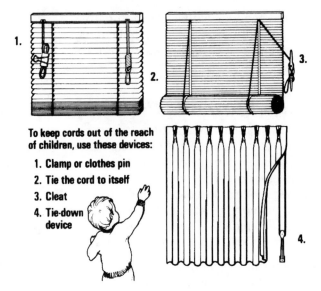

To keep cords out of the reach of children, use these devices:

1. Clamp or clothes pin
2. Tie the cord to itself
3. Cleat
4. Tie-down device

Drawstring Dangers

In 1995, following strangulation deaths associated with drawstrings in clothing, the CPSC developed guidelines with manufacturers to eliminate these strings from outerwear. Clothing makers now use snaps, Velcro, buttons and elastic instead.

Cut all drawstrings on children's clothing. (Courtesy of the Consumer Product Safety Commission)

The danger is that the drawstrings can get caught on playground equipment, cribs, fences, or other items. Some kids have died or suffered serious injuries when their jacket strings got caught in school bus doors or in escalators.

If you have hand-me-downs such as hooded sweatshirts or jackets made before 1995, remove all the drawstrings. Strings around necks cause the most injuries, but jacket bottoms can be hazardous, too.

Tales from the Safety Zone

So many things have changed since our parents raised us. We now know more about how to prevent strangulation and other injuries. Today's grandparents have a lot to learn (which may come as a surprise to them if they successfully raised you!). The savvy ones are getting up-to-date by reading books like this and taking "grandparenting" classes. These special courses offered by some hospitals and senior centers let grandparents learn with their contemporaries—a more comfortable situation than taking parenting classes with the younger generation. And your folks may more readily accept instruction from a teacher than from you.

Learn First Aid

If your child's airway is blocked, every second counts; emergency personnel may not be able to get to him in time. That's why every parent needs to take a course on how to perform first aid on a child who's choking, and how to perform CPR in case your child stops breathing. You need to learn different techniques for use on babies and on older children.

In Chapter 27, "First Aid to the Rescue!" we describe the basic techniques for helping a child who is choking. You also can learn about them through videos, but we strongly recommend that you get hands-on training. You need to practice the skills on a mannequin to really understand what's involved. The more practice you have in a class setting, the more confident you'll be in an emergency.

Watch Out!

If your choking child is able to cough, cry, or speak, don't administer first aid because you could turn a partial blockage into a total blockage. Call your pediatrician for advice. Emergency first aid should be used only in cases where the child can't breathe at all or his airway is so blocked that he's losing color and can only cough weakly.

Basic life-support classes are offered by the American Red Cross and the American Heart Association. Contact one of these organizations or your pediatrician to find out where courses are available in your community. If you have an in-home caregiver, take her with you to the training class. Even if she's already had a course, she might benefit from a refresher.

The Least You Need to Know

➤ Don't put babies to sleep on soft bedding.

➤ Keep balloons and small toys away from young children.

➤ Don't let children under 4 eat hard, round foods.

➤ Never tie a pacifier or teether around a baby's neck.

➤ Keep window-covering cords out of children's reach and/or retrofit with safety tassels.

➤ Learn how to give first aid to a child who chokes or stops breathing.

Chapter 10

Have Gun, Will Be Careful

In This Chapter

➤ Storing guns safely

➤ Safety devices

➤ What to teach your kids

➤ Should you buy them toy guns?

➤ Gun owners' legal responsibility

Gun ownership is one of the most controversial issues in the United States today, but most people agree that children shouldn't have unsupervised access to guns. We think the most effective way to assure this is to keep guns out of homes where children live.

We know that many American families own guns for protection and for recreation. About half of all American homes have some type of firearm. One in four homes has a handgun. If you are a gun owner, it is essential that you take steps to keep your guns out the hands of unsupervised children—yours and other people's.

Keep Them Away from Kids

The most important rule in a house with children is that guns should be stored unloaded and locked up and that ammunition be locked in a separate location. Then make sure your kids don't have access to the keys or the lock combinations.

Tales from the Safety Zone

The statistics clearly point to an epidemic of gun injuries to children. Approximately 150 children 14 and younger die each year from unintentional gunshot wounds and hundreds more are injured or permanently disabled. Handguns account for the majority of these injuries. That's why the American Academy of Pediatrics considers handgun ownership to be a health risk and supports legislation and regulations to remove firearms from children's environments.

People who have firearms for protection are naturally inclined to want their guns to be kept loaded and handy in case of an intruder. Unfortunately, most unintentional shootings of children happen because they are playing with a loaded gun. Kids are curious, and they like to imitate adult behavior. They're also very clever—they can find guns that parents think are well hidden and out of reach. One study found that 75 to 80 percent of first and second graders in homes with a gun knew where it was kept.

Don't underestimate your child's trigger finger. Kids as young as 3 have enough strength to fire many of the handguns on today's market, especially the small, lighter-weight models marketed to women. Pediatricians at Children's Memorial Hospital at Northwestern University tested the hand strength of children ages 3 to 10. The doctors found that a fourth of 3- and 4-year-olds and 70 percent of 5- and 6-year-olds were strong enough to fire nearly all the handguns commonly sold.

Some parents who keep a gun for protection figure they'll keep it loaded and by their bed only at night when the kids are asleep. But can they be sure that they'll remember every morning to lock that gun away?

Safety Savvy

When deciding whether to keep a gun for protection, consider the odds: A gun kept in the home is 43 times more likely to result in the death of a family member, friend, or acquaintance than of a criminal.

Watch Out!

Load your gun only if and when you intend to fire it.

Safe Storage

If you have recreational guns—used for hunting or target shooting practice, for example—consider storing them at a gun club. Or dismantle them and lock them up at home in a separate place from where you lock the ammunition. It's also smart to wait to load them after you leave home, either at the target range or the place where you hunt.

A gun safe is one good choice for locked storage. Display cases with glass windows are not, because the glass can be broken, and because guns that are out of sight are less likely to attract children. The locked boxes in which some handguns are shipped aren't safe either, because determined children can dismantle them.

Even if you don't own a gun, you need to check other places your child spends time. Ask the parents of his friends if they have guns and, if so, how they store them. Don't forget to check with relatives and your family day care provider, if you use one. You may feel awkward about having this conversation, but it could save your child's life.

Gun Locks

A safety device that could help reduce firearms injuries to children is the gun lock. Some local communities require that gun locks be provided with every new handgun purchased.

The most common type of lock encloses the trigger guard on a gun so that the trigger cannot be pulled. Some come with a key, others with a combination lock. Some locks have an alarm system that activates if someone tampers with the lock.

One problem with gun locks is that there are no performance standards for them. Prices and quality vary. Heavy-duty locks can cost $30 to $90, but you can also purchase a plastic one for $1 that could easily break off the gun. Never rely on these cheap, plastic versions, and don't buy a lock that doesn't require either a key or a combination to disengage it.

Watch Out!

Unintentional shootings among children occur most often when they are unsupervised and out of school, according to the National SAFE KIDS Campaign. Peak times are late afternoons, weekends, during summer months, and during the November and December holidays.

Gadget Guide

Not all trigger locks fit all kinds of guns, even though some are marketed that way. Check to make sure the lock shaft does not move. If there is extra space allowing it to move, it's possible the trigger could be activated.

Watch Out!

The concept behind a trigger lock is that if a child found an unloaded handgun, he still wouldn't be able to load and fire it. A trigger lock should not be used on a loaded gun, because it is possible that the gun could still discharge, even with the lock on.

Safety Savvy

Schools in more than 70 cities offer a course called Straight Talk About Risks (STAR). Created by the Center to Prevent Handgun Violence, STAR teaches children in grades pre-K through 12 how to develop victim prevention skills and to manage conflicts without guns or other violence. To learn more, call 202–289-7319, or visit the Web site www.handguncontrol.org.

Messages to Give Your Kids

An important part of protecting your children is talking to them about guns.

➤ **Never touch.** The very first message very young children should hear about guns is to stay away from them. Even if you don't own a gun, it's possible your child could encounter one at a friend's house. Tell your youngster to never touch a gun. If he sees one, he should not pick it up but immediately leave the area to tell a parent or another trusted adult.

➤ **TV vs. real life.** Start at an early age explaining the difference between television and real-life violence. Kids need to understand that real guns can seriously hurt or even kill children. Be careful what your kids watch on television. A steady diet of shoot-'em-ups can give young children—and older ones, too—distorted views of violence and conflict resolution!

➤ **Dealing with disputes.** With older children, there is the added risk of guns being used to settle disputes or to commit suicide. The alarming number of school shootings has brought more attention to the issue of youth gun violence and led to calls for parent and community involvement in prevention. (For more information on school violence prevention, see Chapter 20, "School Days.")

➤ **Be a good role model.** If you own a gun, don't use it in a manner you wouldn't want your child to imitate. You can also be a role model to others by working with your school's parent association to present education programs for other parents on protecting kids from guns.

BB Guns Are Not Toys

Many people think of BB guns or pellet rifles as fairly harmless. You probably knew kids who had them when you were growing up, or you may have had one yourself.

So you may be surprised to know that these guns, especially high-velocity models, kill several people each year.

Given the danger, BB guns should not be thought of as toys. High-velocity BB guns, which can be dangerous up to 350 yards, typically come with warning labels that say "Not a Toy. Adult Supervision Required." The Consumer Product Safety Commission says children younger than age 16 should not use them, and, like other guns, they should never be aimed at another person.

Should You Buy Toy Guns for Your Child?

Child development experts say few kids younger than 8 can reliably distinguish between real guns and toy guns. And they can't fully understand the consequence of their actions. Little wonder, then, that the natural inclination of a child who encounters a real gun that's loaded is to imitate what he has seen on television.

Families' personal values differ on whether they want their kids to have toy guns. Admittedly, it's hard to ban them when everybody else on the block has one, but some parents do. If you let your child have a toy gun, buy one that looks very different from a real one—a brightly colored water pistol, for example. While it doesn't happen often, there have been times when a child has gotten into trouble or has been injured because someone, sometimes even a police officer, thought the toy he was carrying was the real thing.

Lions and Lambs

A grassroots initiative called The Lion and Lamb Project is campaigning against the mixed messages kids are getting about violence. Children are told violence is bad, but they also see violence being glorified on television, in videos, and in computer and arcade games.

Safety Savvy

The Lion and Lamb Project offers a Parent Action Kit to help parents choose alternatives to violent toys. You can reach the group at 301-654-3091, or visit the Web site at www.lionlamb.org.

To counter that, the project helps parents talk to their children about how to have fun in nonviolent ways. To reinforce the message, the project helps community groups hold toy trade-ins where kids turn in one of their violent toys so that it can join other such toys and be transformed into a peace sculpture. Participants get a Lionhearted Certificate and gifts or discounts from local merchants selling non-violent toys.

Toy Gun Dangers

Toy guns that fire projectiles (such as plastic) are responsible for several hundred injuries each year, particularly ones to eyes and faces. Although there are industry-produced voluntary standards covering projectile-type toys, this is no guarantee that an eye, for example, won't be hurt by them. It's best not to take chances; don't let your child play with these toys.

Parents Can Be Legally Responsible

Nearly a third of the states have passed child access protection (CAP) laws. These laws make an adult criminally responsible for deaths or injuries caused by a child who had access to the adult's gun. A study published in the *Journal of the American Medical Association* (1997, Cummings, Grossman, Rivara, and Koepsell) examined the effectiveness of these laws. The researchers found that in states that had CAP laws, unintentional shooting deaths of children 14 and under were reduced by 23 percent from 1990 through 1994. More states are considering such legislation (and so is Congress).

Safer Guns—an Oxymoron?

Much of the legislative discussion around gun control has focused on who can own them rather than whether guns are manufactured with safety in mind.

You might be surprised to know that firearms are not federally regulated consumer products, as are caps for toy guns, fireworks, cribs, baby rattles, and thousands of other products.

Gadget Guide

Technology is being developed that would make a gun inoperable by anyone but the authorized owner. So-called "personalized" guns could, for example, use radio frequency technology so that the gun would only work for a user wearing a tiny transponder with a unique code. Another technology being explored uses a fingerprint to identify the owner.

In 1997, Massachusetts became the first state to declare handguns a consumer product and to establish safety requirements that must be met for a gun to be sold in the state. Other states may follow. This would create a patchwork of different standards around the country—a patchwork that could be avoided if the federal government passed a national standard.

Some of the safety features manufacturers can build into guns include trigger locks, load indicators (which show whether there is ammunition in the firing chamber), and increased trigger resistance to make it harder for a small child to fire a gun.

So How Do I Get Rid of It?

If you own a gun and decide you don't want it anymore because of the threat to your children, one option is to call your local law enforcement agency.

Many will send an officer to your home so you don't have the worry of safely transporting it to the police station. Often these guns are destroyed. Some departments have policies that allow them to sell such guns or recycle them in other ways.

Some communities also have buy-back programs in which cash is offered for guns that are turned in and later destroyed.

The Least You Need to Know

➤ In homes with children, it's best not to have guns—period.

➤ If you have guns, keep them locked up and unloaded. Keep the ammunition in a separate and locked place.

➤ Teach your kids to tell a trusted adult if they find a gun and not to touch it themselves.

➤ BB guns are not for children younger than 16.

➤ Avoid toys that shoot projectiles; they have been known to injure eyes.

Part 3

On the Road

To make sure your child won't become a traffic injury statistic, start with our guide through the complexities of properly restraining a child—baby to grade-schooler—in a motor vehicle. When your child is ready to cross streets or ride a bike, there's a whole new level of traffic issues for you to tackle. Here's how to decide when your child is ready to navigate traffic and how to prepare her for taking to the road on foot and by bike.

Chapter 11

Use Some (Car) Restraint

In This Chapter

➤ Buying safety seats for babies and pre-schoolers

➤ Using booster seats for older children

➤ Installing seats correctly

➤ What to do about air bags

➤ Handling a resistant rider

➤ Buying a safer car

"Buckle up for safety, buckle up ..." Do you remember a catchy jingle sung to the tune of a college fight song that used to permeate the airwaves? Well, maybe we ought to bring it back so it's permanently imbedded in everyone's brain. Despite all the laws and the educational campaigns, too many parents still don't buckle up their kids. The result is that motor vehicle crashes are the leading cause of childhood injuries.

What's more, the National Highway Traffic Safety Administration (NHTSA) estimates that nearly 80 percent of children who are placed in safety seats are improperly restrained—either because the seat hasn't been installed properly in the car or the child hasn't been buckled into the seat correctly.

And, claims NHTSA, at least half of the 1,800 children ages 14 and under who are killed in crashes each year could be saved if they were properly restrained. For infants, car seats reduce the risk of death by more than 70 percent.

Never take a chance. Remember that jingle and buckle your child up on every ride.

Tales from the Safety Zone

Although all states have some kind of child passenger law, loopholes leave a lot of kids un-protected. Some laws only cover passenger cars, not trucks. Some cover only kids in cars reg-istered in that state. Some cover parents and guardians but not baby-sitters. Safety advocates are working in several states to strengthen these laws.

Car Seat Basics

Although there's a lot to know about the proper use of car seats, the most important things to remember are:

➤ Never put an infant in the front seat of a vehicle that has a passenger-side airbag.

➤ All children 12 and under should sit in a rear seat, which, if there should be a collision, is much safer than the front seat.

➤ Never hold your baby in your arms in a moving vehicle.

➤ Until they are 1 year old and weigh at least 20 pounds, babies should ride in a rear-facing infant or convertible seat.

➤ Children 1 and older and who weigh between 20 and 40 pounds can ride in a forward-facing con-vertible seat.

➤ Children between 40 and 80 pounds (usually 4 to 8 years old), should ride in booster car seats.

The last point is especially important because 95 per-cent of kids who should be in car boosters aren't. After they've outgrown the safety seat, they still aren't tall enough to be safely restrained merely by the car's seat belts.

Safety Savvy

To receive free materials on child passenger safety from the National SAFE KIDS Campaign, call 800-441-1888.

Buying a Child Safety Seat

Plan on spending some serious shopping time, because there are many decisions to make and a lot of choices available. After you've determined what type of seat your child needs, you'll find within that category models with a variety of features. From a safety standpoint, the three most important questions to consider are:

Watch Out!

If you have a crash, replace your child safety seat with a new one even if you can't see any obvious damage. The stresses on the seat's parts could have caused structural weaknesses. This is why you should steer clear of seats sold at yard sales unless you know and trust the seller.

➤ Does it fit your child?

➤ Do you find it easy enough to use that you'll do so every time?

➤ Does it fit your vehicle?

All seats sold today should carry labels certifying they meet or exceed Federal Motor Vehicle Safety Standard 213. Those made before January 1, 1981, do not meet this standard and should not be used. You can call the NHTSA auto safety hotline (800-424-9393) or check the Web site www.nhtsa.dot.gov to see if your used seat has been recalled.

Infant-Only Seats

These must be used facing the rear of the car (as opposed to convertible seats, which can be turned to the forward position when the baby reaches the right height and age).

Infant-only seats are for babies up to 1 year of age and generally up to 20 pounds. (A few models accommodate 22-pound babies.) Both criteria must be met before the baby can be switched to a forward-facing convertible seat. The American Academy of Pediatrics says it's especially important for a baby to reach her first birthday before the position switch, because younger babies run the risk of neck and spinal injuries in the forward, more upright position.

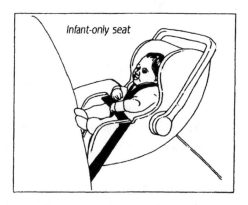

Infant-only seat

This kind of seat fits babies under 20 pounds and always faces the rear. (Courtesy of NHTSA)

Some infants become too tall for their infant seats before they reach the weight limit. The baby's head should be no more than one inch above the top of the seat.

Infant-only seats are light and portable and provide a better fit for a newborn than a convertible seat. Many come with handles made so you can carry your baby around when she's not in the car. Some infant seats have detachable bases that stay in the vehicle for easy installation. A few models can be converted to strollers.

The downside to an infant-only seat is that you can use it only for a year; then you have to buy a bigger car seat.

Convertible Seats

Theoretically, these are for children from birth to approximately 4 years old who weigh a maximum of 40 pounds. We say theoretically because some types don't work well for infants.

Infants less than 1 year old and over 20 pounds ride rear-facing in a seat approved for heavier infants.
(Courtesy of NHTSA)

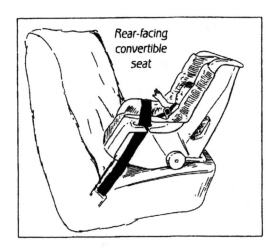

Rear-facing convertible seat

A convertible seat comes with one of three types of restraining harnesses:

➤ The five-point harness, which has straps connecting at the crotch, at each shoulder, and at each hip. This type is best for newborns because it fits them snugly.

➤ The T-shield, which has shoulder straps and a triangular shield that locks in front of the child's crotch.

➤ The tray-shield has a wide tray that swings down over the child's head. In some cars, the roof may be too low to allow you to raise the shield completely.

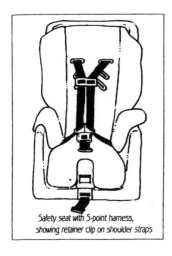

Safety seat with 5-point harness,
showing retainer clip on shoulder straps

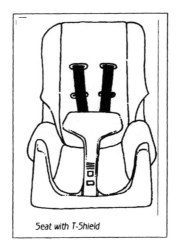

Seat with T-Shield

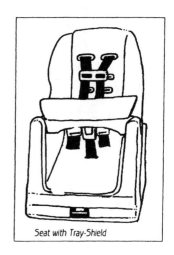

Seat with Tray-Shield

(Courtesy of NHTSA)

Some parents find shields easier to operate than the five-point harnesses, but shields often are too high up on a small infant's body or don't fit closely enough to secure him. If you're skipping purchasing an infant seat and going right to a convertible, buy a five-point harness model.

A few convertible seats can be used as rear-facing infant seats for babies up to 32 pounds. These are good for hefty kids who pass the 20-pound mark before their first birthday, but still must be placed in a rear-facing seat. When you buy a seat, it's smart to look for those with higher weight limits since your baby may be one who grows fast.

Safety Savvy

Be sure to return the registration card that comes with your seat. That way the manufacturer can notify you in case there is a recall.

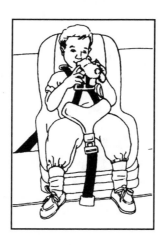

Convertible seat turned to face forward after child is at least 1 year old and weighs at least 20 pounds.
(Courtesy of NHTSA)

Give 'Em a Boost

Booster car seats are for kids who have reached 40 pounds and therefore have outgrown their convertible seats.

Many parents let their children go right from convertible seats to using regular seat belts. This is unsafe, because these kids aren't yet tall enough to fit belts designed for adults.

Even if your state only requires younger kids to be restrained in safety seats, use a booster when he's older. No matter what your state allows, a child isn't ready for lap or lap/shoulder belts until the belts fit really well, usually when the child weighs 60 to 80 pounds, somewhere around age 8.

There are two basic kinds of booster seats. The belt-positioning booster, used with combination lap and shoulder belts, is preferable. The other type, the shield booster (which is used if you have only lap belts) doesn't offer as much protection for the upper body and only protects children up to 40 pounds. Some models come with a removable shield so you can use them as belt-positioning boosters, too. In that case, the weight limit rises to about 60 pounds, depending on the model.

If your car has a low seat back and your child's ears are above it, choose a belt-positioning booster with a high back. This will protect her head.

When you think your child has outgrown the booster and is ready to wear seat belts, here's how to check for proper fit:

➤ The lap belt should fit low over the hips and upper thighs, not across the abdomen.

➤ The shoulder belt should fit snugly over the shoulder, not across the neck.

➤ The child should be tall enough that his knees bend at the edge of the seat without his having to slouch.

Built-Ins

Some cars and vans can be equipped with optional, built-in child safety seats, sometimes called integrated safety seats. They can be used instead of a convertible seat or booster, but they don't work for babies under 1 year who need to ride in the rear-facing position.

Tales from the Safety Zone

It's one thing to put a 4-year-old in a booster, but quite another to convince her to keep using it when she's 7. Other kids may ask her why she's still using a "baby seat." One mother we know explained to her daughter that the height let her see out the windows better. When the girl told this to her friends, they could see her point since their view was limited. The mom also encouraged the parents of her child's friends to use boosters. That way, more kids would ride safely, and her daughter wouldn't stand out from the crowd.

Depending on the car model, the harness works for kids from 20 to about 65 pounds. After 65 pounds, children can use the integrated seat as a booster with the car's lap and shoulder belt.

Built-in seats are simple to use because you never have to worry about installing them. When you don't need them, they can be folded away. Unfortunately, you'll still need to invest in a car seat for those occasions when your car is in the shop, your child is transported in another vehicle, or you want to use a safety seat on an airplane.

For information about using your car seat on an airplane trip, see Chapter 22, "Travels with My Children."

Watch Out!

Never put shoulder belts under kids' arms or behind their backs. The child will not be restrained!

Getting It Right: Installing and Using the Seat

Believe it or not, four out of five car seats are used improperly. This estimate by the National Highway Traffic Safety Administration is derived from the results of numerous checks conducted by safety experts at supermarkets, shopping malls, and other locations.

A 1999 study by the National SAFE KIDS Campaign of 17,500 child seats presented by parents at safety-check events found 85 percent were used incorrectly.

Why all this misuse? One reason is that not every seat is compatible with every car. There are more than 100 models of car seats, 300 models of passenger vehicles and a variety of seat belt systems! In 2002, all new vehicles will be required to have a universal anchor system, which will make it possible for all car seats to be installed the same way in all vehicles. The new equipment began appearing on the 2000 cars.

Tales from the Safety Zone

Maryland marketing specialist Joseph Colella had never heard about the incompatibility problem with car seats until his 3-year-old niece Dana was killed in a 1994 crash when her seat failed to restrain her. According to *The Washington Post,* Colella formed the DANA Foundation and started a vigorous campaign to get the media to educate parents. When NHTSA Director Ricardo Martinez appointed a blue-ribbon panel to study the issue, he named Colella to it. That panel's work led to the requirement for a universal anchoring system.

Installing the Seat

Don't rely on store clerks to instruct you. Before you buy a seat, read the manual and the car owner's manual and then test the seat out by installing it in your car to make sure it's compatible. If it's a convertible seat, be certain you can install it in both the forward- and rear-facing positions.

One of the most common installation mistakes is failure to fasten the seat into the car tightly. The rule of thumb is that the seat shouldn't move more than an inch from side to side or forward and back. Make sure you thread the seat belt through the seat's openings correctly and pull it tight by pressing your knee into the upholstery of the seat of the car and applying force on the belt.

To make your child's safety seat secure, push down on it while you tighten the belt. (Courtesy of NHTSA)

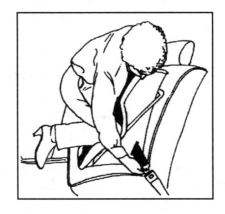

Some seat belts will not secure a car seat unless you use a locking clip. A clip should have come with the car seat when you bought it, but if you need one they are available from stores where you buy seats. Vehicles made after September 1, 1996, do not need clips because they must have belts with locking or switchable retractors.

"Installing" Your Baby

A key mistake here is leaving too much play in the harness that holds the baby into the seat. It's tight enough if you can slip no more than one finger between the harness and the baby's collar bone. The harness retainer clip, which pulls the two straps together on the baby's chest, should be positioned at armpit level.

If your newborn slouches in his seat because of his small size, you can roll up receiving blankets or diapers and wedge them between the side of his body and the wall of the car seat. Or buy a cushiony liner made for this purpose.

If the weather is cold, put a blanket over the baby after you buckle her into the seat. If you wrap her up beforehand, the bulkiness of the blanket could prevent the harness from fitting snugly.

You'll need to adjust the height of the harness as baby grows taller. Carefully follow the manufacturer's instructions on proper installation and use, and check the seat periodically to make sure it still fits the baby properly.

Air Bags

Air bags have saved the lives of many adults in serious crashes. Unfortunately, they can be killers of children, especially babies in rear-facing car seats. The reason is that the bag activates with such force that it hits the back of the child with such force that the shell and padding of the child seat cannot absorb enough energy to protect the child. Older children not in car seats have died because they were too close to the air bag when it activated. This is a good reason why kids 12 and under should always ride in the back seat.

Gadget Guide

Certain cars made by Ford, Toyota, and Nissan prior to 1995 have seat belts that need a "heavy-duty" locking clip. A standard clip is not strong enough to hold the belts in place with a child safety seat. You can get the clip from these auto dealers.

Safety Savvy

General Motors and the National SAFE KIDS Campaign sponsor Car Seat Check Up events at GM dealerships. Experts give parents hands-on instruction, with the child in the seat, to make sure he's properly restrained. For a list of scheduled Check Up events, visit the Web site www.safekids.org. Or check NHTSA's site at www.nhtsa.dot.gov for a list by zip codes of trained car seat checkers.

Safety Savvy

The hot sun beating down on your parked car can heat up your car seat, especially the metal buckle. (Ouch!) Throw a light-colored blanket or oversized towel on the car seat when it's not in use, and try to park in the shade.

Watch Out!

Never let your child ride in the cargo area of any vehicle nor in a truck bed, even if it has a cover. Children must be strapped in at all times. Otherwise they could go flying and get seriously hurt if you stop suddenly.

Since January 1998, consumers have been allowed to install an on/off switch for their air bags if they meet certain criteria. One of these is the need to transport a child in the front seat because the vehicle has no back seat.

Deactivating an air bag is highly discouraged, however, because you could forget to turn it back on when an adult passenger is riding with you. Also, air bag or no, kids generally are safer from crash forces when they are riding in the back.

Buying a Safer Car

We're not suggesting you go out and buy a car for your new baby, but when you shop for your next car, keep child safety in mind.

Here are some tips from the National Highway Traffic Safety Administration:

➤ It's harder to get your child into and out of a safety seat if you have a two-door car.

➤ The back seats of small cars and many pick-up trucks are too small for some car seats, especially for those in the rear-facing, reclining position.

➤ Side-facing jump seats in pick-ups are never appropriate for a child safety seat.

➤ Splits in bench seats can make it tough to install a car seat.

➤ The center, rear seat belts in some small cars are too close together to handle a wide-based car seat, but you might be able to fit one with a smaller base.

➤ Deep bucket seats won't accommodate some safety seats. Try one with a narrow base or top tether strap. (Passenger cars made after January 1989 have holes for anchoring tethers that come with some car seats.)

When Others Drive Your Child

You may consistently put your child in a car seat, but can you be sure that other drivers who transport your child do the same? This isn't as easy as it sounds.

Say another mother offers to bring your child home from nursery school for a play date with her child. Your car seat is in your car, not hers. This is when safety has to outweigh convenience. Either take the mom your seat, offer to drive your child to her house, or turn down the play date.

Another common safety violation is committed by the parent who drives several 8-year-olds to a birthday party and doesn't have enough seat belts to go around—so he doubles up two kids in one belt. A no-no. Before you car pool with anyone, ask if there is enough room for all the children to ride while properly restrained. If not, offer to drive some of the kids yourself.

Tales from the Safety Zone

With laws in all 50 states and the District of Columbia requiring that kids be restrained, why do so many people fail to do so? Enforcement is spotty and often the penalty is merely a token fine. More than 1,000 groups endorse Operation ABC Mobilization: America Buckles Up Children. Around the Memorial Day and Thanksgiving holidays, thousands of police officers across the country fan out to educate drivers and enforce child passenger laws. A survey by the National Safety Council showed fatalities of children and adults were down 35 percent during the first mobilization over Memorial Day weekend, 1998.

There are even occasions when nursery schools let parent volunteers drive kids on field trips without using safety seats. This happens because installing seats in other people's cars is tricky and time-consuming. Parents should draw a firm line with the school: No seats, no field trips. Suggest the trips be scheduled first thing in the morning, and have each parent be responsible for installing his child's seat into the volunteer's car.

Overcoming Kid Resistance

Kids aren't universally thrilled about being strapped into safety seats. That's why it's so important for you to make it a rule from day one that the car doesn't move unless everyone is buckled up.

Safety Savvy

The best way to get kids buckled up is to get their parents to buckle up. A study reported in the journal *Pediatrics* found that drivers who wore seat belts were three times more likely to restrain their children in the car.

Gadget Guide

Some parents have found that allowing kids to play with their car seats at home makes them more willing to use the seats in the car. A resistant child might feel more comfortable with his seat if he can sit in it on the living room floor while watching a video or if he's allowed to decorate it with stickers.

Watch Out!

Be sure to lock your doors when transporting children, and take advantage of childproof locks if your car has them. More than one parent has been surprised by a preschooler who figures out how to open the door while the car is speeding down the highway.

One key is to model safe behavior by making sure you and other adults in your car always buckle up. Also, be consistent. If you let someone drive your toddler home from nursery school without a car seat "just this once," your child gets the message that sometimes it's okay.

As kids grow past infancy and become more mobile, they may start fussing about getting into the seat. Stand your ground. Remind them of the rules. Then turn your attention to something else, such as writing a grocery list or filing your nails. Convey the impression that you can wait forever. If you let on that they are making you late by resisting (even if they are), you'll see repeat performances, because they hope you'll give in out of desperation.

To teach preschoolers effectively, the American Academy of Pediatrics recommends talking about safety as "grown-up behavior" and praising kids when they willingly get in their seats and let you buckle them up.

Sometimes kids get cranky in their car seats because they are tired of being confined in the car, not just in the seat. They'll be more content if you:

➤ Provide some entertainment. Sing with them, play children's tapes, or try the game of spotting things of a certain color along the road.

➤ Buy a car window shade that keeps the sun out of their eyes and makes it easier for them to doze in their seats.

➤ On a long trip, make brief, but frequent, stops to cuddle or nurse a baby or to let older kids stretch their legs and have a snack.

Protecting Kids with Special Needs

Occasionally, children have medical problems—such as breathing difficulties or casts—that make it necessary to use special types of car restraints. Your pediatrician can advise you about the equipment you need.

Special seats can be quite expensive, so check to see if your insurance will cover the cost. Sometimes it does. You also can ask your doctor, your children's hospital or the National Easter Seal Society (800-221-6827) about whether there are any loaner programs in your area.

The Least You Need to Know

➤ Never let your child ride unrestrained in your car or anyone else's.

➤ To be certain that the safety seat you want will work in your car, try it in your vehicle before you buy it.

➤ Make sure the seat is installed tightly and that your child is fastened into it correctly.

➤ Keep your children in booster seats until they grow tall enough to use seat belts alone, usually not before age 8.

➤ Never put a baby in the front of a car that has a passenger-side air bag. Ideally, all children under 12 should ride in a rear seat.

Chapter 12

Where the Sidewalk Ends: Pedestrian Safety

In This Chapter

➤ When your child's ready to cross a street

➤ Teaching street smarts

➤ How schools can encourage safe walkers

➤ Becoming a sidewalk activist

Preventing pedestrian injuries has been one of the toughest challenges for safety advocates. Car seats and bike helmets are major success stories in reducing other types of traffic injuries, but when a child mixes with motor vehicles while on foot, the situation is complex and the safety solutions aren't easy.

Children can be impulsive, and sometimes drivers aren't as attentive as they should be. Combine these with traffic engineering flaws, like no traffic light or stop sign at a busy intersection, and you've got a dangerous situation.

Old Enough to Cross the Street?

All parents eventually must confront this question: Is my child ready to cross the street by himself? Many over-estimate their children's abilities and let them handle traffic before they're ready—physically, behaviorally, or cognitively. The consensus among many child safety experts is that children should not cross streets alone until they're at least 10 years old.

Before that age, children have several physical limitations. Their depth perception is not as well developed as an adult's, so they have trouble judging the speed and distance of oncoming cars. Their limited peripheral vision makes it difficult for them to notice cars turning from the side. Their sense of hearing is not as well developed, either, so they're less able to isolate the direction of the sound from a honking horn or siren.

Tales from the Safety Zone

Parents sometimes say one thing and do another. A study, published in *Pediatrics* (1989, by F. Rivara, A. Bergman, and C. Drake), of parents with children in kindergarten to grade four in a suburban school district revealed that 94 percent didn't think 5- to 6-year-olds could reliably cross streets alone. Yet one third of the parents allowed their kindergarten children to cross streets alone and their first-graders to walk to school by themselves.

Watch Out!

Even though you'll teach your preschooler not to run out into the street, young kids can't be relied on to remember when they are engrossed in playing. Young kids need constant supervision when playing anywhere near traffic!

Another strike against young kids is that they are short, and they can't see as well from a lower vantage point. It's harder for drivers to see them, too. This is especially true when drivers are backing up in tall vehicles such as vans and sport utility vehicles (SUVs). Yet children mistakenly assume that, if they can see a car, the car can "see" them.

Teaching Kids to Navigate Streets

Age 10 is a guideline, but that doesn't mean *your* 10-year-old is ready. Some kids are cautious by nature, but others are impulsive. They may be distracted easily by their friends and may forget to pay attention to what they're doing. You have to decide if and when your child is mature and responsible enough to face traffic alone, based on your observations of how well he's learned the necessary skills and how consistent he is in using them.

When you begin to let your child cross streets alone, start gradually and work up. Restrict him at first to quiet streets. Only after he's established a track record of practicing safe pedestrian skills should he be allowed to attempt busier intersections.

Tales from the Safety Zone

Close to 1,000 child pedestrians ages 14 and under die each year as a result of being hit by motor vehicles on streets and in parking lots and driveways. Pedestrian injury is a leading cause of unintentional deaths in children ages 5 to 9. This is one reason we think children under age 10 aren't ready to deal with traffic. More boys are hit than girls. Their upbringing may make boys bolder about taking risks. Exposure may be an issue, too, since some parents are more likely to allow their sons to walk to school at an earlier age than their daughters.

Long before your child reaches 10, you can be getting her ready for safe street-crossing. Begin as soon as she starts walking. It's much easier to teach her safe habits from the beginning than to have to break bad ones later.

Beginning Lessons

The critical lesson for toddlers and pre-schoolers is never to play in the street or a driveway. Teach them always to stop at the curb or the grass edging the roadway because the street is for cars. Stress especially that they can't run into the street to retrieve a toy.

Teach your child good safety habits while holding her hand and walking with her in your neighborhood. Stop whenever you reach a corner and make a big show of looking left, right and left again before stepping off the curb.

Safety Savvy

Young children imitate the behavior of adults, so it's important to be a good role model. Once you become a parent, you have to resist the temptation to jaywalk, especially when carrying or walking with your child. Always take the extra minute to cross at the corner.

Also, explain that you never run across streets. It's too easy to trip and fall.

Rules of the Road

Continue to reinforce the safety messages once your child is in kindergarten. But now you can add some practical lessons. When you walk to an intersection, ask your child whether it is safe for the two of you to cross. This helps you figure out how well he is grasping the rules.

Safety Savvy

As with all skills, practice makes perfect when it comes to safety. The more opportunities your child has to practice pedestrian skills, the better she'll be, and the lessons have a wonderful side benefit: Walking is great exercise for both you and your child. Plus you save on gas and help the environment every time you skip driving.

Watch Out!

Make it a rule that your children can't clamp on the headphones when they go for a walk. Kids who listen to personal tape or CD players or radios with headphones while they walk can become distracted. They also can miss the sound of a car coming or a siren approaching.

Be patient. Navigating traffic is a complicated process for which he is not yet ready. Praise him when he makes the right call. Remind him, though, that he's still never to cross the street without an adult.

Here are fundamental rules to teach your kids:

➤ Walk on sidewalks or shoulders, not in the street.

➤ If there are no sidewalks and you've got to walk on the shoulder, walk as far off the road surface as possible, facing traffic.

➤ Cross at a crosswalk or corner, not mid-block, and especially not between parked cars.

➤ Look left, then right, then left again before crossing the street, and keep looking all ways until you reach the other side.

➤ Try to make eye contact with drivers before crossing in front of them so you're sure they see you.

➤ Obey traffic lights and "Walk/Don't Walk" signals, and stay within designated crosswalks.

➤ Keep a lookout for cars that are turning or backing up, especially around driveways and garages.

When you're nearing the time you think your child is ready to solo, have him take charge of your walks, making decisions and leading you across streets. This lets him be on his own but with you still nearby to intervene if he makes a mistake.

A Green Light Doesn't Mean "Go"

Learning to handle traffic signals is tricky. Tell your child that a green light means she should stop at the curb and look both ways to make sure the traffic has indeed stopped. The same goes when the "Walk" sign is flashing. You have to allow for the possibility that a driver will ignore the light. Just because one car stops doesn't mean one coming the other way will.

It's also a good idea for a child to wait for a fresh green light or "Walk" sign so she'll have the maximum amount of time to cross. If she didn't actually see the signal change to green, she should wait for the next one.

If a child is in the middle of the street when the "Walk" sign switches to "Don't Walk," the rule is to keep moving at a brisk pace (but not run) to the other side. She shouldn't stop in the middle of the street or turn back the way she came.

If your state allows right turns on red, teach your child that, at some intersections, drivers are allowed to turn even if they don't have a green light and may not always remember to yield to pedestrians.

Special Danger Zones

Parking lots can be even more dangerous than streets. A parent with hands full of groceries may be tempted to let Junior walk on his own. Don't do it. With no sidewalks to separate kids from cars, a young child is easily confused. Hold onto him in parking lots, or have him hold onto you, and at the same time teach him not to walk behind vehicles that are backing up. Small children are not always visible to drivers, especially to drivers in vans.

Driveways are another danger zone. This is where pre-schoolers often are injured. It's best not to let your child play in your driveway. If you do let him play there, use traffic cones to block the entrance and supervise him at all times.

How Schools Can Help

Schools can reinforce the safe-crossing lessons you teach your child at home, especially with children in those vulnerable ages of 5 to 9. Schools also can create maps designating the safest routes for reaching the schoolyard.

Adult crossing guards and student safety patrols stationed at key intersections around the school provide important help for kids. Tell your child to obey the instructions of these "helpers."

Safety Savvy

You can teach pedestrian safety in the car, too. Explain the traffic lights and rules about yielding to pedestrians. Point out to your child when you see drivers who don't yield. This gives kids a better understanding of traffic from the driver's point of view and may help them understand the kind of driver error they should be alert to when walking.

Watch Out!

The ice cream truck draws kids into the street, making them vulnerable to other drivers who pass the truck and don't see the children crossing in front of it. Injuries at ice-cream trucks are so numerous that some states have laws requiring the trucks to have swing arms like the kind on school buses, cautioning other drivers to slow down or stop for kids. A trip to the ice-cream truck should include adult supervision until your child is experienced at navigating traffic.

Safety Savvy

If your child isn't quite ready to walk to school on his own, but the route doesn't have heavy traffic, you might be able to find a responsible older child in the neighborhood who will walk with him.

Watch Out!

See Chapter 20, "School Days," for information on teaching your child about school bus safety. For information on preventing collisions between cars and kids on skates, skateboards, and other moving toys, see Chapter 16, "Wheels and Blades: Recreation Safety."

Schools also contribute to child safety by providing playgrounds that relieve the temptation for kids to play in the street. Make sure your child follows the safest route to the playground and tells you where he is going.

Choosing the Safest Route

When your child starts walking alone, help her pick the safest routes to where she wants to go—a friend's house, a store, or to school. This route may not be the shortest one, but insist that she follow the agreed-upon route every day and not take shortcuts.

Find the route that has the fewest street crossings. Avoid intersections that don't have traffic lights, and pick intersections with crossing guards or safety patrols. You also need to consider your child's personal safety from strangers when picking a route. For more information on this, see Chapter 25, "It's My Body: Personal Safety."

Words to the Weather-Wise

Weather conditions can affect how safe it is to walk outside. Ice and snow are especially hazardous. If sidewalks are icy, your kids may be tempted to walk in the street. Snow can mask where the sidewalk ends and the street begins. Fog can reduce visibility. Streets are slicker and drivers have less control in rain, ice, and snow. Hats and scarves that cover ears can distort the sound of approaching cars, as can a layer of snow.

Explain to your child the need for extra caution during inclement weather. Stress that if roads are slippery, he should not cross a street until there are no cars in sight at all or until traffic has come to a complete stop.

Storms can develop quickly while children are walking somewhere. Teach your child that if he encounters lighting, he should seek shelter in a building—never under a tree. If he's caught in the open, he should lie flat on the ground.

In communities prone to sudden tornadoes, children are taught that if there isn't time to seek shelter, they should lie in a ditch or other low-lying area if possible.

Making Streets Safer

Here are some tips from communities that have tackled pedestrian safety:

➤ Police must enforce pedestrian right-of-way laws and speed limits, especially around schools and playgrounds.

➤ Cameras placed at dangerous intersections can help police enforce traffic safety laws.

➤ Building more sidewalks and bike paths will help keep cars and people separated.

Safety Savvy

When you buy winter outerwear for your child, pick bright colors that will help her be more visible in bad weather.

➤ Speed bumps, "Children at Play" signs, and other "traffic calming" measures can be effective at slowing down cars in residential neighborhoods.

➤ Driver education courses should include pedestrian-awareness training.

How Walkable Is Your Neighborhood?

When you walk with your child on the routes she frequents, notice if there are hazards. Many are easily correctable. Look for:

➤ Bushes, trees, poles, or parked cars that block a pedestrian's view.

➤ Missing stop signs or signals that don't work.

➤ Sidewalks that are broken or blocked by dumpsters or other obstacles.

➤ Traffic lights that don't allow a reasonable amount of time for walkers to cross.

➤ Intersections where drivers frequently run red lights or streets where people tend to speed.

➤ Scary dogs that may be dangerous.

There are a number of actions you can take to correct these problems and make the route safer for your child and others. Politely ask neighbors to trim shrubbery. Ask pet owners to keep dogs on leashes or in fenced yards. If neighbors refuse to comply with polite requests, contact the authorities in your community about enforcing applicable laws.

Contact your public works department about missing signs, poorly timed signals, and impassable sidewalks. Alert police to trouble spots where driving or parking violations are common.

Sidewalk Activism

Some local politicians' careers are being made or broken by the divisive issue of sidewalks in America's suburbs. On one side, parents who want safer places for their children to walk and play join forces with residents who think people are too dependent on cars and too isolated from their neighbors. On the other side are homeowners who don't want to give up part of their yards to sidewalks that have to be shoveled in winter and can cause liability problems if someone falls. Some opponents prefer the country feel of a neighborhood with no sidewalks.

Highway departments are now beginning to look at sidewalks from a safety standpoint. Historically, the car has been king, and road construction didn't include much consideration of pedestrian needs. Some of that's now changing in response to pedestrian injuries and pressure from parents and others for traffic engineers to consider two-footed traffic in the transportation mix.

Safety Savvy

If you want to become a pedestrian safety activist in your neighborhood, check out the information at the Campaign to Make America Walkable, a program of the Bicycle Federation of America, at their Web site: www.bikefed.org.

If getting sidewalks isn't likely in your neighborhood, one low-cost alternative you can push for is an edge strip or fog line, which can be painted at the edge of the road to help delineate for pedestrians and motorists the portion of the road they should be using.

Some neighborhoods have banded together to petition for other safety improvements such as more traffic lights, four-way stops, speed bumps, and stricter traffic enforcement. If your neighborhood has safety hazards, don't wait for a child to be injured. Speak up at meetings of your local government, gather signatures for a petition and contact the media. Enlist allies to join you because many voices will be more likely to produce the government action you seek.

Walk-to-School Days

The Partnership for a Walkable America, coordinated by the National Safety Council, sponsors an annual "Walk Our Children to School Day" in the fall. Parents and caregivers join with community leaders, health care organizations, law enforcement officials, and others interested in pedestrian safety to walk children to school.

These events are organized around the country to promote awareness of the difficulties and dangers children face each day when walking to school. For more information, check on the Web at www.nsc.org or call 630-285-1121.

The Least You Need to Know

➤ Pre-schoolers should always be supervised when they play near traffic.

➤ Children younger than 10 aren't ready to cross streets alone.

➤ Safe crossers look left, right, and left again, then continue to look while crossing a street.

➤ Don't jaywalk; it sets a dangerous example for your kids.

➤ Walk the routes your child takes to see if there are hazards that need correcting.

➤ Consider joining with your neighbors to press for traffic safety improvements.

Chapter 13

A Ticket to Ride: Safe Biking

In This Chapter

➤ The must-have helmet

➤ Buying a bike that fits

➤ Teaching the rules of the road

➤ Restricting where kids ride

➤ Baby as passenger

Remember that important milestone in your life when you got your first bike? Having the ability to get around on your own probably gave you a heady sense of freedom and independence—even if you were only allowed to go to the end of the block! A bicycle provides transportation, recreation, and exercise all rolled into one.

Your child, too, can have many happy hours on her bike—if she learns to operate it safely and ALWAYS wears her helmet.

Helmets: Buying Them, Using Them

Bike helmets have saved many children from serious injury or death. Indeed, the National Highway Traffic Safety Administration (NHTSA) says helmets are 85 percent effective in reducing head injuries and 88 percent effective in reducing brain injuries.

Helmet usage continues to climb as a result of better-fitting and better-looking helmets, public education, and state helmet laws.

They're also a real bargain, selling for as little as $15 in discount stores. And unlike clothes, kids don't outgrow them every year. Helmets usually come with two or three sets of foam fitting pads so you can change to thinner padding and make more room in the helmet as your child's head grows.

Tales from the Safety Zone

Kids—and adults—are getting the message. Bicycle helmet usage climbed from 18 percent of riders in 1991 to 50 percent in 1998, according to a joint survey by McDonald's and the Consumer Product Safety Commission (CPSC). The bad news is that the other 50 percent seldom or never wear a helmet. Compliance is better among kids than adults. The survey found that, according to their parents, 69 percent of children under 16 wear a helmet on a regular basis while riding a bike. (This figure probably is somewhat high since kids report wearing helmets less than their parents think they do!) Only 38 percent of adult riders wear helmets regularly.

What to Buy

Today's helmets are more comfortable, thanks to lightweight materials and ventilation holes that allow for better air flow to keep heads cool. Some even have openings that a ponytail can fit through. Today's helmets are also safer. The Consumer Product Safety Commission's mandatory helmet standards took effect in March 1999. Any helmet made after that date must meet that standard and should carry a label saying it is CPSC-compliant.

Watch Out!

Anytime a helmet has been in a serious fall or crash, it should be replaced even if you can't see actual damage. The stress on the materials from the impact could make the helmet less effective the next time.

Prior to that date, helmets typically met the voluntary standards set by the American National Standards Institute (ANSI), the Snell Memorial Foundation, or the American Society for Testing and Materials (ASTM). These helmets will still be available in stores until March 2002. If you have one of these helmets, the CPSC says it provides sufficient protection; it's not necessary to replace it with one that meets the 1999 federal standard until your child outgrows it or the helmet has been in a crash.

Bike helmets also should be worn by children on tricycles and are recommended for such other sports as in-line skating and skateboarding. If your child engages in aggressive skateboarding or skating maneuvers, consider buying a multi-sport helmet sold specifically for those activities. The multi-sport helmet covers more of the back of the head for protection during backward falls. These are not de-signed for biking, however, and shouldn't be used as a substitute for a bike helmet.

What About Toddlers?

Toddler-size helmets are made for kids who ride in seats on their parents' bikes or for young tricyclers. They are very light-weight because toddlers don't have strong neck muscles. Under the 1999 CPSC standard, helmets for kids ages 4 and under must provide extra coverage at the back and sides. These helmets are not for babies under 1 year of age, however. No youngster that age should travel by bike, either in a child seat or trailer.

Watch Out!

Kids shouldn't wear their bike helmets while playing on the playground. The helmet can become trapped in playground equipment and cause strangulation. CPSC is aware of at least two children who have died this way.

It's difficult to get a toddler to tolerate a helmet, but it can be done. Ease into it well before taking a bike ride. Try having him wear it for short periods around the house, maybe with a Darth Vader or pro-football type costume. Put yours on, too, so he can see that it's something everybody does. With luck, when he has his first ride, he'll enjoy the outing so much that he'll forget he's wearing the helmet. If he absolutely refuses to wear it, then delay bike riding until he's ready.

Proper Fit

You'll have an easier time getting your child to wear his helmet consistently if it fits comfortably. Ask for a salesperson's help to get the right size, and have your child try it on in the store before you buy it.

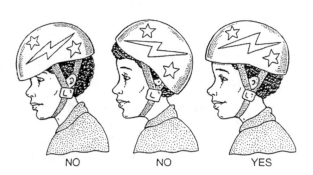

NO   NO   YES

A helmet should sit on top of the head in a level position and should not rock back and forth or from side to side. (Courtesy of the National SAFE KIDS Campaign)

It's very important that the helmet be worn level on the head. If it's tilted back, the forehead is left unprotected. If it's too low on the forehead, the back of the head becomes vulnerable. The chin strap should fit snugly.

Getting Your Child to Wear It

Bicycle safety requires tough love. From the first day your child gets on her bicycle, the message should be clear: no helmet, no bike riding. If you make this non-negotiable, and punish a violation by taking away her wheels for a few days, she'll likely choose to cooperate. If she doesn't, she can walk.

Safety Savvy

CPSC has a "Get in the Helmet Habit" Web site with activities for kids and information for parents at www.bikehelmet.org. You also can get the material by calling 800-638-2772.

Watch Out!

Some states and local jurisdictions have passed laws requiring that children wear bike helmets. Age limits differ. Find out whether there is a law in your area. The possibility of a fine is an added incentive for kids to keep their helmets on.

To make your child more willing to wear his helmet, set an example by always wearing your own helmet. This is especially effective with younger children because they like to imitate adult behavior. Wearing your helmet could save your life, too!

Point out to your child that professional athletes wear helmets—including members of the Olympics bicycle racing teams.

Also, let your kids help you pick out their helmets. Some prefer particular styles or colors, or ones that come with a variety of stickers so kids can decorate them themselves.

Be sure to choose a helmet with good ventilation. Kids on bikes work up a sweat. The helmet will stay more comfortable—and be less likely to be removed—if it has adequate openings to let in cool breezes.

Many community groups work with parents to get kids to don helmets. Police officers in some towns give ice cream cone coupons to helmet-wearing children they see on bicycles. Bicycle safety is becoming part of many schools' curricula, and some schools require students to wear helmets if they ride to school. Community groups hold bike fairs at schools or other locations to teach safety rules and distribute free or discounted helmets to kids who need them.

Positive reinforcement works: Don't forget to praise your child for wearing a helmet, especially when she's first getting used to the idea. You might reward her with special treats occasionally for wearing the helmet without being reminded.

Buying the Right Bike

The typical 3-year-old can master a tricycle. When kids get to be about 5 or 6, they're usually ready—and anxious—to try a two-wheeler.

Although it's nice to surprise your child with a bike for his birthday, it's better to take him along to pick out one that fits him. Because bikes are expensive, it's tough to have to keep buying bigger ones as the child grows. For this reason, you might be tempted to buy a bike that's a little too big so your child can grow into it. This is a bad idea because a too-big bike is harder for the child to control. It's safer to keep him on his smaller one until he's big enough for the next size.

A good used bike may be a more cost-effective answer while your child is still growing. But if you buy a new one, don't necessarily go for one of the cheaper ones. A more expensive bike could actually save you money in the long run if it's more adjustable so your child can use it longer.

Gadget Guide

For maximum safety, equip your child's bike with a safety flag. Often used by adults who bike on busy roads, flags are also a good idea for young cyclists who aren't as visible to drivers, especially if bushes or other obstacles block the view. A warning bell is a another good safety gadget; teach your child to ring it when he's passing another cyclist, skater, or pedestrian on a bike path.

A child should be able to put his feet flat on the ground when sitting on the bike seat. (Courtesy of the Consumer Product Safety Commission)

Proper Fit

Here's how to tell if a bike is the right size for your child:

➤ When he sits on the seat with his hands on the handlebar, he should be able to place the balls of both feet on the ground.

➤ When he straddles the top bar and puts both feet flat on the ground, he should have at least an inch of clearance between his crotch and the bar. (Obviously this is only for boys' bikes, which have such a bar.)

Safety Savvy

Coaster brakes are best for a first bike because they're easier for a young child to coordinate than hand brakes. Wait until your child is around age 8 before considering hand brakes, and make sure he can grasp them easily and apply enough pressure to stop the bike.

Watch Out!

Your child should be allowed to ride on his own only after you have supervised and observed him long enough to feel certain he has mastered all necessary skills including braking, using hand signals without swerving, and following all traffic rules. Limit him initially to streets with light traffic, and require him to walk his bike through busy intersections where cars may be making turns.

I See by Your Outfit

Kids don't need special bicycle clothes for riding, but it's smart to wear bright colors so it's easier for drivers to see them. Also, baggy pants are out because they can get caught in the chain. A rubber band or pants clip can be used to keep normal-width pants tight around the ankle.

Avoid loose or slip-on style shoes. Athletic shoes are better, as long as the laces are tucked in under the tongue.

Ticket to Ride

Teaching your child to stay on a two-wheeler without falling off and to use the brakes is just the beginning. Then you have to teach her the rules of the road.

How old should she be before she's allowed to ride in the street? It depends on the child's maturity and how busy the street is. The American Academy of Pediatrics says some 8- and 9-year-olds may be capable of riding safely on some streets, but many others are not. We think, as a general rule, kids younger than 10 should not be on roads that are used by motor vehicles.

While your child is a novice rider, you'll want to restrict her to sidewalks or paths where there are no cars. Eventually, you can ride with her on streets with little traffic.

Rules of the Road

Many communities have bicycle safety education programs. Find out if there is one in your area and enroll your child. Your local bike store, police department, health department, or school may know of such courses.

If you're teaching her yourself, here are some of the basic rules:

➤ Obey all traffic signs, signals, and markings on the pavement.

➤ Stop and look left, then right, then left again before entering the roadway or an intersection.

➤ Ride on the right side of the road with the traffic flow and in a straight line—no swerving.

➤ Use appropriate hand signals when turning.

➤ If you're with other bicyclists, ride single file, and don't tailgate.

➤ Never carry a passenger on your bike.

➤ Always keep your hands firmly on the handlebars.

➤ Stay alert for drainage grates, pot holes, loose gravel, low tree branches, leaves, and other obstacles that could cause a spill.

➤ Watch out for opening car doors.

➤ Don't listen to headphones while riding.

➤ Ride defensively—many drivers don't notice bicyclists.

Once your child is allowed to venture out on her own with her bike, be sure to talk to her about how to avoid situations that put her at personal risk. See Chapter 25, "It's My Body: Personal Safety," for more information.

Riding to School

When your child wants to bike to school, help him map out the safest course. It might not be the same route he uses if he walks to school.

Children are usually encouraged to walk along well-traveled routes where there are people or vehicles nearby, making kids less vulnerable to personal threats. Your child biker, on the other hand, needs a route with little traffic and as few obstacles as possible. Avoid routes over loose stones or gravel, for example. Also pick streets with lower speed limits or speed bumps.

Safety Savvy

Once you give your child the green light to travel on his own, keep monitoring his biking habits. If you find he is failing to follow the rules, take away the bike for a few days to reinforce the importance of riding safely in traffic.

Watch Out!

Children should never ride their bikes at night. Bike lights and retro-reflective clothing recommended for adult riders are not enough to make night biking safe for children. Night riding is risky enough for adults and takes special skills that children don't have. Don't let your child ride in bad weather, either, when visibility is limited and slippery surfaces can cause falls.

Tales from the Safety Zone

Bicycles are associated with more childhood injuries than any other consumer product except cars. Cyclists ages 14 and under have a risk of injury five times greater than older bike riders, with more than 200 deaths in this age group annually. A few injuries are the result of falls or collisions with stationary objects, but most deaths involve a collision with a motor vehicle.

Kids as Passengers

If you love to bike, you may be anxious to take your baby along. But you'll have to wait until he's at least a year old. Children younger than that don't have the neck muscles to support a helmet—a must for bike passengers—or to withstand the jolts of bike riding.

Tales from the Safety Zone

An increasing number of cities have "cops on bikes" programs. One reason is that bikes are often more maneuverable for chasing a suspect who is on foot than is a police cruiser. Another benefit is that police officers on bikes can have more personal contact with citizens who are biking or walking. These officers wear helmets and promote bike safety, especially with children. They're also more approachable, so a child is more likely to ask them questions and get to know police officers as their friends.

Bike Seats

Between 12 months and 4 years, some parents use a rear-mounted child carrier. (Beyond age 4, the typical child's weight makes the bike unstable and difficult to operate.) If you do use one of these carriers, be careful to attach it securely to the bike and fasten your youngster in with the safety straps. The carrier should have a guard to keep the child's hands and feet from getting caught in the wheel. It also should have a high back and a safety harness sufficient to support the child if he falls asleep.

Even when you use the proper equipment, there are many risks with having young children as passengers. The ride for a child can be very rough, especially if he dozes off, and his head lolls to one side. The passenger makes the bike unstable and increases braking time. Obstacles such as broken pavement or wet leaves become more likely to cause the biker to lose control. Only very competent adult riders should carry little passengers. If you decide to do it, go slow and ride on bike paths or quiet streets, not in busy traffic.

Bike Trailers

Some parents use bike trailers to pull their children instead of carrying them in bike seats. Trailer passengers need bike helmets, too. Because trailers are low to the ground, they are hard for motorists to see and therefore are best restricted to use on bike trails. A tall bike flag makes the trailer more visible.

As fun as it is for you, remember that the ride for a small child can be very rough. Some kids have better developed neck muscles and can withstand the bumps better than others, so it's a good idea to talk with your pediatrician about whether riding as a bike passenger, in either a seat or a trailer, is appropriate for your child.

BMX Basics

Since bikes were invented, kids have enjoyed racing them. In the mid-1970s, some California kids invented a whole new racing sport similar to motorcycle motocross. Now BMX (bicycle motocross) has swept the country and the number of tracks—both indoor and outdoor—is growing. The dirt tracks feature jumps, turns, and other challenging obstacles.

Kids of all ages enjoy the sport, and parents appreciate having a place other than the street for their children to ride. The National Bicycle League (NBL), the largest non-profit sanctioning body, has adopted a number of safety measures required of competitors. Even if your child isn't into competition, here are some of the NBL's safety rules you might want to follow if your child rides on a nearby track:

Gadget Guide

Don't be tempted to carry your baby in a front-pack or back-pack instead of a bike seat. Use only seats—and helmets—designed for child bike passengers over age 1. Before that age, leave your child with a sitter if you want to go biking.

Safety Savvy

Little bike passengers can get hurt even before the ride starts if, for instance, you let go of the bike while putting on your own helmet. Your child could move around, causing the bike—and himself—to fall over. Once your child is in the seat, hold on to that bike.

Safety Savvy

For a brochure on safety and BMX competition, contact the National Bicycle League at 800-886-BMX1. The Web site is www.NBL.org.

➤ Wear a special helmet that covers the ears, and that has a mouthguard attached. Regular bicycle helmets, which don't cover the ears, aren't acceptable.

➤ Wear long pants and a long-sleeve shirt to protect against scrapes during falls.

➤ A 20-inch bike is used for competition and must have pads on the handlebar's crossbar, on the frame, and on the handlebar stem.

➤ Kick stands, chain guards, reflectors, and other gadgets must be removed from the bike before racing (and put back on before street riding).

The Least You Need to Know

➤ Enforce the rule "no helmet, no ride."

➤ Don't be tempted to buy a bike that your child can grow into; one that's too big offers little protection.

➤ Bike riding at night is a no-no for kids.

➤ Wait until your baby is 1 year old before taking him out for a ride in a bike seat or trailer.

➤ In general, kids under age 10 don't have sufficient control of the bike nor enough good judgment to ride on streets.

Part 4

Sports and Recreation

Okay, sports fans, time to watch the kids line up for the big game! And they'll win, no matter what the score, if they have fun and don't get hurt. The keys to success are following the rules, using the right equipment, maintaining a safe playing field, and making sure coaches teach safe play. In this section, you'll also learn how exercise can help prevent injuries and how kids can enjoy non-competitive sports, such as in-line skating or skateboarding, without getting hurt.

Life's a Playground

Remember the thrill of swinging up in the air? Of flying down the slide? The hours kids spend on playgrounds can be some of the happiest of childhood.

Today's playgrounds look a lot different from the ones we remember. There are new types of play structures, some of which have been created with the help of children who know a heck of a lot more than adults about what kids find fun. Some of the pieces we played on as youngsters are gone or have been modified to make playgrounds safer. (Liability concerns are a driving force behind many of these modifications.)

Though kids think strictly in terms of entertainment, playgrounds provide important side benefits. Children develop large motor skills, exercise their bodies and imaginations, improve their social skills, and have opportunities to take risks in a relatively safe environment. Throw in fresh air and sunshine, and you've got an all-around childhood necessity.

Some argue that safety concerns have gone too far—that they've eliminated all elements of risk-taking that playgrounds can offer. Given the high number of injuries that occur on America's playgrounds, however, we think it's possible to remove hazards without eliminating children's ability to take reasonable risks. Kids deserve a safe environment in which to play.

Public Playgrounds

Public playgrounds can provide more variety and challenge than your backyard version, but you also have less control over safety there. When you spot something dangerous, you can do two things: Make that area off-limits for your child, and contact the owners or operators of the playground to have the problem corrected.

The Consumer Product Safety Commission (CPSC) offers these tips for checking the safety of a public playground:

➤ Inspect the surface underneath the equipment. Ideally, it should be at least 12 inches of wood chips, mulch, sand, or pea gravel, or be covered with mats made of safety-tested rubber.

➤ Check for potentially dangerous hardware, such as open "S" hooks or protruding bolt ends.

➤ Make sure spaces that could trap children, such as openings in guardrails or between ladder rungs, measure less than three and a half inches or more than nine inches.

➤ Check for sharp points or edges in equipment.

➤ Look out for tripping hazards such as exposed concrete footings, tree stumps, and rocks.

➤ Make sure elevated surfaces, like platforms and ramps, have guardrails to prevent falls.

➤ Check playgrounds regularly to see that equipment and surfaces are in good condition.

There are no mandatory regulations with which all playgrounds must comply, but some state and local jurisdictions require playgrounds to meet CPSC guidelines as well as the technical standards devised by the American Society for Testing and Materials.

Metal and Wood

If the equipment is metal, it should be painted or galvanized to prevent rusting. Otherwise, the structure can become weakened or develop sharp, broken edges. Parts used for climbing and gripping are safest if covered with slip-resistant material.

Check hot surfaces on metal equipment—such as steel decks, slides or steps—before you let your young child play on them. In direct sunlight, the temperatures can become high enough to cause contact burns. The CPSC knows of incidents in which kids suffered second- and third-degree burns on their hands, legs and buttocks because they unknowingly sat down on hot metal equipment. Young children are at particular risk because, unlike older children who pull away quickly from something hot, little ones may not react promptly.

Wooden equipment can deteriorate and become splintered. Bolts can loosen. If you notice these maintenance problems, report them to whomever is in charge of the playground.

Some of today's play equipment is made of space-age plastics that don't get as hot as metal and need less maintenance.

Gadget Guide

Because of numerous injuries, the CPSC recommends playgrounds not have heavy metal swings such as animal figures or gliders, on which more than one child can ride at a time. Also avoid free-swinging ropes (which can fray or form loops) and swinging exercise rings and trapeze bars designed as athletic equipment. Overhead rings with short chains that children use in progression to span a distance are okay.

Moving Parts and Nets

Moving parts can pinch or crush a child's finger. Give special scrutiny to merry-go-rounds, seesaws, and suspension bridges. Exposed mechanisms, such as joints or springs, are prime places for injury. Moving parts should be kept lubricated.

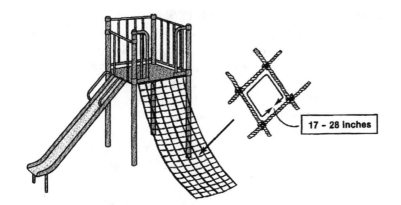

17 - 28 inches

Before you allow your child to climb a playground net, make sure that the holes' parameters are smaller than 17 inches or larger than 28 so that her head can't get caught.
(Courtesy of the Consumer Product Safety Commission)

Cargo nets are a popular component of some play equipment, but they pose risks if the holes are big enough to allow a child's head to get caught. A child's head can be trapped, risking strangulation, if the net's openings have a perimeter length (the sum of the length of the four sides) of between 17 and 28 inches. (The CPSC has reports of

157

incidents on play equipment at fast-food restaurants where the nets had to be cut to release children's heads.) Before letting your child play, check to make sure the openings are too small for her head to go through or large enough that she can pull it back out easily.

Watch That Clothing!

Kids should never wear clothing with drawstrings. The strings can get caught on playground equipment—and other places—and strangle children. Also, avoid long scarves or necklaces and ponchos. Kids should remove bike helmets before climbing onto playground equipment. Not only can the strap get caught, the helmet itself can become trapped in an opening that the rest of the child's body has already gone through and possibly hang the child.

Tales from the Safety Zone

Data from the CPSC's National Electronic Injury Surveillance System reveals that the most common playground injuries to children younger than 5 involve swings and slides. For children 5 through 14, climbing equipment tops the list, followed by swings and slides.

It's What's Underneath That Counts

The number one safety measure playgrounds need—but the majority lack—is a shock-absorbing surface under the equipment. No matter how well you supervise your child and how well the equipment is designed with safety in mind, occasional falls are inevitable. In fact, of the approximately 200,000 children treated in emergency rooms each year for playground injuries, about three-fourths were hurt in falls to the ground or onto other equipment. Falls often result in broken bones. Most serious are those falls that result in head injury.

Gadget Guide

Permanent rubbery mats are typically installed over concrete or asphalt as a foundation. Loose fill, like wood chips or gravel, however, should never be installed on concrete or asphalt.

Equipment with asphalt or concrete underneath can lead to serious head injuries if a child falls. Grass or dirt, while a little softer, can become hard-packed and dangerous, too. The safest alternates are loose-fill materials or cushioning mats. While these surfaces can't totally protect a child from getting hurt, they can reduce the severity of the injury.

The height of the play equipment determines how deep the loose fill underneath should be. Children falling from greater heights need more cushion in a fall. The CPSC-recommended depth is at least 12 inches for equipment in typical public playgrounds. If your backyard equipment is not as tall, you won't need it quite as deep. Detailed information on depth needed for the height of specific equipment is available from CPSC. (See the accompanying Safety Savvy.)

Some playgrounds have soft surfaces but they don't cover a wide enough area. The soft surface, or "fall zone," under a swing, for example, should extend out twice as far as the height of the swing in both the front and the back. The "fall zone" under stationary equipment should extend at least six feet in all directions from the edges of the equipment.

If loose fill material is used, it must be maintained. This includes replacing the material as needed and raking, leveling, and sifting to maintain an adequate depth and to remove foreign matter. Good drainage underneath the fill is necessary to maintain the surface.

Safety Savvy

The Consumer Product Safety Commission has worked with the American Society for Testing and Materials to produce detailed guidelines for playground surface depths as well as equipment safety. Call the CPSC hotline, 800-638-2772, to request its *Handbook for Public Playground Safety*. Other sources of playground safety advice are the American Academy of Orthopaedic Surgeons (800-824-BONES or www.AAOS.org).

Tales from the Safety Zone

The Iowa-based National Program for Playground Safety issued a report in 1999 rating America's public playgrounds, and it gave them an average grade of C-minus. In the 31 states where playgrounds were studied, Delaware earned the highest rating—a B—and Michigan and Florida were worst with D-minuses. The researchers found that soft materials under the equipment was not applied to the right areas in 62 percent of playgrounds and wasn't deep enough in 56 percent of the cases, even though the CPSC guidelines have been in place since 1981.

Mulch and Chips

Shredded mulch and wood chips are popular loose fill surface materials because they are easy to obtain, easy to install, and inexpensive. A retaining barrier is required to contain the material, and the loose fill has to be replenished often because it decomposes and compacts. The disadvantage is that it is subject to microbial growth when it's wet. It also can conceal sharp objects such as broken glass.

Sand and Pea Gravel

Sand and pea gravel also are inexpensive and easy to install. Maintenance is required similar to mulch and wood chips. Disadvantages of sand are that it can blow into children's eyes and can become hard-packed when wet. Kids also can track it out of the intended area, making regular replacement necessary, and of course there's the danger of it being used as a litter box by cats and other animals. Gravel can be hard to walk on. If it gets thrown onto walkways, it can cause falls.

Mats and Tiles

Rubbery mats and tiles come in a variety of synthetic materials and require little maintenance. They don't hide sharp objects or animal waste as loose fill can. The disadvantage is that mats cost a lot more initially and require professional installation.

The Well-Designed Playground

Equipment placement is another key to playground safety. Play equipment for preschoolers should be separate from the equipment for older children. Popular pieces that attract many children have to be spaced far apart. There also needs to be adequate space for getting off slides and merry-go-rounds. Swings and other active-play equipment should be separated from quieter play areas such as sandboxes.

If slides face north, they won't absorb as much sun and become so hot. Trees are a playground asset because they provide shade, but limbs must be kept trimmed so that they don't grow too close to equipment.

A fence or other barrier, such as shrubbery, around a playground prevents children from running into the street. Equipment should be installed at least six feet from fences.

Gadget Guide

If you have a cellular phone, take it to the playground with you in case you have to summon help in an emergency. It's also a good idea to carry a few first-aid supplies such as adhesive bandages and antiseptic.

Playground Rules and Etiquette

Using good manners on the playground isn't just a way to make friends; it also promotes safety. Kids who push or shove others while on or near equipment can cause a fall or other injury. Taking turns is an important safety rule, too. Teach your child that if he encounters a problem with other children's behavior on the playground, he can ask you or his caregiver for help.

Children respond to rules better if they have a hand in making them. In your backyard, you can help them decide how long each child's turn on the swing will be, for example. Day care centers and schools often use similar tactics.

Kids sometimes get hurt if they don't use play equipment the way it was designed to be used. Climbing up a slide instead of using the ladder, stepping outside the railings at the top or using the teeter-totter as a balance beam are examples of misuse that can be dangerous. In their exuberance, children may forget to use handrails when they climb steps, so you'll need to remind them.

No matter how well constructed and maintained, not all playground equipment is safe for all ages. If your playground has play pieces your child isn't old enough for, set rules on what can be used and supervise carefully. Kids younger than 5, for example, should not use slides higher than about four feet off the ground.

Watch Out!

Teach your kids to not jump from swings and to not walk in front of or behind a moving swing; they should walk around it. Don't let them swing an empty seat or wind it up, either. Swings with lightweight rubber or plastic seats are safer than heavy metal or wooden ones. For toddlers, bucket seats are ideal for providing support on all sides.

In Your Own Backyard

Many of the same safety rules for public playgrounds apply to your home playground, too. You'll need a six-foot buffer zone between the equipment and any obstructions such as garages, fences, trees, utility poles, or wires. Soft surfaces—typically wood chips or sand—should extend several feet out from the equipment.

Don't buy play equipment too big for your preschooler. Buy pieces that are the right size for her now and add larger pieces later, rather than buying something she'll grow into. If your play

Safety Savvy

Position your play equipment so you can see it from the house. A view from the kitchen window, for example, allows you to watch the kids while you cook dinner.

equipment must accommodate older siblings, too, supervise the younger one carefully.

Prices for backyard play sets vary, with metal generally costing less than wood. A higher price doesn't necessarily mean you're getting safer equipment, though. Regardless of what you buy, if you install it yourself, make sure you follow the manufacturer's directions carefully.

Metal Sets

Manufacturers of metal swing sets recommend that the legs be anchored so they cannot tip over when energetic kids swing on them. Most companies suggest setting the legs in concrete.

Plastic Equipment

Plastic climbing equipment is popular with the pre-school set. However, hundreds of children have been hurt, a few fatally, because the climbing gyms were used indoors in homes or day care centers The CPSC and manufacturers warn that climbing gyms should not be put on wood or cement floors and that even carpeting doesn't provide adequate injury protection. This equipment should be placed outdoors on sand, mulch, or another shock-absorbing surface.

Climbing gyms should be placed outdoors on mulch or sand, not hard floors or carpeting.
(Courtesy of the Consumer Product Safety Commission)

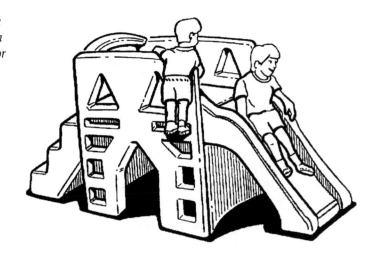

Building Playgrounds

You see it all over: fabulous playgrounds built by local parents in community endeavors akin to old-fashioned barn-raisings. Neighbors join forces to raise funds and provide labor to clean their local park, repair existing equipment, and install new play structures. Also, it's not unusual, when school funds aren't available, for parent-teacher associations to step in and collaborate to improve school playgrounds.

If you're interested in getting involved in a playground project like this, do what some other savvy groups have done: Instead of using an equipment dealer with a vested interest in selling you his products, use a neutral consultant for help in designing a safe play area that kids will enjoy for years to come. He or she can also help provide access for disabled children under the guidelines of the Americans with Disabilities Act.

You may be able to find one through the National Program for Playground Safety (800-554-PLAY or www.uni.edu/playground) or through the National Recreation and Park Association 703-858-0784 or www.nrpa.org), which certifies playground safety consultants.

Watch Out!

Think twice before buying a trampoline for your backyard play area. They're really not safe for home use. See Chapter 17, "Flex Those Muscles!" for more information.

Tales from the Safety Zone

Darrell Hammond grew up in an orphanage and overcame dyslexia to graduate from college and pursue his dream of helping other kids have happy childhoods. As *The Wall Street Journal* (April 2, 1999) reported, Hammond started with a few inner-city neighborhoods to help residents clear space, raise money, and install equipment. Gradually his Washington, D.C.-based non-profit group, KaBoom, has grown by recruiting corporate sponsors to help build playgrounds across the country. The sponsors not only provide funds and building materials but volunteers, too. Seems they discovered that playground construction can serve as an employee team-building exercise!

The Least You Need to Know

➤ Soft surfaces under play equipment are a must to prevent serious injuries from a fall.

➤ Kids should never wear clothing with neck drawstrings.

➤ Steer pre-schoolers away from play equipment designed for older children.

➤ If a piece of equipment poses a safety hazard, keep your child off it, and notify the playground operators.

Chapter 15

On the Waterfront

In This Chapter

➤ Using backyard pools and hot tubs safely

➤ Teaching your kids swimming rules

➤ When to start swim lessons

➤ Avoiding diving injuries

➤ Swimming safely in ponds, lakes, and oceans

➤ Avoiding thin ice while skating

Most kids love to play in water. They get their first lessons in splashing from their daily bath and gradually move on to jumping in rain puddles, taking dips in the wading pool, and running through the sprinkler.

We want kids to love water but also to have a healthy respect for it. It's up to the adults in their lives to supervise them and teach them how to enjoy water safely.

Drowning is the second leading cause of death in children ages 14 and under. In Chapter 2, "Caution: Household Danger Zones Ahead," you read about ways to eliminate drowning hazards in the home. For infants and toddlers, the dangers include bathtubs, toilets, diaper pails, buckets, and even large coolers of melting ice. It surprises some parents to learn that a tiny child can drown in as little as one inch of water.

Watch Out!

Even small wading pools can be a threat to very young children. Dump the water out when the pool is not in use. If there are fountains or ornamental fish ponds near your home, watch closely if your little one plays near them.

As children get older, swimming pools become the biggest danger. The majority of deaths and injuries occur in residential pools, usually when a child is left unattended. Safety measures, including adult supervision, putting up fences, and learning first aid, are critical to preventing drowning. Many submersion victims can be saved if adults know how to rescue them quickly and restart the breathing process.

Residential Pools

Fencing around backyard pools has been a key to the decline in child drownings. Guidelines on pool safety developed by the Consumer Product Safety Commission (CPSC) are not mandatory under federal law, but many communities have incorporated them into their building codes.

The reason pool barriers are so important is that even when parents are conscientious about supervising their little ones, drowning can happen in an instant. Toddlers are inquisitive and impulsive. They're also unpredictable, and their abilities change almost daily. By the time a child's absence is noted, it may already be too late. A very young child is unlikely to splash or scream, so the parent or caregiver may not be aware that a child's in trouble.

When you aren't around, pool fences deter other neighborhood children who might wander into your yard.

In a CPSC study of swimming pool mishaps, most of the submersion victims were being supervised by one or both parents. More than three quarters of these children had been missing for five minutes or less from their homes or yards when they were found in the pool.

Tales from the Safety Zone

We're making headway in protecting kids from drowning and near-drowning. The National SAFE KIDS Campaign reports that child drownings declined 30 percent in the last decade. The rate of bathtub-related drownings has declined even more, in part because parents have gotten the prevention message. Children ages 1 to 4 are at greatest risk for drowning, with a rate 2.5 times that of other children.

Barriers provide extra time. They can be the margin of safety that lets you locate your child when he has strayed from you. They're not only needed around pools but also around spas, hot tubs, and whirlpools.

Fences and Gates

A fence or wall at least four feet high should be installed completely around the pool. It's safest to enclose the pool on all sides with a fence rather than using your house as part of the barrier. Otherwise, your youngster could wander out the back door and make her way to the pool on her own. (See the following sections, "Door Alarms," and "Power Safety Covers.")

Safety Savvy

The CPSC has prepared detailed guidelines for constructing barriers around pools. To obtain them, call the CPSC hotline at 800-638-2772 or visit the Web site www.CPSC.gov.

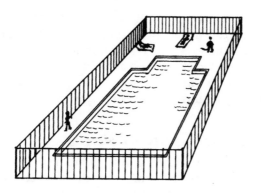

Fences enclosing backyard pools, not just yards with pools, can save many lives.
(Courtesy of the Consumer Product Safety Commission)

Whatever barrier you use, it should not provide places for a child to squeeze through or to get a foothold and climb over. If it's a chain link fence, for example, the diamond-shaped openings should be no larger than 1¾ inches. If the fence is made of vertical slats, the space between them should not exceed four inches. Spacing larger than that could allow a toddler to squeeze through.

The fence will do no good if the gate allows a child access. The gate should be self-closing and self-latching with the latch out of a child's reach. Never prop it open.

Watch Out!

If you notice your child is missing, check the pool first. Seconds count. Go to the edge and scan the entire bottom, then check the rest of the pool area before searching other parts of the house or yard.

Watch Out!

Be careful where and how you store the chemicals you use to keep your pool clean. They can be harmful to children if handled or swallowed.

Gadget Guide

Don't allow standing rain water to accumulate on the top of the power cover. A toddler could possibly drown in that, too.

Door Alarms

If your house is one part of the pool barrier, it's smart to put alarms on the doors that lead from the house to the pool. These operate with batteries or electricity, and can be temporarily deactivated when an adult needs to open the door. The key pad, which you use to deactivate them, should be placed high enough on the door to be well out of children's reach.

Power Safety Covers

Instead of alarming the doors, you can cover your in-ground pool with a power safety cover, a motorized barrier that easily opens and closes over the water in the pool. With the cover in place, small children will be protected from the water.

Power safety covers, if they meet standards set by the American Society of Testing and Materials, can withstand the weight of two adults and a child. This allows for a rescue in case an individual falls on the cover. The cover only works, of course, if it is closed completely after each use of the pool.

Above-Ground Pools

To protect your children from falling into an above-ground pool, secure and lock the steps and ladders or remove them when the pool is not in use. Consider fencing these as well.

Using the Pool Safely

Up to now we've talked about protecting your kids when you *aren't* using the pool. But kids can drown while adults are pool-side, too. If you're having a social gathering, ask an adult to be the designated pool watcher, giving full attention to the task. Rotate the duty.

Here are some more pool rules:

➤ If you have a pool cover, remove it completely before using the pool. A partially covered pool can trap a child.

➤ Don't leave chairs or tables near fences that a small child could stand on to climb over.

➤ Remove toys from pools so kids won't be tempted to reach in to retrieve them.

➤ Don't allow tricycles or wagons in the pool area.

Keep rescue equipment by the pool: a life preserver, rope, shepherd's crook, and a phone for calling rescue personnel if necessary. If there is an emergency, yell for help, then start cardiopulmonary resuscitation (CPR). If there's no one else present who can call 911, perform CPR for one minute, then quickly call 911, and then resume CPR.

The American Academy of Pediatrics recommends that even if your child acts normal after being revived, she should still be seen by her doctor right away.

Safety Savvy

If you learn cardiopulmonary resuscitation (CPR), you could save your child's life. Many children have been revived because an adult was able to begin CPR *immediately*, rather than have to wait for the arrival of emergency personnel. Baby-sitters, grandparents, and older siblings who supervise your child should learn it, too.

Hot Tubs, Spas, and Whirlpools

Locked covers should be put over hot tubs, spas, and whirlpools when they are not in use. Never leave children on their own in them. Children have drowned because their hair became entangled when it was sucked into the drain of the spa, hot tub, or whirlpool. Some of these incidents have occurred when kids were playing a game to see who could hold their breath under water the longest. When they leaned over to submerge their heads, their hair fell near the drain where the suction was strong enough to pull the hair in, trapping them.

These incidents led to the development of a voluntary standard for drain covers to reduce the risk of hair entrapment. Check with your dealer to be sure your drain covers meet the standard. Got an older spa? Consider getting your drains replaced with the new, safer models. If your drain cover is missing or broken, shut off the spa until you can have the cover replaced.

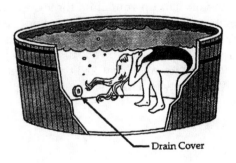

Drain Cover

Keep hair away from drain covers. (Courtesy of the Consumer Product Safety Commission)

Watch Out!

High temperatures in hot tubs, spas, and whirlpools can lead to heat stroke or even death. The heat affects younger children more quickly than teens or adults. The American Academy of Pediatrics recommends parents not let young children use these devices before consulting their pediatricians. Spa temperatures should never exceed 104°F.

Watch Out!

Even if your child knows how to swim, she still needs adult supervision. She might be able to swim to the side of the pool under normal circumstances, but she could get confused or scared if she falls in with her clothes on and not be able to save herself.

There have been a few instances in which a part of a young child's body was trapped in a drain. To eliminate this hazard, the CPSC helped develop a standard requiring dome-shaped drain outlets and two outlets for each pump, to reduce the powerful suction if the drain ever gets blocked. Again, if you've got an older spa that doesn't have these features, you may want to consider updating yours with these dome-shaped outlets and the new two-drain models.

When to Start Swimming Lessons

The American Academy of Pediatrics discourages parents from signing kids up for swimming lessons until at least the age of 3. One reason is that parents who start kids earlier can develop a false sense of security that their children can swim, leading to lax supervision. The kids, too, can become over-confident. Another reason is that young children have a higher risk of getting sick from swallowing too much water. They're also more at risk of getting infections if the water is dirty.

If you want to start early, choose a class where your child is not required to put his head under water and one in which you will be assisting him in all the activities. The Red Cross, for example, has baby and toddler classes that help children get used to the water. Then you can sign him up for formal lessons when he's ready—usually between ages 4 and 5. At that point, most kids have the motor skills needed for beginner swimming classes and also have the ability to understand water safety rules.

When you sign up your child for lessons, make sure the instructor is nationally certified under Red Cross or YMCA standards. To learn more about swimming courses for children and CPR/first aid courses for adults, contact your local Red Cross chapter or visit the Web site www.crossnet.org.

Swimming Rules

Whether in a pool, a lake, or the ocean, many of the same basic rules apply:

➤ Teach your child never to swim anywhere alone. (That's good advice for adults, too.)

➤ Always have school-age children supervised by a lifeguard or other adult when they swim. The adult needs to know how to swim and how to perform CPR. Teenagers should be advised to swim with a buddy, never alone.

➤ Don't let kids push or jump on top of someone else in or near water. Walk, don't run, near pools or docks.

➤ Your child should never dive into water unless permitted by an adult who knows how deep the water is.

➤ Going down a pool slide head first is a no-no.

➤ At the first sign of thunder or lightening, everyone should leave the water.

➤ Warn your kids not to pretend to be drowning and call for help in jest.

Diving Off the Deep End

Adolescents are especially in danger of spinal cord injuries from diving because they're more likely to take risks. They should:

➤ Never dive into above-ground pools because they usually aren't deep enough.

➤ Dive into in-ground pools only from the ends of diving boards, never from the sides of the board or pool.

➤ Never dive when more than one person is on the diving board because horseplay can lead to injury.

➤ Wait until the area is clear before diving, and then swim away promptly to avoid being hit by another diver.

➤ Never dive from piers or docks.

➤ Go into water feet first to check the depth before considering diving. Water should be at least nine feet deep.

Diving is a skill. Encourage your child to take lessons so she can dive safely without risking injury.

Flotation Devices

The majority of states have laws requiring that children wear personal flotation devices (PFDs), also known as life jackets, when on boats or near open bodies of water. The laws vary as to age requirements and exemptions. The U.S. Coast Guard requires recreational boats to carry one approved PFD of the correct size for each person in the boat. To find out what the law is in your state, contact the state's Department of Natural Resources or Attorney General's office.

Life jackets are designed to float a child face up in the water. They are not, however, intended to substitute for adult supervision.

Life jackets are sized according to weight. Some also specify a chest size. It's best to take your child with you when you buy one so he can try it on and be sure it fits snugly. Make sure the straps are fastened properly. Teach him how to put on the life jacket himself. Have him wear it at all times when he's on a boat or near the water. And be sure to replace the life jacket when your child outgrows it.

Gadget Guide

Don't rely on inflatable toys, rafts, or water wings to keep kids afloat in water over their heads. It's okay for non-swimming children to use them as long as parents are supervising and are within reach of the child.

Tales from the Safety Zone

Of the children ages 14 and under who drowned in boating-related incidents over a four-year period, the National SAFE KIDS Campaign estimated that more than 70 percent could have been saved if the children had been wearing PFDs.

Natural Bodies of Water

Ponds, rivers, lakes, and other natural bodies of water require special precautions. In these places, kids should swim only in designated areas and only with adult supervision.

Ponds

Besides the dangers from drowning, farm ponds can also harbor disease if they receive fertilizer or pesticide runoff. They also may contain broken glass or jagged rocks.

Children should swim only in ponds that have been maintained for that purpose and that have rescue equipment nearby. They should never swim there alone.

For information on maintaining a pond for swimming, see Chapter 24, "Down on the Farm."

Down by the Beach

At the ocean, children should swim in areas with lifeguards and obey warnings about high surf and strong undertow. Also caution your children not to overestimate their swimming ability. If they go out too far, they may tire before they can get back to shore. Relying on a raft isn't safe either because it could deflate or be swept out of reach.

Tell your child that if he drifts or swims out too far, he should call for help, remain calm, and float on his back or tread water until help comes. He will drift with the tide at an angle to the shore. The wave action will gradually bring him near the shore but some distance from where he first entered the ocean. If he encounters an undertow or riptide, he should not fight it but rather go with the flow to catch his breath and then swim parallel to the shore.

Watch Out!

Small children have drowned when they wandered near farm ponds, drainage ditches, wells, and irrigation canals. If you have any of these near your home, extra supervision is necessary. You might also urge the owners of the land on which these bodies of water are found to put up fences and post "No Trespassing" signs. You can warn them about legal liability should a child be injured there.

You're on Thin Ice

Kids don't drown only in warm weather. Those who walk or skate on frozen bodies of water are at risk if the ice breaks. This is an especially dangerous situation because hypothermia can keep an otherwise strong swimmer from saving himself. Also, the hole to climb out of may be hard for the victim to find once he's gone under.

Let your child skate only on lakes or ponds where local officials have determined that the ice is strong enough. Typically, safe skating requires a depth of at least five to six inches. It's best to steer clear of the pond's edges or places where logs or rocks stick out of the water, because those are the first places where the ice will melt.

The Least You Need to Know

➤ Don't allow children to go into a pool, hot tub, spa, or whirlpool without adult supervision.

➤ CPR can save a child's life; learn it.

➤ Backyard pools should be enclosed by a locked fence or other barrier.

➤ Start swimming lessons early, but not before age 3.

➤ Life jackets are a must for children on boats.

➤ In ponds, lakes, and other natural bodies of water, swim only in designated areas and never alone.

➤ Skate only where local officials have determined that the ice is thick enough.

Chapter 16

Wheels and Blades: Recreation Safety

In This Chapter

➤ The in-line skating craze

➤ Skateboarding the safe way

➤ Taking to the ski slopes

➤ Tubing and water skiing

➤ Motorized recreation isn't kids' stuff

Shoe leather doesn't get kids where they want to go fast enough. That's why they love all manner of activities involving equipment that speeds them along the pavement, ice, snow, and water. Here's how to help them stay safe in the process.

In-Line Skates

Its popularity with kids is one reason in-line skating is among the fastest-growing sports in America.

Once kids discovered how much faster they could go on in-line skates, traditional roller skates became passé. Cruising speeds on these skates average 10 to 17 miles per hour. Kids don't like being confined to indoor rinks, either, which has been the traditional venue for roller skating. And in-line skating is versatile. It has spawned a whole new sport: roller hockey, which is similar to ice hockey but without the ice.

Safety Savvy

If you don't skate yourself, consider asking an experienced parent or teenager to give your child some pointers. Many communities have formal classes for both in-line skating and roller hockey. To find out if there are certified instructors in your area, call the International In-line Skating Association (IISA) at 910-762-7004 or visit the Web site www.iisa.org.

How Young Can They Start?

Most experts agree that when kids reach 7 or 8 years old, they have the muscle coordination and mental maturity to learn to skate safely.

While your child is learning, take her to an empty parking lot or other paved area where surfaces are smooth and there is no traffic. Or you may have access to a rink with space set aside for beginners. The skills she needs to master include steering, controlling her speed, and—most important—braking.

Buying Skates

The rule on skates for kids is not to buy a "too large" pair that they can grow into. If the skates are too big— or too small—your child can develop blisters. Some models come with removable liners in two sizes so the skates can be used longer. Another option is to shop at consignment stores where you may find a pair in your child's size that are in good condition because some other child outgrew them.

Necessary Safety Gear

Practiced properly and with the right gear, in-line skating is a relatively safe sport. Safety gear is designed to work together, so it's important to wear all of it, which includes:

➤ A helmet labeled ANSI, ASTM, or Snell approved. A bike helmet is acceptable. (See Chapter 13, "A Ticket to Ride: Safe Biking.") If your child engages in aggressive maneuvers, however, consider buying a multi-sport helmet sold specifically for use with in-line skates and skateboards. It covers more of the back of the head for protection during backward falls. Multi-sport helmets are not designed for biking, however, and shouldn't be used as a substitute for a bike helmet.

➤ Knee pads securely fastened so they won't come off during a slide.

➤ Elbow pads for protection during a sideways fall.

➤ Wrist protectors with hard plastic linings that allow a skater to slide on the pavement during a fall.

What best-dressed in-line skaters wear: helmets, wrist protectors, and knee and elbow pads. (Courtesy of the Consumer Product Safety Commission)

When your child outgrows his skates, check his protective gear in case he's outgrown that, too.

Children who play in organized roller hockey leagues need additional protective equipment because of the risk of getting hit with a stick or the puck. This means helmets with face shields, shin guards, and mouthpieces. Protective cups are required for boys.

Rules of the Road

Along with requiring your child to wear safety gear, establish these safety rules:

➤ Don't ride in the street. Most in-line skating fatalities have involved collisions with motor vehicles.

➤ Don't ride after dark.

➤ Don't ride on wet or rough pavement, gravel, or dirt.

➤ Don't wear headphones or anything else that obstructs hearing or vision.

Skater Etiquette

To avoid streets, many skaters are taking to bike paths and areas set aside in public parks. They may be sharing the road with cyclists, joggers,

Safety Savvy

If your child wants to play roller hockey, she can find out about the rules, local instructors, and leagues from USA Hockey at 800-566-3288 or www.usahockey.com.

Watch Out!

Don't buy a child's argument that he no longer needs to wear as much protective gear because he's become an experienced skater. He actually may need it more, because confidence breeds the inclination to go faster or try more daring stunts.

and even parents pushing strollers. For that reason, your child should be taught to stay alert and to be courteous to others. He should keep to the right on sidewalks or paths and pass others on the left. In situations where their paths cross, skaters should yield to pedestrians.

The National Skate Patrol

Members of the National Skate Patrol are trained volunteers who patrol public skating areas and provide assistance to skaters, including on-the-spot instruction, advice, and maps. They carry two-way radios to summon help for injured skaters. Kids can get safety tips from patrol members, who are identified by their NSP T-shirts. For information, contact the IISA at the phone number or Web site mentioned earlier in this chapter.

Tales from the Safety Zone

A generation ago, in-line skating was unheard of. Michael Zaidman, director of the National Roller Skating Museum, writes in an IISA publication that, in 1960, a Chicago company tried to market something resembling today's in-line skate, but it took Scott Olsen, a young Minneapolis hockey player, to perfect it. Looking for a way to play hockey during warm months when there was no ice, he bought a pair of the Chicago skates at a used sporting goods store and modified them by adding better wheels and a heel brake. In 1984, a Minneapolis businessman bought Olsen's fledging company, Rollerblade, Inc., and broadened the market from hockey players to millions of skating enthusiasts.

Skateboards

The risk of getting critically hurt is twice as high for skateboarders as it is for in-line skaters. Among the reasons: skateboarders are less likely to wear protective gear and they are more likely to perform dangerous stunts that result in falls. (They tend to fall backward more often than in-line skaters, risking head injuries.)

Your child can reduce his chance of injury by learning how to fall. Tell him that if he loses his balance, he should crouch down so he won't have so far to fall, then try to roll rather than put his arms out to catch himself.

All decked out for safe skateboarding, with helmet, knee and elbow pads, and wrist guards. (Courtesy of the Consumer Product Safety Commission)

Safe Skating Places

Irregular surfaces are a common cause of falls, so kids should check the area for obstructions be-fore skateboarding. Skateboarding in the street is a no-no, as is riding with more than one person on the same board.

If your kids don't have safe places to skateboard, do what other parents have done: Petition your community leaders to create skateboarding areas away from pedestrians or traffic.

Tubing and Water Skiing

In Chapter 15, "On the Waterfront," we talked about safe swimming, but there's more to water recreation than just swimming. Take water skiing and tubing, for example.

In tubing, you sit on an innertube, or other tube designed just for the purpose, that's connected by rope to a power boat.

Watch Out!

The American Academy of Pediatrics says children younger than 5 should not ride a skateboard because of their high center of gravity, immature neuromuscular system, and poor judgment skills.

For a safe ride, tubers and water skiers should always wear life jackets. Before beginning either sport, participants should check their equipment including the rope which can become frayed.

Some injuries have occurred when the rider or skier hit a floating dock, debris, or some other obstacle such as a rock sticking out of the water. That's why the driver should be knowledgeable about any obstructions in the water and know where the water becomes shallow.

For both these sports, there should always be a second person in the boat beside the driver to watch the tube rider or water skier and to keep the tow rope from going slack so the rider doesn't get tangled in it.

Winter Wonderland

Snow? Yippee! Get out those sleds, skates, snowboards, and skis! Here are some safety tips to keep these winter sports injury-free.

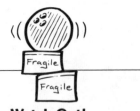

Watch Out!

Know how to protect your little snow bunnies from both frostbite and winter sunburn. For information on skin protection, see Chapter 23, "The Great Outdoors."

Gadget Guide

Inflatable snow tubes are popular because they go fast and can become airborne when they hit a bump or small hill. For these reasons, they also cause more injuries than standard sleds. Kids should take care to use them only on wide slopes that have no obstructions.

Sledding

For safe sledding, pick snow-covered (as opposed to ice-covered) gentle slopes that are far from traffic and free of trees and fences. Also, check for snow-covered obstacles, such as large rocks or tree stumps.

The safest sleds and toboggans have steering mechanisms so kids can maintain some measure of control. Snow disks, which go very fast and can be steered only with weight shifts or dragging of feet, cause many injuries. The safest position on a sled is sitting upright rather than lying flat on the stomach, which increases the chance of head and abdominal injuries.

Ice Skating

The primary risk in ice skating is falling through a break in the ice. This is an especially dangerous situation because hypothermia can keep an otherwise strong swimmer from saving himself. Let your child skate only at rinks or on lakes or ponds where local officials have determined that the ice is strong enough. Kids should skate with friends, never alone. That way, should there be an emergency, someone can go for help.

When there are lots of others on the ice, remind your kids to skate in the direction of the crowd and not dart across the ice.

Skiing

You can see kids as young as three on the ski slopes these days. This popular sport has become a real family affair.

When you take your child skiing, your first stop probably will be the ski rental shop where personnel should be able to help you find equipment to fit your child's size. This is important because kids sometimes get hurt using equipment that is too big for them and therefore harder to control. The skis, boots, and bindings all need to be the proper size.

Gadget Guide

Skaters who keep their blades sharp are less likely to fall than those with dull blades.

Your child also should wear a helmet. More common in Europe, wearing helmets on the slopes is catching on here due in part to some high-profile skiing fatalities and because of a publicity campaign launched by the Consumer Product Safety Commission (CPSC).

Ski helmets cost between $50 and $100 and have a rigid outer shell and a soft inner layer with thermal insulation to keep the head warm. The brow area is shaped to allow room for goggles. Helmets also can be rented. CPSC recommends them for all skiers and snowboarders, not just children. Set a good example for your kids by wearing one yourself.

Tales from the Safety Zone

A study by the CPSC concluded that helmet use by skiers and snowboarders could prevent or reduce the severity of 53 percent of head injuries to children under age 15. The proportion of skiing and snowboarding head injuries is higher in children than in any other age group. Interestingly, the CPSC study found that, while hospital-treated skiing injuries overall declined substantially between 1993 and 1997, head injuries remained relatively constant. The decline was attributed to redesigns in ski equipment, particularly bindings, that have reduced leg injuries.

If your child hasn't skied before, enroll him in a class. He'll probably learn more that way than if you try to teach him, and he'll enjoy being with other kids who also are

Safety Savvy

Some ski areas are so crowded that it's hard for kids to find their parents for periodic check-ins. A few resorts rent cell phones and beepers to keep families in touch. At the least, you should pin your name and your hotel's phone number and address onto your child's jacket so you can be reached if there is a problem.

Gadget Guide

Not all helmets are right for all sports. This poses a dilemma for parents whose children engage in several. Although manufacturers have developed some multi-sport helmets, the designs are still evolving. When you buy a helmet for any of the activities described in this chapter, check the label to see whether it is suitable for the sport in which it is to be used.

learning. Classes for children are geared to their ages and attention spans. Instructors use techniques that make skill-building a game. Safety is an important part of the lessons.

You can reinforce the safety lessons by reminding your kids to:

➤ Stop only on the edges of the slope, not in the middle.

➤ Stay alert for other skiers, especially when crossing trails.

➤ Always ski with a buddy or a parent so one can go for help if the other is injured.

➤ Ski only in designated areas.

When your child is first learning, have him stick to the beginner trails. If he isn't skiing with you, require periodic check-ins. Kids don't always notice when they are getting too cold or too tired, so you need to monitor their condition. More are injured at the end of the day when fatigue affects their ability to stay in control.

Snowboarding

An innovation of the 1970s, snowboarding has rapidly gained a large following. The board resembles a skateboard and the activity is similar to surfboarding. Participants don't use poles and their boot bindings don't release as with skis.

Snowboarding requires a fair amount of lower-leg control, and young children don't have the balance and muscular development to manage it safely. The American Academy of Pediatrics recommends parents not let their children try snowboarding until they are at least age 7.

Play it safe and have your snowboarder wear a helmet. Lessons are important, especially in safe jumping since jumps are a key part of the sport and also a leading cause of injuries. Snowboarders should not be on the slopes alone.

Motorized Sports

Motor power means going even faster, but with greater speed and power comes greater danger.

All-Terrain Vehicles

All-terrain vehicles (ATVs) are motorized recreational cycles with oversized tires that are designed for off-the-road use on a variety of terrains. They can reach speeds from 30 to 50 miles per hour.

Although there has been a significant reduction in ATV deaths and injuries since the 1980s, these vehicles remain a major hazard for children.

One reason for the injury reduction has been the ban on manufacturing three-wheeled models, which aren't as stable as four-wheeled ATVs. A 1988 consent decree between the CPSC and ATV distributors halted sales. Some sold prior to that are still in use, however.

The decree also required safety improvements in the four-wheeled versions and recommendations that adult-size ATVs (engines of 90 cc or greater) not be used by children under age 16.

Although smaller versions of ATVs are marketed for 12- to 15-year-olds, the American Academy of Pediatrics and others are urging the passage of legislation to restrict all ATVs to people 16 and older.

Watch Out!

Many states have enacted laws governing the use of ATVs. Find out what yours requires, if anything, before letting your adolescent drive one. Some states require drivers to take a safety course, but you should require it of your child, even if your state doesn't. Ask your local dealer about classes or contact your state maternal and child health agency.

Gadget Guide

ATV riders need motorcycle helmets, not those designed for bicycle riding.

If your adolescent rides an ATV, he should wear a helmet and protective clothing such as a long-sleeved shirt, long pants, boots, and gloves. Also, caution him not to take a passenger. The large seats are designed to allow drivers to shift their weight to maintain their balance, not to carry other people.

Personal Water Craft

Personal water craft look similar to ATVs except that they have runners that skim the water. As with ATVs, we question the ability of children to manage any vehicle with this much power. Personal water craft should be restricted to persons 16 and over, in our view. This is now the requirement in some states.

Safety Savvy

The National Children's Center for Rural and Agricultural Health and Safety, part of the Children's Safety Network, offers information on ATV, personal water craft, and snowmobile safety. Call 888-924-SAFE (888-924-7233) or visit www.marshmed.org/nfmc/children/.

Snowmobiles

Snowmobiles are powerful motorized vehicles that can achieve high speeds. It's common for children in rural areas to operate them, but we believe no child under the age of 16 should drive one. This also is the age recommendation of the American Academy of Pediatrics.

Snowmobile dangers include colliding with fixed objects, falling through thin ice, and suffering hypothermia after breaking down in a remote area.

If your child is a passenger on a snowmobile, he should wear an approved helmet. Make sure he also wears goggles, gloves, boots, and other warm clothing.

Kids often are hurt when an adult snowmobile driver takes risks such as speeding, driving at night, or driving under the influence of alcohol. Don't let your child ride with anyone whose training, skill, or judgment you doubt.

The Least You Need to Know

➤ Helmets aren't just for cyclists; they should be worn by in-line skaters, snow skiers and snow boarders, skateboarders, ATV riders, and snowmobilers, too.

➤ Enjoying recreational activities with a friend is safer because there's someone to help in an emergency.

➤ It's best to stick to areas designated for a particular activity.

➤ Training courses help children learn skills and safety.

➤ Kids younger than 16 should not drive ATVs, snowmobiles, or personal water craft.

Chapter 17

Flex Those Muscles!

In This Chapter

➤ Sedentary children face injury and health risks

➤ The phys ed crisis

➤ Starting kids on the road to lifelong fitness

➤ The dangers of adult exercise equipment

➤ How to prevent your child from becoming obese

Exercise has more to do with injury prevention than you might think. This is because out-of-shape children are more prone to injury when they engage in a sport or other physical activity.

It's the reason professional athletes work so hard in the off-season to stay in shape—they know they could be seriously hurt if their muscles lose their tone and strength. Some experts estimate that half of all youth sports injuries could be eliminated if kids were better prepared to play their games.

Unfortunately, we're raising a generation of sedentary kids. With this comes a steady rise in the number of obese children who face a variety of health risks. We need to get kids moving again and help them have fun in the process so they'll stick with it. It's never too late to start kids on the road to lifelong fitness.

How Did Kids Get So Out of Shape?

Just how out of shape are they? One study comparing national fitness test scores of 6- to 14-year-olds from 1980 to 1994 found today's children have significantly less endurance than their counterparts 15 years ago. For example, the number of boys ages 10 to 14 who can't perform a single push-up has risen 64 percent.

Safety Savvy

The Centers for Disease Control and Prevention report these benefits of regular physical activity in childhood and adolescence: It improves strength and endurance, helps build healthy bones and muscles, helps control weight, reduces anxiety and stress, increases self-esteem, and may improve blood pressure and cholesterol levels.

The situation gets worse as kids grow into adolescence. The landmark Surgeon General's Report on Physical Activity and Health released in 1996 found that almost half of all youths age 12 to 20 were not vigorously active on a regular basis and 14 percent were completely inactive. Girls are twice as likely to be inactive as boys.

In some ways, safety concerns have actually *contributed* to the problem. Fearing harm from strangers or traffic, today's parents are more likely to drive their kids everywhere rather than let them walk or ride their bikes, as previous generations did.

Many children who stay home alone after school are required by their parents to stay inside with the doors locked rather than play outdoors. It's easy to understand, then, why kids fill their hours with television and computer games. And once they're hooked, it's hard to break the habit.

Phys Ed Classes Are Woefully Inadequate

One logical place for kids to get in shape is at school. But physical education (phys ed or PE) classes have been so eroded that some elementary children get less than an hour a week. Too many budget-crunched school systems look at PE as a frill that can be cut along with music and art. Many overcrowded schools have too many students and too little space for kids to move around even when they do have PE class.

The "Shape of the Nation" report issued by the National Association for Sport and Physical Education (NASPE) found that only one state, Illinois, required daily PE for all students K–12. Most states mandate some PE, but, in elementary schools, for example, the times range from only 50 to 200 minutes per week. NASPE found the majority of high school students take PE during only one year from ninth through twelfth grades.

Tales from the Safety Zone

In 1987, Congress passed a resolution encouraging state and local governments and local education agencies to provide high-quality, daily physical education programs for all children in K–12. In 1996, the Surgeon General issued a report recommending the same thing. So did the Centers for Disease Control and Prevention the following year, in its guidelines for schools. Yet, despite these and other national recommendations, there is no federal mandate or funding targeted to physical education.

A New Approach to PE

One reason parents may not be up in arms about the lack of PE classes in school is that many of them didn't get much out of PE when they were kids. If you didn't do well on the annual fitness test, if you didn't have a knack for fielding balls or using the gymnastics equipment, PE was mostly a humiliating experience. In games such as dodge ball, where the least-skilled are eliminated first, only the athletically gifted got the playing time.

The male-oriented, competitive approach has been especially tough on girls, because many of them tend to enjoy cooperative activities more.

There's also little "physical" in too many of today's physical education classes. The U.S. Department of Health and Human Services says kids in PE class should be active for at least 50 percent of the time. Researchers have found, however, that kids engage in vigorous activity for only a few minutes in a typical class. The rest of the time is spent standing around while the teacher takes attendance, or waiting for a turn to shoot a basket or hit a ball.

PE class in the majority of today's schools is taught the same as it was in the 1950s. Fortunately, PE reformers have created new programs that are being tried in a few innovative schools. The emphasis is not on competition but on helping kids build skills and develop an interest in some activity they will enjoy doing on their own, even into adulthood.

Anything to keep the heart pumping—from doing the hula hoop to in-line skating and biking—can be found in the new-style PE class. Games are adapted to de-emphasize competition and replace it with cooperation. In one curriculum, for example, a kickball game requires the whole team to run the bases in order to score. Instead of running races, kids run at their own pace while hooked to heart rate monitors so they can see the fitness progress they are making.

How to Get More PE for Your Kids

Your school can put more focus on fitness if you and other parents make it clear this is a priority. Find out how much time children spend in PE each week. Just as you get academic test scores, ask to receive annual fitness scores. Find out how many kids are in a class and how much time is actually spent in vigorous activities. Find out if all kids are playing all the time in team sports. Ask whether the teachers in charge of PE classes are actually PE specialists or have received adequate training.

Armed with this information, go to your parent-teacher association to discuss ways your school can improve its program. If funding is an issue, you may have to elevate the discussion to the district level.

How to Get Your Kids Moving Again

How your child spends his out-of-school hours has a direct impact on his fitness. One way you can encourage him is to set a good example. If you can find physical activities to do together, your child might be more motivated.

Here are some specific steps you can take:

➤ Limit TV-watching and video game playing—no more than two hours a day—for both kids and adults in the family.

➤ Give your child "fitness" gifts for birthdays—anything from jump ropes to in-line skates.

➤ Make his birthday party something physical. Indoor climbing gyms are popular with the younger set. Older kids might like ice skating, bowling, or facilities with climbing walls, which have become the "in" thing.

➤ Walk with him instead of driving whenever possible.

➤ Make family weekends and vacations active ones. Take a bike ride, swim, or go hiking.

➤ Offer him lessons in tennis, horseback riding, or some other activity he wants to try.

➤ Get exercise tapes with fun music that kids and adults can do together.

Strength Training, Kid-Style

Another way to work out with your child is to take her with you to the gym. Some YMCAs and health clubs now offer special equipment and classes just for kids.

The demand for children's fitness programs has even led to a health club in Chicago that is exclusively for kids. It plans to open franchises in other cities.

Tales from the Safety Zone

A device invented by obesity researchers at St. Luke's–Roosevelt Hospital Center in New York could become the next hot trend in exercise for kids. According to *USA Today,* the researchers hooked a stationary bike to a TV that would work only if the bike were peddled. Overweight children ages 8 to 12 were randomly assigned either to the TV-bike or to a TV that simply had a stationary bike in front of it. The kids who had to pedal to run the TV chose to bike an average of an hour a week, the others only eight minutes.

A key part of these programs is strength training to improve muscles and build bones. Although strength training was long thought to be unnecessary—and perhaps even unsafe—for children, current research shows that if done correctly it's beneficial for all ages, from kids to seniors.

What's Strength Training?

Moving against resistance, such as when you lift weights or do push-ups, are types of strength training. This is not the same as body-building, an adult competitive sport.

Safety Savvy

Both the American Academy of Pediatrics and the American College of Sports Medicine promote youth strength training. They caution, however, that there is the potential for injury unless programs are designed specifically for children and are supervised by a qualified instructor.

Girls who shun the idea of lifting weights for fear of developing bulging muscles shouldn't worry. Their bodies don't have the hormones necessary for it. Strength training is especially important for helping girls build strong bones and prevent osteoporosis later in life.

A strength training program includes a series of exercises aimed at increasing the strength, endurance, and power of muscles. Kids who do this will be less likely to be injured in sports and will have more stamina when they play. Research shows kids ages 7 to 12 can increase their strength by approximately 40 percent in an 8- to 12-week program of two or three weekly sessions.

Home Gym No-Nos

Although we think it's important for kids to see their parents maintaining a fitness regime, the equipment you use at home is potentially dangerous to younger ones.

Try to limit young children's access to gym equipment. It's best if you can keep it in a room with a locked door. But, if the equipment is in the family room, keeping kids away can be difficult.

Gadget Guide

To retrofit a bike you already have, you can buy special wheel covers and chain guards at sporting goods stores or from many manufacturers.

Children's fingers can be amputated if they touch moving parts of exercise equipment.
(Courtesy of the Consumer Product Safety Commission)

Stationary Bikes

Stationary bikes are one of the biggest hazards. Small children who don't realize the danger can get their fingers or toes caught in the spokes, chain, or sprocket while a parent or older sibling is pedaling. To eliminate this hazard, buy a model that has enclosed chains, wheels, and sprockets, or that uses some form of resistance other than a wheel. Find a way to immobilize the bike when you are not using it.

Treadmills

The conveyor belt on a treadmill is hazardous because a child can fall off while it's moving, or his clothes can get caught and pull him into the mechanism.

The safest models require keys to turn them on. Unplug your treadmill when you aren't on it. Don't use it when your child is around and can see how it works or might try to climb on. If you have the kind that collapses, fold it up and store it out of your child's sight.

Free Weights and Jump Ropes

Weights can fall on a child's head or crush his hands or feet if he manages to lift them. A few kids have actually been strangled with jump ropes they found hanging from exercise equipment or hooks. Lock these items away when you aren't using them.

Gadget Guide

Any kind of exercise equipment that has moving parts—from rowing machines to skiing simulators—have the potential to crush fingers or cause other serious injuries. Ask your sporting goods store about child safety features and add-ons with any equipment you purchase.

The Connection Between Obesity and Injury

By rearing a generation of sedentary children, we've produced a lot of overweight children—as many as 25 percent of them by some estimates.

The National Center for Health Statistics reports that more than twice as many kids are overweight today than 30 years ago. Lack of physical activity is one of the major causes of overweight children. (Another is poor eating habits.)

Kids who are heavy are more likely to suffer from stressed lower joints and other orthopedic problems. If their excess weight leads to less physical activity, they will be more likely to get hurt when they exert themselves. Obesity also puts kids at risk of diabetes, cardiovascular diseases, and other illnesses.

Tales from the Safety Zone

A 1996 study by the Federal Interagency Forum on Child and Family Statistics reported that most American children have diets that are rated "poor" or "in need of improvement." As children get older, the report said, the quality of their diet declines. Twenty-four percent of 2- to 5-year-olds had a good diet compared with only 6 percent of kids ages 13 to 18, mostly because the teenagers drink soda instead of milk and eat less fruit.

The Role of Calcium

Calcium is essential for building strong bones and preventing fractures. Drinking milk is the easiest way to get enough calcium, but most children and teens don't get the recommended amount.

Children 4 to 8 need 800 mg of calcium (two to three glasses of milk per day). Kids 9 to 18, whose bones are growing rapidly, need 1,300 mg of calcium or four to five glasses of milk per day. Low-fat milk has as much calcium as whole milk and is healthier.

Watch Out!

Milk and milk products contain other important nutrients, including vitamin D, which assists calcium absorption. That's why you shouldn't rely on calcium-fortified juices as your child's main source of the mineral. They lack adequate amounts of vitamin D.

Instilling Good Eating Habits

Here are some tips for getting kids to eat healthier:

➤ Cut down on your family's fast-food meals.

➤ Keep healthy snacks handy at home instead of junk food.

➤ Don't talk about dieting; talk about healthy eating.

➤ Don't use dessert as a reward.

➤ Let kids learn to stop eating when they're full. Don't make them clean their plates.

➤ Limit soda; offer low-fat milk to children after age 2.

➤ Set a good example by eating healthy yourself.

If you start offering healthy foods when your children are very young, they'll be less likely to develop bad habits when they get older.

The Least You Need to Know

➤ Sedentary kids are at risk of injury, obesity, and other health dangers.

➤ Schools should put more emphasis on physical education for lifelong fitness.

➤ Kids will be more inclined to be physically active if you make it fun and join in.

➤ Home gym equipment poses hazards for young children.

➤ Teach your kids how to eat healthy.

Chapter 18

Preventing Sports Injuries

In This Chapter

➤ What parents and coaches can do to reduce injuries

➤ Treating injuries at home

➤ How to know if an injury needs medical attention

➤ Getting the right shoes and protective gear

➤ Safety tips for eight specific sports

Sports and children are a natural match. Kids who participate in sports get exercise and develop coordination while learning sportsmanship, team work, discipline, and other skills valuable throughout life.

Children's participation in sports, both formal and informal, has been growing in the United States, especially among girls. But along with the benefits come risks. More players means increasing numbers of sports injuries, and children are more vulnerable than adults because their bodies are still growing and their athletic skills aren't fully developed.

Minor injuries are almost inevitable. Cuts, scrapes, bruises, and the like are part of the game, so to speak, and the risks of getting them are outweighed by the benefits sports offer. Serious injuries, especially to the head and neck, are another matter.

They're not worth the risk, and luckily there are ways to reduce the chances of them happening. The use of helmets and other safety gear, improvements in sports rules, and adherence to participants' age and weight recommendations are examples. In this chapter, you find ways to keep your kids in the game and away from the injured reserve lists in the most popular kids' sports today.

For more information on other recreational activities, such as in-line skating, see Chapter 16, "Wheels and Blades: Recreation Safety." For more about the importance of physical fitness, see Chapter 17, "Flex Those Muscles!"

Making the Playing Field Safe

Sports organizers, officials, coaches, and parents all have responsibilities for keeping young athletes healthy.

The American Academy of Orthopaedic Surgeons (AAOS) recommends that team organizers group athletes by size, skill level, and physical maturity rather than by chronological age, especially in contact sports. If this isn't possible, coaches should modify the sport to accommodate kids with varying ability levels. Game officials can make sure kids play fair, and they can call fouls or otherwise sanction players who engage in unnecessarily rough or dangerous play that can injure others.

Watch Out!

Overzealous parents and coaches can be so bent on winning that they push kids to extremes that may lead to injury. In particular, some parents pressure their children to play competitively at very young ages, when they're more vulnerable to injury. Let your child play for the fun of it. If he develops a competitive spirit through his participation, it should be without adult pressure.

Coaches can also minimize injuries if they:

➤ Check playing areas regularly to make sure conditions are safe. Note especially if there are any holes in the turf or if glass or other debris is scattered on the playing surface.

➤ Insist that children wear appropriate safety gear.

➤ Have kids bring water bottles to practices and games and make sure they take breaks to avoid dehydration when playing in hot weather.

➤ Require kids to warm up their muscles before play and stress to them the importance of staying in peak physical condition.

➤ Don't let kids overexert themselves on the playing field. For example, baseball pitchers should be limited to a certain number of pitches or innings.

➤ Ensure that all participants know the rules—and play by them.

Parents can support their athletes by encouraging them to eat a healthy diet and get enough sleep. Before your child starts a new sport, you should consult with your pediatrician about the need for a physical.

Get to know your child's coaches so you're assured that they are not sacrificing safety by pushing kids to win.

Boys and Girls Together

Until they reach puberty, it's generally okay for boys and girls to play sports together. After puberty, however, boys become larger and stronger as they gain more muscle mass. At that point, doctors usually recommend they not play on the co-ed teams. Exceptions are made occasionally for an outstanding female player for whom there is no girls' team.

When Injuries Happen

Kids are more prone to athletic injuries than adults because their muscles, tendons, and ligaments are still growing. The AAOS says an injury that causes a bruise or strain in an adult could cause serious damage to a child's growth plate—the developing cartilage where bone growth is occurring.

Injuries fall into two categories: acute, which are caused by sudden trauma, and overuse. An example of the latter is what's called "Little League Elbow," that describes a common injury to young throwers in several sports, not just baseball.

Is It Serious?

Any child or adult experiences occasional minor aches and pains from physical exertion such as playing sports, but pay attention and seek a doctor's opinion if your child's pain persists or if his playing is affected. An injury that is left untreated can cause permanent damage.

What to Do for an Injury

The typical treatment orthopedic surgeons recommend for simple strains and sprains is "RICE." That stands for **r**est, **i**ce, **c**ompression, and elevation. With a sore ankle, for example, the child might be advised to avoid walking on it, apply ice to reduce swelling, wrap it with elastic bandages, and elevate it as much as possible.

Safety Savvy

Kids need adequate calcium to build strong bones and help avoid fractures later in life. Milk is one of the best sources and also contains vitamin D, which helps calcium absorption. Encourage your kids to drink at least three glasses a day. If they won't drink milk, try other dairy products such as yogurt and cheese.

Watch Out!

Never encourage your child to "play through the pain." Kids who are overly tired or in pain should stay on the sidelines.

Depending on the type and severity of an injury, the doctor might recommend braces, physical therapy, strengthening exercises, and reducing or suspending athletic activity.

Coaching the Coaches

Coaches should be certified in cardiopulmonary resuscitation and first aid and have first-aid equipment with them at all practices and games. Also, they should have a plan for summoning help in an emergency. Cellular phones are a good idea for this purpose.

Ideally, your child's coaches have been trained in coaching techniques for their particular sport, but coaches of children's teams often are parent volunteers with no formal training. Many youth sports organizations offer weekend coaching clinics that novice coaches can take advantage of. Training makes coaches better able to teach fundamental skills and keep players safe.

If the Shoe Fits

Along with sports-specific safety equipment, a shoe that fits properly can prevent injuries. Sometimes it's hard to know if a shoe fits your child's foot properly. Here are some tips from the AAOS:

➤ Go shoe-shopping right after your child has been running or practicing her sport. That's when her feet are largest.

➤ Have her wear the same type of sock she wears to play sports.

➤ Have the sales clerk measure both feet. One usually is a little larger than the other. Fit the new shoes to the larger foot.

➤ Buy a pair of shoes that allow a half inch of space between the longest toe and the end of the shoe.

➤ Have your child walk around the store to make sure the shoes feel comfortable. She shouldn't have to "break them in."

Sports Specifics

Different sports call for different types of safety measures and equipment. When you buy equipment, look for labels indicating the equipment has been approved by the

American Society for Testing and Materials or the National Operating Committee on Standards for Athletic Equipment.

Following is a brief run-down on safety measures for several popular sports.

Tales from the Safety Zone

Each year, more than 775,000 children under age 15 are treated in hospital emergency rooms for sports-related injuries: mostly from falls, collisions, being struck by an object, or overexertion. Approximately 60 percent of the injuries from organized sports occurred during practice rather than a game. In one Canadian study, almost three fourths of sports injuries occurred while children participated in unorganized athletic activities rather than organized sports.

Soccer

Millions of American kids have taken up soccer. Because there is not as much physical contact as in other sports, children can begin play at very young ages and on co-ed as well as single-sex teams. It's also a sport that children of all body sizes can learn to play. And the constant running provides an excellent cardiovascular workout.

The Right Soccer Equipment

All players should wear shin guards that cover the leg from below the knee to just above the foot. Knee-high socks are worn over the shin guards. Avoid shoes with screw-in metal cleats; molded plastic cleats are softer and therefore less likely to cause injury.

As children become more experienced and skilled at the game, they will want to learn about headers (bouncing the ball off their heads). They should be taught to hit the ball only with the forehead and not the temple.

Balls come in various sizes for players of different age groups. Check with your coach to make sure your child practices with the right size ball.

Safety Savvy

For more soccer information, contact the U.S. Youth Soccer Organization at 800-4-SOCCER (800-476-2237) or visit the Web site www.youthsoccer.org.

Movable Soccer Goals Can Be Dangerous

The Consumer Product Safety Commission (CPSC) is aware of 23 deaths since 1979 from soccer goals that tipped over and crushed children who climbed on them or hung from the cross bars.

Most of the goals that caused injury were "homemade" by school shop classes, custodians, or local welders. They can be heavy and unstable. The CPSC offers these injury-prevention tips:

➤ Instruct kids never to climb on the net or the frame of the soccer goal.

➤ Use extreme caution when moving the goals.

➤ To prevent goals from falling over during use, they should be anchored to the ground.

➤ Check all connecting hardware before each use and replace damaged or missing fasteners immediately.

➤ When goals are not in use, anchor or chain goals to fence posts, dugouts or other permanent structures.

➤ For storage in the off-season, take the goals completely apart.

➤ Use the goals only on flat fields.

Soccer goals must be anchored to prevent them from falling on children. (Courtesy of the Consumer Product Safety Commission)

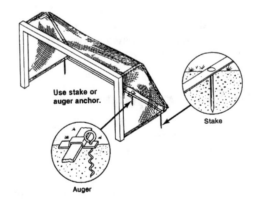

Use stake or auger anchor.

Stake

Auger

Baseball

According to the National SAFE KIDS Campaign, of all youth sports, baseball has the highest fatality rate, even though it requires much less safety equipment than such high-risk sports as football or hockey.

Getting hit in the head with a ball is one of the potentially serious injuries a child can suffer playing baseball. Players should wear a batting helmet when batting, running bases, or waiting to bat. Some youth leagues also require players to wear helmets with face guards to reduce injuries to eyes, noses, and mouths. You also should remind your child to keep his eye on the ball, not only to improve his performance but to keep him from getting hit.

Boys should wear protective cups. Mitts should fit players well; they shouldn't be so loose that they might fall off. Don't let children play with bats that are too long or too heavy: Your child should be able to hold the bat at shoulder length, pointed straight out, with a steady, not shaky, arm.

Gadget Guide

If your child's team has helmets that are too large for your child, buy him his own. A helmet that slips doesn't offer much protection.

Catchers should use a catcher's mitt and wear protective gear on their heads, faces, throats, chests, and shins.

The Consumer Product Safety Commission says break-away bases, which yield on impact, could reduce large numbers of leg and foot injuries kids suffer when sliding into bases. Soft-core balls are also recommended. Cleats made of molded plastic are safer than metal ones.

Pitchers are vulnerable to repetitive stress injuries to their arms. If your child's pitching arm hurts, he should stop playing and tell the coach. Little League rules limit the number of innings a player can pitch per week, depending on his age, as one way to prevent such injuries. For example, 12-year-olds can pitch up to six innings a week and 13- to 16-year-olds can pitch nine. Baseball associations' rules vary, so check with the organization your child plays in for more information.

Softball

Although softball doesn't have as high a rate of injuries as baseball, there's still plenty of potential for head injury and falls. Players should wear batting helmets and cleats and follow the same safety rules described in the section on baseball. Breakaway bases should be used, too.

Hockey

Because there is so much contact in ice hockey, players are required to wear a lot of protective gear including helmets with face masks; pads for shoulders, shins and elbows; padded pants; gloves; jerseys; mouth guards; and athletic supporters.

Don't buy adult equipment or youth equipment that is too big for your child. Over-sized equipment won't protect properly. The same goes for equipment that's too small. Check your child's equipment at the beginning and in the middle of the season to make sure he hasn't outgrown it.

Safety Savvy

When buying hockey equipment, look for the Hockey Equipment Certification Council (HECC) label, which indicates that the equipment has been tested and meets the requirements of amateur hockey governing bodies. For more information on hockey safety equipment, call USA Hockey at 800-566-3288 or visit its Web site at www.usahockey.com.

Football

Protective gear has helped reduce many of the serious injuries associated with this sport. Youth football leagues have specific requirements for the various kinds of protective gear that players must wear.

Most critical is a well-fitting helmet with a face mask and mouth guard. Youth leagues also wear thigh guards and shoulder, hip, tail, and knee pads under their pants and jersey. If your child wears glasses while playing, they should be made of non-shattering glass. Or you can buy prescription sports glasses.

Volleyball

Two kids going after the same volleyball can sometimes spell c-o-l-l-i-s-i-o-n. It doesn't have to if players learn to call for the ball so their teammates can back off. Kids also should be warned never to hang on the net or the net supports, which can fall on them.

A volleyball court should have overhead clearance so that objects like tree limbs and basketball hoops don't deflect the ball during play.

Basketball

Collisions are a problem in this sport, too, but they can be minimized if children learn to play their positions properly. Make sure your child wears shoes and socks that provide adequate support. Because the game is fast-paced, kids need to be in good condition and remember to drink water during breaks in practices or games so that they don't get dehydrated.

Watch Out!

Because of the high number of serious injuries and deaths associated with trampolines, they're no longer recommended for home use or for phys ed classes. If they're used by gymnastics programs, it should be under strictest supervision.

Gymnastics

Gymnastics is associated with many types of serious injury. The main protective gear in gymnastics isn't *on* the individual but *underneath* him. Properly secured padding under equipment and around landing areas is a must. Equipment should be spaced far enough apart so that gymnasts don't run into each other, and it needs to be checked regularly and maintained properly.

But in this sport, it's the supervision that can play the most critical role in preventing injuries. Each new move a gymnast undertakes should be with the careful instruction and supervision of an experienced coach. When you enroll your child in a program, ask about the coach's qualifications, the coach/child ratio, and the program's injury rate.

Tennis

Players of tennis and other racket sports such as racquetball and squash are prone to chronic elbow and shoulder injuries. Most can be prevented with proper conditioning and training. As with other sports, warming up and stretching muscles before play will help prevent injuries. It's also important to wear shoes and socks that provide good support.

Gadget Guide

Eye injuries are also common in racket sports because of the ball's small size and its fast speed. The American Academy of Pediatrics recommends that children use protective eyewear when playing.

The Least You Need to Know

➤ Whether you're a parent or coach, don't be shy about insisting that children wear appropriate shoes and safety gear during practices as well as games.

➤ Age is not as important as size, skill level, and physical maturity when grouping kids for sports teams.

➤ Be certain that playing areas—indoors and out—are inspected regularly for hazards.

➤ Coaches should be certified in CPR and first aid.

➤ Parents or coaches who pressure kids to win at sports can cause increases in injuries.

Part 5

Beyond Home: Safety in the Community

Once your child ventures beyond home, you won't always be there to make sure he's protected. But you can do a lot from afar. You can check out child-care providers, day care centers, schools, and camps using the questions in this section. There's also help here for teaching a child to protect himself from people who want to do him harm. We also give you tips for traveling safely with children and for enjoying the great outdoors without getting hurt.

Chapter 19

Child Care: May I See Your License Please?

In This Chapter

➤ Finding quality day care

➤ Evaluating the staff

➤ Checking the safety of the facility

➤ Preventing physical or sexual abuse

By the time most children reach school-age, they've already been in some form of group care. Some attend day care centers or family day care homes. Others go to nursery school.

Sending your little one off to day care for the first time can be fraught with anxiety. You may worry about how she'll adjust, whether she'll miss you, how well she'll get along with the teacher and the other children. Those concerns are natural—and probably, inevitable. But you don't want to worry about her safety. You can do a lot to ease your mind about that. In this chapter, you'll learn how to assess the safety of a variety of child-care settings. Chapter 26, "Nannies Need to Know," will help you handle safety concerns if your child is cared for in your home.

Day Care Centers

Many parents assume that, because states license day care centers, these facilities are safe and don't need parental scrutiny. Wrong!

Requirements vary from state to state. Some state codes are more stringent than others, and there are safety measures that aren't addressed by codes at all. Carbon monoxide (CO) detectors, for example, are recommended for all homes—and should certainly be in all day care centers—but most states don't require them in centers.

Enforcement varies, and inspections may be spotty. Even if a center passed its last inspection, that's no assurance that it's still in compliance. That could have been two years ago! All these are reasons you should check out for yourself the center's safety features before leaving your little one there. After you've enrolled your child, stay alert to how well safety measures are followed, and don't hesitate to speak to the director if you suspect they aren't.

A thorough evaluation of a day care center takes time. Plan to make at least two visits at different times of the day. That way you'll see how well the children are supervised during class time, mealtime, and outdoor play.

If all this seems like an enormous time commitment, think of it this way: If you invest the time upfront to find the right place, you'll be less likely to have to go through the whole process again because you made a mistake the first time!

Tales from the Safety Zone

Some parents spend more time choosing a car than selecting a day care center. The Child Care Connection, a resource and referral agency in Montgomery County, Maryland, conducted a survey of child care providers—both family day care and day care centers—and reported that 75 percent of parents spent less than an hour observing a program before enrolling their children. More than 11 percent signed up their children without even visiting the program first!

How Many Kids Is Too Many?

Staff-to-child ratios are an important safety consideration. If a caregiver has too many to look after, the risk of injury is increased. The size of the group in a room is also important. Too many kids in one area creates more noise and chaos, making supervision more difficult.

Every group of children in a center should have at least two caregivers. The national health and safety performance standards published jointly by the American Public Health Association and the American Academy of Pediatrics provides these guidelines for desirable child-to-staff ratios:

How Many Caregivers Are Enough?

Children's Ages	Child-to-Staff Ratio	Maximum Group Size
Birth–12 mos.	3:1	6
13–24 mos.	3:1	6
25–30 mos.	4:1	8
1–35 mos.	5:1	10
3 years old	7:1	14
4 years old	8:1	16
5 years old	8:1	16
6–8 years old	10:1	20
9–12 years old	12:1	24

(The two oldest groups typically apply to facilities providing before- or after-school care.)

Find out, too, about the staff's experience and qualifications—as well as the rate of turnover. Day care jobs are generally low paying, and some centers have high turnover rates. Try to find one with a stable staff, because changing caregivers is upsetting to a young child.

A Safety Checklist

When you tour a center, notice whether it has the kinds of safety features that you read about in Chapter 2, "Caution: Household Danger Zones Ahead"—the ones that you need in your own home. (Take along the tearout card in front of this book to remind you.)

Some important features to look for include:

➤ Smoke alarms, CO detectors, and fire extinguishers

➤ Safety covers on electrical outlets

➤ Furniture with no sharp corners

➤ Window covering cords that can't be reached by kids

➤ Hinged child gates at stairways

➤ Safe storage areas that keep cleaning supplies, medications, and other potentially toxic substances out of reach.

Safety Savvy

All centers must meet minimum standards for licensing, but some exceed them. One sign of quality is a center that has voluntarily sought and earned accreditation from the National Association for the Education of Young Children (NAEYC), the nation's largest organization for early childhood professionals. For a list of accredited centers in your area, visit NAEYC's Web site at www.nayec.org, or call 800-424-2460, ext. 601.

➤ Tap water no hotter than 120°F

➤ Equipment that is clean and well maintained

➤ Soft surfaces under outdoor play equipment

Notice whether the toys are age-appropriate, clean, and in good condition. Make sure there are no small toys or parts that could choke children.

If your child is an infant, see if babies are put to sleep on their backs, and if the cribs with napping babies are free of soft bedding and toys. Check whether highchairs and infant seats have safety straps and that they are used consistently. Infants should be fed while sitting up.

Centers should have written policies regarding discipline. Ask to see a copy, and discuss with the director any questions you have.

Tales from the Safety Zone

Two thirds of child care–settings examined by the Consumer Product Safety Commission in 1998 had at least one safety hazard. The 220 facilities across the country included federal, non-profit, for-profit, and in-home facilities. The most common hazard was children wearing outerwear with drawstrings at the neck. Others, in descending order, were: unsafe playground surfaces, loops on window blind cords, cribs with soft bedding, lack of safety gates, cribs that didn't meet safety standards, and products in use that had been recalled.

Playgrounds

A study by the Centers for Disease Control and Prevention found that about half the injuries occurring in day care centers happen on the playground. Give this area close scrutiny, noticing especially whether there is cushioning material under the equipment (such as wood chips or mulch, sand, or a rubberized surface). Falls, most often from climbing equipment, are by far the most common cause of injury.

Notice whether the play equipment is well maintained and is appropriate for the age groups using it. Also notice whether the playground is free of broken glass, loose rocks, and poisonous plants. If there is a sandbox, it should be kept covered when not in use to prevent animals from turning it into a litter box.

As you observe children on the playground, notice whether the center has rules for playing safely and if the rules are enforced consistently. A child who shoves others can cause serious harm to his classmates if left unchecked.

Ideally, the playground should have some shade in the summer. Even so, you should put sunscreen on your children or send in hats and other protective clothing.

See Chapter 14, "Life's a Playground," for more information on playground safety.

Happy Mealtime

When you visit a center to check it out, join the kids for lunch. Notice whether the caregivers make sure the kids don't eat hard, round foods (refer to the list in Chapter 9, "Why Is Junior Turning Blue?: Airway Obstruction"). Babies and toddlers should have food cut in small pieces. Also, a caregiver should always be with the children while they're eating in case a child chokes. Ask if all the caregivers have been trained to administer first aid to a child whose airway is blocked.

Check out the food preparation area for cleanliness. Also look at how food is handled. For example, perishables such as meat, poultry, milk, and eggs should be kept refrigerated until just before they're used.

In an Emergency

Is there a written policy manual for handling emergencies at the center? There should be, and all staff members should be familiar with it. See that it includes procedures for handling a medical emergency as well as phone numbers for fire, police, ambulance, and the nearest hospital. There also should be a well-stocked emergency kit.

Watch Out!

Some day care centers in cities don't have room for play equipment, so they use public playgrounds nearby. It's quite likely that some of this equipment is too big for pre-schoolers. Visit the playground when the day care center kids are there so you can see how well the caregivers restrict them to age-appropriate play structures. Also check the condition of the equipment and surfaces underneath.

Watch Out!

To prevent the spread of germs, caregivers should wash their hands before and after serving meals and should have the kids wash, too. The caregivers also should wash their hands every time they change a diaper or help a child go to the toilet.

Find out if the caregivers have been trained in cardiopulmonary resuscitation (CPR) and pediatric first aid. Adult first aid is not an adequate substitute because, for example, the procedure for handling a choking baby is different from that used for treating an adult. Also ask about the center's fire evacuation plan and how often drills are conducted. Is syrup of ipecac available in case of poison ingestion? And is the poison control center number posted by the telephone?

On the Road

If the center takes children on field trips, ask about safety provisions, especially for transportation. You'll want to make sure that every child is restrained in a safety seat approved for his age and weight and that the staff takes an emergency first-aid kit with them.

Safety Savvy

For a double-check of what centers should be doing to protect children's health and safety, visit the Web site of the National Resource Center for Health and Safety in Child Care. It's got detailed guidelines for writing child-care regulations, which are used mostly by state licensing agencies but which can be helpful to you, too. Look for "Stepping Stones" on the Web at http://nrc.uschsc.edu.

Checking References

Don't rely solely on your observations. Ask the center director for the names and phone numbers of a few parents who use the center. When you call them, understand that they may be inclined to paint a totally rosy picture and not be forthcoming with complaints about the facility. After all, they've put their own child there. The best way to elicit an honest appraisal is to ask open-ended questions, especially what they like best about the center and what they like least. The latter is likely to surface any nagging concerns they may have. These may be minor and have nothing to do with safety, but the responses will give you a fuller view of the facility.

If you like what you see and hear, and decide to enroll your child, your assessment job doesn't end there. You have to keep monitoring the quality and the safety of the care.

Safety Savvy

The CPSC offers a Child Care Safety Checklist for child-care providers and parents to use. To get a free copy, send a postcard to Child Care Safety Checklist, CPSC, Washington, DC, 20207, or access the Web site at www.cpsc.org.

Family Day Care

Family day care—sometimes called home day care—refers to care provided in someone else's home, not in a day care center. Often, the provider is a mother who wants to earn money while taking care of her own children.

Although a licensed home is preferable, finding one can be difficult. Not all states require licensing, and in those that do, most providers operate without licenses anyway. Some states allow various combinations of voluntary licensing, registration, or self-certification.

Screening Family Day Care Providers

Family, friends, co-workers, and neighbors often are your best source of referrals to quality care. Once you have a list of providers to screen, call them in the evening when they aren't caring for children. Ask each one basic questions: whether she has openings, her experience, the hours, costs, and the age and number of children she cares for.

Safety Savvy

To find licensed home day care (as well as other types) in your area, contact your local child-care resource and referral agency. Some offer referrals free and others charge small fees for printouts of caregivers. You can get the local number by calling the National Association of Child Care Resource and Referral Agencies' toll-free phone service, Child Care Aware, 800-424-2246, or visit www.naccrra.net.

In communities where family day care is regulated, a provider typically is limited to six or fewer children, including her own pre-schoolers, with generally no more than two children younger than two. These are minimum, not optimum, standards. One of your first considerations should be whether a prospective caregiver can adequately supervise the number of children in her care. The younger the children, the fewer she can handle safely.

When you've narrowed the list, schedule visits. On the initial visit, go without your child and just observe. If you like what you see, follow up with a lengthier interview with the caregiver when she isn't caring for the children. Then go back with your child. Be sure to check the caregiver's references before making a final decision.

Part of your visit should include a safety inspection of the home and outdoor play area. You'll be looking for the same things outlined for day care centers, but, because this is someone's home as well as a day care facility, you'll have to pay special attention to how well the provider has protected the children from the kinds of home hazards described in Chapter 2.

You'll also want to make sure she has adequate equipment for the ages of the children in her care, such as multiple cribs and highchairs. Also, ask if she transports children on field trips, and if so, what vehicle she uses and how she restrains the kids.

After you've sifted through the information you've gathered from the interviews, visits, and reference checks, add one more element to your decision—gut instinct. Don't settle for a caregiver who makes you even slightly uneasy. Hard as it is, it's better to keep searching for the person whom you feel you can trust with your most precious possession than settle on someone you're not completely confident in.

Watch Out!

Back-up care for emergencies is important for someone who is alone when caring for children. Ask about her plans for someone to care for the other children if she has to take one to the hospital for emergency treatment. Also find out about her first-aid and CPR training. If she is ill, does someone else care for the children, and is that person also trained?

Safety Savvy

If your caregiver doesn't have a standard consent-to-treat form, use the one in Chapter 26. Make copies of the form so you also can fill in one when you leave your child in the evening with a baby-sitter or when the grandparents care for your child over a weekend.

Information Just in Case

Before you leave your child with a family day care provider, give her phone numbers where you can be reached and a back-up person in case she can't contact you. (See Chapter 26 for a sample form you can use.) She also needs medical information about your child, including any allergies or other special problems. And make sure the caregiver has a signed consent-to-treat form to ensure that an emergency room will treat your child if you can't be reached immediately.

Smoke Gets in Their Eyes—and Lungs

Children who breathe secondhand smoke are more likely to suffer from a range of health problems, according to the American Academy of Pediatrics, including bronchitis. Secondhand smoke has been linked to ear infections and increasing numbers of asthma attacks. Insist that your child's caregiver refrain from smoking when caring for your child.

When the Caregiver Is a Relative

For some parents, having a relative, such as a grandparent, care for their child is the ultimate in peace of mind. Who better to keep Baby happy and safe than someone who loves him?

Love isn't enough if the relative isn't also safety savvy. A 1999 survey by the National SAFE KIDS Campaign found that grandparents rate unintentional injury their number-one concern when caring for grandchildren. Despite their concern, many grandparents surveyed lacked important information and safety devices in their homes.

Don't assume that just because your parents raised kids, they know the safest ways to do it. The safety field is constantly changing. It may be news to them that babies should be put to sleep on their backs or that children who've outgrown their child safety seat need to use boosters.

Having discussions with relatives about safety practices—or child-rearing in general—can be done delicately. Respect their views, but don't compromise on safety matters. Share this book with them, and make the safety discussion an ongoing one. The same applies to friends who care for your child.

Hiring Mary Poppins

Many of the safety measures we've already described for out-of-home care apply to caregivers in your home as well. The safety of the facility—your house and yard—is something you can control. So your focus is on hiring a qualified person and then preparing her to handle safety issues that might arise.

In Chapter 26, we describe how to select a nanny and then prepare her so she can keep your child safe. She needs to know, for example, your fire evacuation plan, how to reach you in an emergency, and where to find your fuse box and the first-aid kit. Chapter 27, "First Aid to the Rescue!" has valuable information on handling emergencies if they occur.

Protecting Your Child from Abuse

Because of a few high-profile cases, many parents fear their children will be sexually abused by a day care provider; yet studies show that day care is relatively safe. If you've followed the advice in this chapter about choosing a quality day care program, that should ease your mind, but you should also know the signs to look for in the rare cases where children are physically or sexually abused.

Always listen to your kids and take them seriously if they tell you about something at day care that makes them uncomfortable. With kids who are not talking yet, or who seem reluctant to talk, you'll have to watch for other cues.

Watch Out!

Never put your child in a day care facility or home that does not have an open-door policy for parents. You should not have to call first, and no areas that children have access to should be off limits to you.

Warning Signs

The National Center for Missing and Exploited Children says parents should be alert to these indicators of abuse:

➤ Changes in behavior or extreme mood swings.

➤ Changes in bed-wetting, nightmares, fear of going to bed, or other sleep disturbances.

➤ Acting out inappropriate sexual activity or showing an unusual interest in sexual matters.

➤ Sudden acting out of feelings, or aggressive or rebellious behavior.

➤ Regression to infantile behavior or clinging.

➤ School problems, behavior problems.

➤ Changes in toilet-training habits.

➤ Fear of certain places, people, or activities; an excessive fear of going to the day care center.

Choosing a Responsible Provider

Many day care centers conduct background checks on potential employees to see if they have criminal records. Screening also can turn up substance abuse or a history of emotional instability. Ask the center director how it screens prospective day care providers. Ask also about others who may have contact with your child, such as janitors or bus drivers.

In family day care, it's less likely that you'll have this information. The majority of these homes are not licensed so you have to rely more on the provider's references, including the recommendations you receive from people you know, such as friends or neighbors.

You also need to know who besides the family day care provider will come into contact with your child. Some abuse cases have involved relatives, such as the fathers or sons of providers.

Safety Savvy

During your interview with a prospective day care provider, ask detailed questions about her philosophy of discipline. On your visit, observe how she handles behavior problems, including punishments she uses.

Go to the Source

To see how caregivers are treating their charges, you can volunteer to go on field trips or help out occasionally. But for real day-to-day information, your child is probably your best source.

As soon as they start to talk, kids can tell you what happened at school. If your child isn't very verbal yet, he might enjoy acting out the day's events at day care. For kids, it's a game—like playing house—only this is called playing school. You can play the teacher and he can tell you what to do. This gives you an idea of how comfortable he appears to be with the adults in his day care program.

It's also important to create an open atmosphere in which your child feels he can talk to you about anything without fear of being ridiculed or blamed. Start when he's very young and maintain the dialogue as he grows, so he knows he can trust you to be supportive and open, even if he needs to talk about something he finds embarrassing.

Messages for Your Child

Kids can learn to protect themselves if you give them the tools. Young children can be taught some basic lessons that you can elaborate on as they get older.

The National Center for Missing and Exploited Children (NCMEC) offers these messages for kids:

➤ You have the right to say NO to anyone who asks you do something painful, embarrassing, or wrong.

➤ No one should touch you on the parts of the body covered by a bathing suit, nor should you touch anyone else in these private places.

➤ Don't be tricked if someone says to keep something a secret by threatening you or bribing you.

➤ Don't remain alone with an adult in an isolated place, such as a bathroom or bedroom, if it makes you feel uncomfortable.

If You Suspect Abuse

If your child reveals something to you that makes you suspect he's been abused either physically or sexually, try not to over-react in front of him. Just let him know that you're glad he's told you about it. If you're not sure whether abuse has occurred, the NCMEC recommends consulting a doctor, social worker, or law enforcement officer. Don't take your child back to the day care facility until you're convinced it's safe.

If you're pretty certain your child has been harmed, seek medical attention and immediately alert the police and the appropriate social service organization in your community. The NCMEC recommends against dealing directly with the day care provider. Leave that to the authorities. Also, be prepared to provide for professional counseling for your child.

Safety Savvy

The NCMEC maintains a 24-hour, toll-free hotline that can help parents whose children have been exploited. Call 800-THE LOST (843-5678), or check the Web site at www.missingkids.com.

The Least You Need to Know

➤ Make at least two visits, and spend several hours observing a day care program before choosing one.

➤ Pay attention to the ratio of children to adults.

➤ Always check references for a day care center or family care provider you are considering.

➤ Don't rely on licenses; do your own safety check, especially of the playground.

➤ Don't pick a provider that doesn't have an "open-door" policy for parents.

➤ If relatives or a friend care for your child, don't assume they know what they need to about safety precautions. Discuss safety with them.

Chapter 20

School Days

In This Chapter

➤ Getting safely to school by foot or bike

➤ Staying safe while boarding and riding the bus

➤ Environmental hazards lurking in school buildings

➤ Preventing school violence

When your children are ready for school, they face a whole new set of safety issues. How they get to school safely is one of them. Staying safe on the playground is another. So are personal threats from bullies.

We expect schools to be safe places for children and, mostly, they are. Parents working with the staff can help insure they stay that way, and schools can teach kids to keep themselves safer by making safety education part of the curriculum. In many classrooms, children are learning about everything from escaping a fire to performing the Heimlich maneuver on a choking victim.

Getting to School Safely

From fall to spring, millions of children are on the streets every day making their way to and from school. They walk, bike, ride the bus, or are driven by parents. When hundreds converge on one building—or sometimes a complex of buildings—the traffic can be a nightmare and the risks to kids can be numerous.

Ideally, every school would have one loading zone for buses and another for cars. Bike racks would be located in an area that allows safe and easy access. The parking lot would be designed to allow cars to enter without crossing paths with students who walk or bike. In reality, many schools are cramped for space and are located in high-traffic areas. Separating all these vehicles and children can be a real challenge.

We've already discussed in earlier chapters what you can do at home to make your kids street smart. But what about your school? What can it do?

(For more on teaching kids street-crossing skills, see Chapter 12, "Where the Sidewalk Ends: Pedestrian Safety." You might also want to review Chapter 13, "A Ticket to Ride: Safe Biking.")

Form a Committee

Safety measures can take a variety of forms, everything from stepped-up traffic enforcement to in-class education. Your school already may be using some of these effectively. Many schools have adult crossing guards and school safety patrols, for example. Still, there probably are traffic situations that could use improvement. To get a comprehensive look at the issues, your school could do a safety audit with the help of a school safety committee that includes staff, parents, police, and someone from your community's traffic engineering department.

The engineer can look at signs, traffic lights, street markings, and other features of the streets around your school and make recommendations on additional traffic control measures that might be needed, for example.

Safety Savvy

The American Automobile Association has materials for parents and school staff on working together to make the school trip safer. To get information for your school, check your phone book for the number of the chapter near you.

Safest Route Maps

One project of the school safety committee should be preparing maps that show the safest routes to school. The maps would indicate, for example, which intersections have crossing guards and therefore are the best places for children to cross. The maps should be big enough to incorporate the entire enrollment area. That way parents can plan the entire route for their children to follow, either to school or to the bus stop.

Once you pick a route, walk it with your child and point out any hazards he should watch for. You also may notice places where you might need to modify the route, because of large bushes that obstruct the view of an intersection, for example.

The Problem with Parents

Many of the traffic problems around schools are caused by parents. Some ignore the pick-up zones, double park, or block the buses. One dangerous, and all too common, practice is dropping children off on the wrong side of the street and jaywalking with them mid-block. Traffic troubles usually are worse in bad weather, as more parents drive their kids and everyone tries to take short-cuts to hurry into the building without getting wet.

Schools can alleviate congestion by taking such steps as staggering the dismissal of walkers and riders, having them exit on different sides of the building, and creating more pick-up-lane space if possible.

Traffic rule violations put kids in danger. If this is a problem at your school, talk to the parent-teacher association or the school staff—both about ways to ease congestion and to enforce the rules.

Watch Out!

The safest route for your walker to take may not be the same one your child should use to bike to school. The walker could be safer on a route with intersections where there are traffic lights, but the biker might be better off on streets with less traffic.

Bus Rider Basics

Most children injured by buses aren't riding inside during a crash. They're outside the bus in the blind spots around it where they are hidden from the driver's view; kids don't realize that the driver can't seem them.

Watch Out!

If your caregiver drops off your child at school, make sure she has a copy of the school traffic rules and abides by them.

Sometimes a child in the roadway is hit by a passing car whose driver fails to stop for the bus as required by law.

Kids should be taught to stay away from the wheels and the back of the bus. If they cross in front of the bus after deboarding, they should move to at least 10 feet in front of the bus and wait for a signal from the driver that it's safe to cross.

When he waits for the bus, your child should stand on the same side of the street as the bus stops and back up several steps from the edge of the roadway. Explain to him that he should stay back until the bus comes to a complete stop and the door opens. If there are several kids at his stop, they should board single file and use the handrail to avoid falls.

Children should stay 10 feet away from the bus if possible and never go behind it. They should take five giant steps in front of the bus before crossing so the driver can see them.
(Courtesy of the Consumer Product Safety Commission)

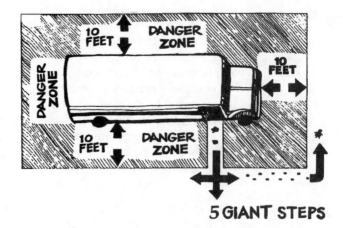

Don't Get Caught

In 1995, following strangulation deaths associated with drawstrings in clothing, the Consumer Product Safety Commission (CPSC) developed guidelines with manufacturers to eliminate these strings from outerwear. One cause of several deaths was drawstrings snagging on the handrails of school buses and causing children to be dragged or to fall under the wheels. Makers now use snaps, Velcro, buttons, and elastic instead of drawstrings, but scarves, backpack straps, and other items also can get caught. Explain to your child why he needs to be careful that his belongings don't dangle when he exits the bus.

Watch Out!

Caution your child that if she drops something near the bus, she shouldn't stoop to get it but should move away and wait until the bus has passed. Or she should get the driver's attention and permission before picking it up. If she leaves her backpack on the bus, she shouldn't run after it. Assure her that it's better to lose something than be hurt. (And most likely her pack will be waiting for her on the bus or in lost and found the next day.)

Don't Play Around

It's hard for drivers to keep their attention on the road when kids are goofing around on the bus. Schools and parents need to work together to establish and enforce bus behavior rules including these:

➤ Don't stand up in the bus while it's moving.

➤ Keep the aisles clear.

➤ Don't toss things around in the bus.

➤ Keep the noise down so the driver isn't distracted.

➤ Don't stick hands or arms out the window.

➤ While waiting at the stop, don't run around or shove each other.

Tales from the Safety Zone

Seat belts are not required on school buses in most jurisdictions, and this has generated years of controversy. Opponents of belt installation contend that buses are designed to minimize injury during a collision, and that some children might not be able to unhook their belts in the event an emergency evacuation is necessary. Proponents—including the American Academy of Pediatrics, the American Academy of Orthopaedic Surgeons, and other medical groups—argue that belts could prevent injuries, especially in collisions where buses roll over. The National Highway Traffic Safety Administration announced in September 1999 that from research studies it conducted, the agency concluded that seat belts on buses should not be required.

"Sick" School Buildings

If you send your child to school healthy but he frequently comes home sick, it might not be just the latest germ that's going around. Parents at a few schools have found it's the school building that's the culprit.

One Congressional report estimated that as many as one in five schools has unsatisfactory air quality. Some children can suffer reactions to anything from chemicals used for cleaning or bug control to mold caused by leaky roofs.

Many factors contribute to bad air in schools: construction of tightly sealed buildings, reduction of ventilation to save energy, lack of maintenance, and use of synthetic building materials and furnishings, to name a few.

Safety Savvy

Students should know how to evacuate a bus in case of an emergency. Ask if your school's bus drivers conduct drills so kids won't be confused if they ever have to make an escape.

How to Diagnose an Unhealthy Building

The tricky thing about contaminated air is that it may produce symptoms in just a small percentage of students and staff, so the cause may go unnoticed.

If your child frequently has symptoms similar to a cold, an allergy, or the flu—and if your doctor has eliminated other causes—watch your child to see if the problem clears up on the weekends. Another sign is when people with asthma or allergies have more reactions to these conditions when they are inside the school building than outside it.

If you suspect the problem is at school, contact the principal and request an air quality test. If school offi-cials don't respond to your concerns about school air contamination, canvas other parents or faculty to find out if others are having symptoms. If they are, you can raise the issue as a group with your parent-teacher organization.

Pesticides in School

Because their young bodies are still developing, chil-dren are more susceptible than adults to harm from pesticides and other lawn-care products. Some schools are employing firms that use safer alternative pest con-trol methods. Find out what precautions your school takes.

Asbestos

Many schools still contain asbestos because it once was used so widely in insulation, ceiling tiles, and other building materials and it's not easy to get rid of. Environmental Protection Agency (EPA) regulations require that schools containing this hazardous air pol-lutant have regular inspections and file reports on the results. The reports are available to the public.

Removal of asbestos is considered the last resort. It's costly and must be done by experts because of the danger in handling the material. The alternative is reg-ular observation and maintenance or, if necessary, containment. The EPA has issued guidelines for schools to use when dealing with asbestos.

Unsafe Drinking Water

Occasionally, schools are found to have contaminants such as lead in the drinking water. Lead pipes in older buildings can be one of the culprits. All schools should have their water tested periodically.

Check Out the Playground

More than a third of school injuries are related to sports or recreation. Proper maintenance and supervision of playgrounds and athletic fields are the keys to prevention. (For more information, see Chapter 14, "Life's a Playground," and Chapter 18, "Preventing Sports Injuries.")

Table and Cart Hazards

This may surprise you, but some children have been fatally injured when they helped move folding tables, commonly found in school cafeterias and meeting rooms. These tables can weigh as much as 350 pounds.

Safety Savvy

To find out more about drinking water, call the EPA's Safe Drinking Water Hotline at 800-426-4791, or visit its Web site, www.epa.gov/safewater.

The Consumer Product Safety Commission says most of the injuries have occurred during after-school or non-school sponsored activities. The tables sometimes over-turned when one of the wheels hits the foot of a child pulling it.

Caution your child that only adults should move these tables. Children should not play with the tables nor be near them when they're being moved.

Children should not move folding tables. (Courtesy of the Consumer Product Safety Commission)

(Courtesy of the Consumer Product Safety Commission)

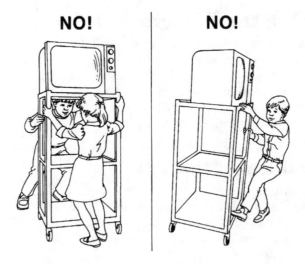

Audio-visual carts—the high rolling ones designed to hold a television on the top shelf—also can tip over on a child. Children should not be allowed to move them or play near them.

School Violence

Highly publicized incidents of school violence have heightened awareness of the need to deal with this complex problem. Such cases actually are quite rare, but schools commonly deal with smaller acts of "violence" all the time: students harming other students, whether it's the kindergarten bully or the junior high sexual harasser.

To put things in perspective, the National SAFE KIDS Campaign cites studies showing school-age children are nine times more likely to sustain an unintentional injury than to be the victim of an intentional injury while at school.

You can teach your child how to avoid becoming a victim. He can learn to be assertive without being aggressive. Help him learn to speak up confidently if he doesn't like something another student is saying or doing to him. Bullies are less likely to pick on children who don't back down easily. However, if he feels another student is about to harm him, it's better to walk away and seek the help of a teacher than get into a physical confrontation.

Many children are reluctant to tell on a bully for fear of retribution. But threatening situations can escalate, and adult intervention is usually the only way to stop the problem. Keep the lines of communication open so your child will be more likely to confide in you. Give him plenty of opportunities to discuss what's on his mind, especially if you sense he's worried about something at school. Then you'll be in a position to make school officials aware of problems, relieving your child of that burden.

Lessons in Compassion

One of the most important things you can do is teach your child to be compassionate to others. Help her understand that teasing another child is a form of verbal abuse that can cause real harm. So is ignoring or snubbing a classmate who's different. Teach your child to stand up for others who are being tormented, too.

Take bullying seriously. When a first grader taunts a classmate, parents may be inclined to think that "it's just the way kids are." But the values you impart at this age will affect how your child will treat others when he moves into higher grades.

(For more information on teaching kids how to protect themselves, see Chapter 25, "It's My Body: Personal Safety.")

Safety Savvy

For more tips on keeping your school safe, contact the National Parent-Teacher Association (PTA) at 800-307-4782 or visit its Web site at www.PTA.org. Other sources include the U.S. Department of Education, 800-USA-LEARN (800-872-5327), www.ed.gov, and the National School Safety Center, 805-373-9977, www.nssc1.org.

When Your Child Is the Bully

If your child is quick to anger, gets into frequent fights at school, and is often rejected by other children because of the way he acts, you should discuss your concerns with a professional who can suggest ways to curb his violent tendencies.

What Schools Can Do

Find out what steps your school is taking to keep students safe from violence. Many are turning to surveillance cameras, metal detectors, and security guards, but the foundation of a violence-prevention program should be early intervention with troubled students. Here are some questions to ask of school administrators:

➤ Are staff and students trained to identify early warning signs?

➤ Is the staff responsive when a student complains about abuse from another student?

➤ Is action taken swiftly to avoid continuation of the problem?

➤ Are there interventions, such as referrals to counselors, rather than just punishments for students with behavioral problems?

Watch Out!

Kids who behave aggressively may be imitating what they've seen on television. While TV violence may not cause aggression, it certainly doesn't help kids who watch a lot of it. Limit the amount of it your child sees by noting which TV shows are rated V for violence. Find out about the ratings on the movies he wants to see, too.

Safety Savvy

Training programs in how to spot troubled students should be extended to all staff, not just teachers and administrators. Sometimes it's the bus driver or the cafeteria worker who witnesses kids harassing others.

Involving Students in Problem-Solving

Some elementary schools are adopting programs to deal with bullying on a regular basis. The formats vary but usually involve a regular time in each classroom where students sit in a circle and bring up any situations that bothered them. This helps children understand how what they do affects the feelings of others. The teacher moderates and keeps the discussion from becoming accusatory.

Some middle schools and high schools have created peer mediation programs—sometimes called student court—to help classmates resolve differences. Student volunteers are trained to hold mediations between classmates who are in conflict. If the parties come to an agreement, they can avoid administrator-imposed sanctions.

What Your Community Can Do

The underlying causes of school violence are complex and require multi-faceted approaches. Working with your school administration and parent-teacher association, you can tackle school safety on many fronts by creating a community dialogue. Participants should include law enforcement officials, social workers, volunteer service groups, religious organizations, and social service agencies, among others.

Together you can:

➤ Create conflict-resolution programs for students.

➤ Review school discipline policy and enforcement.

➤ Develop after-school activities so children have adult supervision and positive things to do with their time.

➤ Pass laws and promote enforcement of provisions to protect children from gun violence at school.

➤ Provide community mental health resources for children and families in need of them.

The Least You Need to Know

➤ Every school should undergo periodic safety audits of traffic, fire prevention measures, and playground facility maintenance.

➤ Teach your child the safe ways to board and exit the school bus.

➤ Poor air quality in a school may be a cause of a child's chronic respiratory ailments, headache, and fatigue if symptoms go away on weekends.

➤ Students should never move audio-visual carts or heavy folding tables like those used in cafeterias.

➤ Find out what your school is doing to prevent student violence.

Chapter 21

It's Off to Camp We Go

In This Chapter

➤ Finding camps that meet your criteria

➤ Questions to ask about the camp's operation

➤ Examining the risk in high-risk activities

➤ How camps combat violence

➤ Deciding which camp is right for your child

Summer for kids isn't what it used to be. Gone are the days when most children idled away the school vacation in their neighborhoods, playing from dawn until dusk with their friends. Today's children, most of whom have working parents, are more likely to be in structured programs with adult supervision.

The demand for summer camps, both day and resident, has grown significantly, and so has the number of camping programs. Enrollment in the estimated 8,500 camps in the United States has been increasing at the rate of 8 to 10 percent a year since 1992. Approximately nine million children enroll in them each summer.

Just as you thoroughly checked day care facilities when your child was younger, now you'll be examining a prospective camp's safety and program content. The difficulty is that this time you probably won't have an opportunity to observe the camp in operation before you sign up your child. That means you'll have to do your research in other ways.

What Are My Choices?

There are two basic kinds of camps: day camps and resident (sometimes called sleep-away or overnight) camps. Day camps tend to have younger children, sometimes as young as pre-school, and, of course, campers don't spend the night. At resident camps, kids usually should be at least 7 years old, and they stay from one to several weeks, sleeping in cabins or tents.

Some camps are single-sex, but the majority are co-ed. Some offer a variety of activities while others have a special focus, such as performing arts, sports, horseback riding, or sailing. Many have begun offering popular adventure activities in recent years. There are even space camps for budding astronauts, and at least one for kids who want to become race car drivers!

Then there are trip and travel camps, which are becoming very popular.

In a trip camp, groups of campers get to their campsite by transportation other than motor vehicles—hiking, canoeing, or riding horseback, for example. The destinations tend to be state or national parks, where the campers pitch tents.

At travel camps, participants go by car or bus to scenic places of interest. Sometimes the two types of trips are combined so that the campers first travel by bus to a location and then begin the trip camp.

Tales from the Safety Zone

A 1998 survey by the American Camping Association found that 55 percent of campers are girls. It also found that campers are getting younger. Three fourths of camp directors reported adding new activities to their programs in response to increased interest in adventure activities, the arts, and sports. Some of the additions included mountain biking, rock climbing, kayaking, photography, in-line skating/roller hockey, gymnastics, soccer, and golf.

Beginning the Search

High demand means camps fill up fast. If you wait until May, you could be left with few or no options. Start your search months in advance. Some day camps make their enrollment applications available as early as February or March. Popular camps can fill up soon after enrollment begins.

To find out what's available, start by asking other parents. You also can inquire at your child's school because some programs, especially day camps, distribute information to them.

Camp Fairs

Fairs provide one-stop shopping for camps. They're held in schools, community centers, or even hotels, usually in late winter or early spring. Some communities also have camp fairs in the fall. The regional offices of the American Camping Association (ACA), an organization of camping professionals, can provide you with information on camp fairs scheduled in your area.

At a fair's information booths, you can browse the displays, pick up literature, and talk to camp representatives. Some booths have slide shows or videos.

A number of resident camps sponsor their own individual events in large metropolitan areas where parents can view more in-depth presentations. If you would rather sit in front of your own TV and take a tour of a camp you're interested in, some of the larger, more established camps do indeed have videos that prospective campers and their families can watch. Contact the top camps on your list to ask about these sources of information.

Watch Out!

If you use a referral service, find out how much direct knowledge it has about the camp. Ask, for example, if the service has visited all the camps it recommends, or if it gets evaluations at the end of the summer from campers it has placed. Also ask how many camps it represents.

Other Sources

In some communities, organizations publish camp directories —particularly day camps—and place them in schools and libraries. Parenting publications often put out a special camp issue listing camp offerings. These aren't necessarily comprehensive, however, as they may be limited to camps that buy advertisements.

Can you go online? Many camps have their own Web sites where you can get additional information.

Some sections of the American Camping Association publish free directories listing ACA-accredited camps in their region. For a copy, phone the nearest ACA office. You also can search for ACA-accredited camps nationwide at www.acacamps.org, or order a printed copy of the annual guide for $19.95 (at the time of this writing) by calling 800-428-2267. Many libraries carry the guide, too.

Referral Services

If you're thinking about a resident camp and want help in knowing what your options are, check to see if there are camp referral services available to you. They help families find camps that meet their criteria, such as program type, cost, and location. They are usually listed in the Yellow Pages under "camps." These services usually are free to families, because the camp consultants earn a commission from the camps they represent. This means the services recommend only their client camps, so you'll get a limited picture of what's available. But those choices might be all you need.

The ACA offers a free referral service through its regional offices, where experienced staff will counsel parents in person or over the phone and match them with ACA-accredited camps. (See the section, "Other Sources," earlier in this chapter, for its 800 number.)

What to Ask About a Camp

Once you've narrowed down your list of possibilities, the real detective work begins. Don't make your decision solely on a glossy brochure, a slick video, or a bubbly camp representative. Check it out for yourself.

Obviously, you can't see a summer camp in action during the winter, but you can find out a lot about the facility by asking the right questions of parents whose children have gone there and of the camp director. The following checklist will help in your search.

Questionnaire for Evaluating Summer Camps

General

❑ Is the camp accredited?

❑ Do the schedule, location, and price meet our family's needs?

❑ What is the camper return rate?

Staff

❑ What are the qualifications of the director?

❑ What are the qualifications and average age of the counselors?

❑ What percentage are returning from past years?

❑ What is the camp's procedure for staff background checks, training, and supervision?

❑ What are the qualifications of specialized staff such as lifeguards, riding instructors, coaches, bus drivers, etc.?

❑ What is the staff-to-camper ratio?

Medical Accommodations

❑ Does the camp have a full-time nurse?

❑ Is there a doctor on call?

❑ How close is the nearest hospital and ambulance service?

Facilities

❏ Is the facility, clean, well maintained, and free of hazards?
  ❏ Buildings
  ❏ Playground equipment
  ❏ Swimming pool
  ❏ Athletic field
  ❏ Buses (if your child will be riding one)

High-Risk Activities

❏ When children are engaged in canoeing, horseback riding, baseball, gymnastics, or other high-risk activities, what protective equipment and safety procedures are used?

Accreditation

One question to ask is whether the camp you're considering is accredited by the American Camping Association. To earn accreditation, a camp must comply with up to 300 industry standards for health, safety, and program quality. These standards address everything—from the director's background to how foods are prepared and stored. There are additional standards applied to aquatics, horseback riding, travel, and trip programs. At least once every three years, a team of trained ACA representatives observes the camp in session to verify compliance.

Of the approximately 8,500 camps, only about 2,200 have earned ACA accreditation. Those numbers include more resident than day camps. Lack of accreditation does not mean a camp isn't good, but if a camp isn't accredited, it's worth asking why. It might not be as important to you if the camp you are considering is in your community and you can check it out for yourself. If you are sending your child to a resident camp for part of the summer, it's reassuring to know that it meets certain standards.

Staff Qualifications

Key to your child's safety at camp are the qualifications and experience of the staff.

The Director

Find out the camp director's educational and career background. ACA suggests he or she have earned at least a bachelor's degree, have completed in-service training within the last three years, and have at least 16 weeks of camp administrative experience.

Counselors

Ask the average age of the counselors and what certification and experience they have. Many camps hire high school and college students. ACA recommends that at least 80 percent of the program counselors be 18 or older. Any counselor under 18 should be at least two years older than the camper she is supervising.

Watch Out!

It's especially important to find out the qualifications of staff in charge of high-risk areas—the lifeguards, horseback riding instructors, and athletic coaches, for example. They should have specific training in their specialties and be well-versed in appropriate safety measures.

Find out what percentage are returning counselors from past years. Some staff turnover is natural, but the ACA reports that at most camps, between 40 and 60 percent of the staff return each year. If the rate is lower, ask why.

Inquire about the camp's procedure for background checks as well as the training and supervision the counselors receive. Camp policies to protect children from physical or sexual abuse generally dictate that counselors work in pairs.

Staff-to-Camper Ratios

Ask about the ratio of counselors to campers. It should be based on the ages of the campers and their special needs. (Campers with disabilities, for example, need more staff.)

Here are the ACA recommendations for resident camps:

➤ One staffer for every six campers ages 6 to 8.

➤ One staffer for every eight campers ages 9 to 14.

➤ One staffer for every 10 campers ages 15 to 18.

For day campers the recommendations are:

➤ One staffer for every eight campers ages 6 to 8.

➤ One staffer for every 10 campers ages 9 to 14.

➤ One staffer for every 12 campers ages 15 to 18.

Do Their Campers Return?

Inquire about the camper return rate. Not every camper wants to go back to the same place the following summer, but a large number of returning campers probably is a sign that the children and their parents were highly satisfied with the camp's offerings and the way it is operated.

This is more important to know when evaluating resident camps than day camps. Children change their choice of day camps more frequently in order to find more variety or to be with their friends.

Medical Accommodations

Find out about the camp's medical resources. Is there a full-time nurse? Is there a doctor on call? How close is the nearest hospital and the nearest ambulance service? What are the camp's protocols about when parents are called if their child is ill or injured?

Watch Out!

When campers are engaged in risky activities such as swimming or horseback riding, there should be additional adult supervision.

If your child has special medical requirements, ask the camp staff how they would be handled. Is there appropriate storage for medications, for example? Can the cafeteria provide special foods for children on restricted diets? What accommodations are made for children with allergies? If, for example, a student carries an injection to be administered in case of bee sting, will all his counselors know how to use it so that precious minutes aren't wasted taking the child to the nurse?

Ask if the staff is trained to recognize the difference between homesickness and depression.

Transportation

Many day camps provide bus transportation to and from their facility morning and afternoon. Buses also may be used for field trips. Some resident camps provide bus service from metropolitan locations. If your child will be using the camp's bus or van, ask how often the vehicles are inspected by mechanics. Find out the drivers' qualifications and if there are any ongoing training or safety programs.

Watch Out!

If your child will ride the bus to day camp and must wait alone at his stop, make sure he knows what to do if the bus doesn't arrive by a certain time. Also, ask what the drop-off policy is. Younger children may not be allowed to be dropped off at a stop where no parent is waiting unless the parent has provided written authorization.

The Facility

If you want to take the extra step of visiting the camp before enrolling your child, find out if any open houses are scheduled. You won't see the camp in operation, but you can observe firsthand whether the facility is well-maintained and possibly meet some of the staff.

Water Safety

Whether you visit or not, find out where kids will be swimming—either a pool or a natural body of water—and if the water is monitored for bacteria. Is there a shallow area marked off for kids who are still learning to swim? Are swimming lessons offered? Are lifeguards certified in lifesaving always present when campers are in the water?

If boating is offered, ask whether counselors are always in the boats with campers. Do campers have to pass a test before they take boats out on their own?

Safety Savvy

If you don't know any families whose children have attended the camp, get references from the director. Ask these parents their overall impressions of the camp, what they liked best, and what they liked least.

Other High-Risk Activities

For any high-risk activity your child might engage in at camp—from rock climbing to white-water rafting—make a point of asking questions about protective equipment, staff training, and safety precautions.

If your child will be riding horses, for example, he should wear a helmet. Ask if the camp requires this. (For more information on safe horseback riding, see Chapter 24, "Down on the Farm.")

Food Handling

State health departments or other regulatory bodies should be responsible for making sure camps prepare and store food safely, but enforcement may be spotty. Ask about food handling, both in the camp cafeteria and when meals are sent out with campers on trips.

Personal Safety

Recent incidents of school violence have heightened concern about camp safety, too. It's wise to ask how behavioral and disciplinary problems are handled. Teasing and practical jokes often can escalate to bullying and fights.

Communicating and Enforcing Rules

The camp should have clear rules of behavior that are communicated to campers at the beginning of the session. For instance, children need to know the penalties for breaking the rules. Camp counselors should be trained in how to defuse tense situations and how to mediate disputes between campers.

Searches

Camps are understandably concerned about the possibility of weapons being brought in by campers. Once essential equipment, a scout knife, for example, now is considered a potential risk.

For this reason, the camp may have a search procedure that involves searching all bags for contraband when campers arrive. Others may do it only if they suspect a camper has something with him that's inappropriate.

The camp's search procedures should be explained to parents. Some camps ask in advance for permission to search campers' personal belongings. This may appear on the enrollment form.

Safety Savvy

Weapons aren't the only kind of contraband. Some resident camps may restrict campers from bringing food that could attract wildlife. Or they tell campers not to bring hair dryers or electronic games. Go over the packing rules with your child and make sure she doesn't take something that will be confiscated.

Safety from Strangers

Camps should have policies that require camp visitors to be escorted by staff. Additionally, the staff should require that the person who picks up a child from camp be on an approved list of names provided by the parent at the time of enrollment.

Making the Final Decision

Your child will surely want a say in choosing a camp. She may be most interested in going where at least one of her friends will be. For that reason, you might want to work with her friends' parents when checking out the options.

At the beginning of the camp selection process, discuss with your child her preferences, factoring in concerns you might have such as distance and cost. You'll probably find it best to let her pick from two or three options that are acceptable to you.

Don't send your child to a camp you have reservations about, no matter how much your child wants to go there. Trust your instincts!

The Least You Need to Know

➤ Start your camp search early so you'll have the widest array of choices.

➤ Ask if the camp has American Camping Association accreditation and if not, why not.

➤ Find out about the staff's qualifications and training as well as staff-to-camper ratios.

➤ Inquire about instructors' qualifications and safety procedures for any high-risk activities offered.

➤ Ask about the camp's procedures for handling illnesses and injuries.

Travels with My Children

Vacations with kids are nothing like the ones you took before you became a parent! The phrase "getting away from it all" has less meaning when you have to take it all with you—crib, stroller, diapers, and all manner of other baby or child gear. On the plus side, though, are the family memories you'll make while experiencing favorite vacation spots through the eyes and mind of your child. Some thoughtful pre-planning and a few precautions along the way will insure your trip is both fun and safe.

Getting There by Car

Few kids relish long hours in the car, and babies and toddlers can become especially cranky, but don't be tempted to unbuckle your crying baby to nurse her or let your toddler stretch out across the back seat when the car is moving. Instead, plan to make frequent stops to feed the baby or let older children run off steam. Pack a ball they

Safety Savvy

Carry an up-to-date photo of your child in case you become separated during your trip. Notice what he's wearing each day. If he's too young to remember them, put his name and the address and phone number where you'll be staying on a piece of paper in his shoe or pocket. Teach him that if he gets lost, he should stay put and you'll come to him.

can kick around at a rest stop. Bring games and toys to occupy them in the car, too, including a few small surprises.

Keep an Emergency Kit

A car's road survival supplies should include jumper cables, flares, flashlight and batteries, first-aid kit, fix-a-flat solution (so you can drive to a safe area for a tire change), small tool box, portable fire extinguisher, and a cell phone to call for help.

Getting There by Airplane

Until your child is 2 years old, airlines will let her fly free as long as you hold her in your lap. We strongly urge you to buy her a ticket, however, so you are assured of having a seat in which to properly restrain her.

The Federal Aviation Administration (FAA) recommends that parents of under-2s buy a ticket and use a car seat on the plane. The federal government has been weighing the benefits and disadvantages of requiring this through government regulation.

We realize that this adds to the cost of travel, but it could save your baby from serious injury if the plane encounters sudden turbulence. It makes no sense to us that everything except babies must be secured in an airplane for takeoffs and landings. During turbulence or a crash, it could be impossible for you to hold onto your child.

Some airlines offer discounts up to 50 percent on tickets for children under age 2, so tell them you have a baby when you make your reservation.

The Right Seat for the Right Child

The FAA advises parents to:

➤ Use a rear-facing child safety seat for babies under 20 pounds.

➤ Use a forward-facing child safety seat for children between 20 and 40 pounds.

➤ Use the plane's seat belt if your child weighs more than 40 pounds. Booster seats and harness or vest-type restraints are not permitted by FAA regulation. If you bring a booster seat to use in a car at your destination, you can check it as luggage.

➤ Make sure your child safety seat is labeled as "certified for use in motor vehicles and aircraft."

The FAA also requires that a child safety seat be placed in a window seat so in an emergency it will not block the escape path for someone sitting next to the child. The seat can't be used in an emergency exit row.

When you haul a car seat through an airport, you'll need all the help you can get. Try to avoid flights on which you have to make a connection. If you can't avoid them, most airlines will provide personnel to help you get to your connecting flight, but you've got to arrange for it in advance. If you schedule flights in off-peak hours, when the planes are less crowded, you'll usually have more time to strap your car seat into the plane seat and stow away your diaper bag and other baby paraphernalia.

Gadget Guide

Measure your child safety seat to make sure it is no wider than 16 inches. If it's wider, it's unlikely to fit in a coach seat in a plane. Even if the armrests are moved out of the way, a wider seat is unlikely to fit the seat frame properly.

Listen Up!

In the event of an emergency evacuation, you'll be responsible for both your child and yourself. Pay attention when the flight attendant describes safety features of your plane, noting especially the location of the exits and how to use the floatation devices.

Safety Savvy

For more information on safe flying, call the FAA's consumer hotline at 800-FAA-Sure (800-322-7873) or visit the Web site www.faa.gov.

Kids Flying Alone

Many kids are veteran flyers who travel solo. It's common for unaccompanied children to fly to their grandparents for a visit or, in the case of a divorce, spend summers with a parent who lives far away.

If your child will be flying alone, check with your airline for its specific rules about unaccompanied children. In general, airlines don't let children fly alone until they're 5. Unaccompanied children between ages 5 and 7 can fly only on direct flights, but children age 8 or over may take a connecting flight. You may be charged an extra fee for an unaccompanied child in addition to the regular fare ticket price.

You or another responsible adult must stay with your child until he has boarded the plane, and you should remain in the airport until the plane has departed. Another adult must meet your child at the arrival gate. Tell everyone, including the reservations clerk and the gate attendants, that your child is flying alone.

When kids reach age 12, they don't get special assistance, such as help with making a connection, unless you specifically request it when you make your reservation. Be sure your child knows that if flights are delayed or canceled, she should seek help

Safety Savvy

Arrive at the airport early and bring the name, address, and phone number of the person who will meet your child at the end of the flight. That adult must show the flight attendant a picture ID, so don't give the airline Grandma's name and expect that Grandpa can pick your child up instead. Make sure your child is carrying this information, too.

Safety Savvy

A portable changing pad is a useful travel accessory. Restrooms don't always have sanitary changing facilities, and a pad lets you change the baby anywhere. Just make sure you use it in a spot where your baby won't fall.

from the airline personnel and never leave the airport with a "helpful" stranger.

What to Take

If your child still sleeps in a crib, buying a portable version for traveling is a good idea. Various models fold easily, are lightweight, and come with carrying cases.

If you're in a hotel, you can usually rent a crib if you reserve one before your arrival. But these are not always well maintained and may, for example, have loose hardware from being frequently set up and re-folded. Some may not be new enough to meet federal safety standards (see Chapter 3, "The Well-Equipped Parent"). Finally, your child may not sleep as comfortably on an unfamiliar mattress and crib sheet.

If you're visiting relatives, they may borrow a used one from a friend or bring down from the attic the one you slept in, which won't meet CPSC standards.

A portable crib also can serve as a playpen and is a good way to confine a baby on the beach.

Some other items you might consider taking on a trip include:

➤ Inflatable infant tub

➤ Night light

➤ Portable highchair

➤ Stroller

➤ Blanket or quilt to cover the ground where your baby might play

Safe Rooms at the Inn

Some savvy hotels that cater to families offer so-called "child-proofing" services. When you make your reservation, let the staff know you have a small child. At minimum, the maids can remove breakable or heavy objects such as ashtrays and table lamps. Some will put shields in the electric outlets, tie up electric cords and make sure window covering cords are out of reach or have been modified so they don't form loops. Ask about anti-scald devices to keep tub and sink water below 120°F. If windows can be opened, low furniture should not be placed in front of them, giving kids something to climb up (and out!) on.

Don't take a room that opens onto the swimming pool unless your children are good swimmers. Even then, make sure they are supervised when they go to the pool.

Where's the Nearest Fire Exit?

When you check into a hotel, locate the fire exit nearest your room. If possible, request a room on the first floor. It will be easier for you to get your child out in case of emergency, and you won't have to worry about him falling off a balcony.

Rental Properties

Whether you rent a lake-side cottage, a beach house or a cabin in the woods, it's unlikely to come with the child safety measures you have in your home. Take the checklist from the front of this book and inspect the rooms to see how you can eliminate as many hazards as possible. You probably can't make a rental property as safe as your home, so extra supervision will be essential.

Pay special attention to where you place your crib—not near a window or window cords. Keep the doors locked if there's a chance your child could wander outside.

At the Grandparents'

When visiting grandparents or other relatives, be prepared to do some basic hazard removal with the checklist from the front of this book. Be especially cautious about medications, because seniors often have several and they may not have requested child-resistant caps. The medicine bottles may not be safely stored either, if the grandparent normally keeps them handy as a reminder to take them. Ask to put the medicines out of your child's reach during the visit.

You don't have to transform your relative's home for your brief visit, but do a quick sweep of the rooms to put away sharp kitchen utensils, heavy objects on low tables, household cleaners, tablecloths, small refrigerator magnets that could be swallowed, and anything else hazardous that you can stow away easily.

With several adoring adults around, supervision should be easy, but make sure someone is in charge at all times. If one person thinks the other is watching the toddler, Junior could get into trouble before anyone notices. In unfamiliar surroundings, he may be in the mood to explore.

Child–Care Programs

Just because the kids are traveling with you doesn't mean you can't have time alone. More and more hotels, resorts, and cruise lines are

Watch Out!

Make sure your rental property has working smoke alarms on each floor, including near the bedrooms.

offering child care—from simple baby-sitting for parents who want to dine out together, to activity-filled programs akin to summer camp.

If you're considering registering for a children's program, ask about the age requirements, credentials of the staff, the child-to-counselor ratio and the activities available.

Amusement and Theme Parks

Safety Savvy

Some families bring their own baby-sitter on vacation. A teenager your kids already know might be happy to have a week at the beach, for example, in exchange for watching your kids for a few hours each afternoon or evening.

With all the noise, people, and excitement, it's easy for families to become separated at amusement parks. Lost children are commonplace at these attractions, so good parks have well-trained staff to handle young wanderers. Tell your children that, if they become separated from you, they should go to the nearest park staff member (wearing a uniform and name tag) and ask for help.

If you lose sight of your child, tell a staff person and request that security officers be notified immediately.

One way to make it easier to keep track of your kids is to dress them in matching shirts and hats in an unusual color or distinctive design.

It's also a good idea to attach a covered luggage tag to your child's clothing or place it in a pocket. (The cover prevents a stranger from seeing your child's name.) Include your name as well as your child's and the name and number of your hotel. Some parks issue special tags for young children; ask about this when you enter the park.

Safe Riding

Don't assume that amusement rides are safe, especially in traveling carnivals where the rides must be taken down and put up at each stop. Look for an inspection notice at the entrance to the ride. If a ride looks poorly maintained, skip it. Also avoid rides that have only one operator. There should be two—one to operate the equipment and one to make sure kids are securely fastened in.

Remind your kids that they must meet the height and weight requirements of a ride and must follow all rules—keeping their hands inside the cars, for example.

Medical Care at the Amusement Park

If you need medical assistance, most large facilities have walk-in clinics or first-aid stations. Check the map so you'll know where to go if you need help.

It's smart to carry a few first-aid supplies with you, such as adhesive bandages and antibiotic cream to treat minor cuts and scrapes. Also, if it's summer, use plenty of sunscreen, take breaks, and make sure your kids get enough liquids so they won't be overcome with the heat.

Medical Care While Traveling

When your child is still a baby, your pediatrician may suggest that you travel only to destinations where good quality medical care is nearby. This is because babies can get a high fever or come down with an ailment quickly.

Carry your pediatrician's number with you when you travel. That way if your child has a minor illness or injury during your trip, your own doctor can advise you on whether you need to seek medical help.

International Travel

If a trip abroad is in your travel plans, you can contact the U.S. Department of State's Bureau of Consular Affairs for travel advisories on the countries you're going to visit. The advisories will tell you what immunizations are required and about any unusual security or health concerns.

You can also request a publication with detailed advice for traveling safely. (Although it is targeted to travelers going abroad, some of the information also could be useful for people traveling in the United States.) You can ask for advisories by calling 202-647-5225, request a fax by dialing 202-647-3000 from your fax machine, or visit the Web site http://travel.state.gov. The Centers for Disease Control and Prevention has health information for international travelers on its Web site, www.CDC.gov/travel.

When you are abroad, the nearest U.S. embassy or consular office can provide you with the names of doctors and nearby medical facilities.

Before taking young children to developing countries, ask your pediatrician for advice.

Bring medicines and simple first-aid items with you whenever you travel, but especially overseas where some items may be harder to buy. Especially important are

Watch Out!

The day can be ruined if your child has trouble walking because of blistered feet. Make sure she wears comfortable shoes with socks. Carry some bandages in case a blister develops. A toddler might not notice one forming, so check her feet once or twice a day so you can deal with a spot that's getting rubbed before it becomes a blister.

Safety Savvy

Don't forget to bring along your health insurance card, any prescription medicines your child needs, extra eyeglasses, a thermometer, children's pain reliever, and something your doctor recommends for stomach upsets and motion sickness if your child is susceptible.

Safety Savvy

If your kids will be wading in creeks, take along extra tennis shoes they can wear to protect their feet from broken glass and sharp rocks. Or buy water shoes or socks with tough soles.

Gadget Guide

Have your child carry a whistle so he can summon help if he becomes separated from you. Carry one yourself so you can call him, too. Also, issue everyone in the family a flashlight—in different colors to avoid ownership battles—for those inevitable night-time treks to the restrooms.

prescription drugs you or your child might be taking, a thermometer, and fever-reducer. See Chapter 27, "First Aid to the Rescue!" for more information.

Camping Cautions

Families who rough it on vacation consider camping a great adventure. It takes kids away from the television and exposes them to the unique pleasures of seeing nature up close, catching fish for dinner, building a campfire, or bathing in a pristine lake. Plus, camping is a heck of a lot cheaper than a resort.

On a camping trip, kids need extra supervision around campfires, grills, fishing hooks, matches, knives, hatchets, and other camping equipment. They also need to be watched near lakes, rivers, or streams close to your campsite. (For tips on water safety, see Chapter 15, "On the Waterfront." Chapter 23, "The Great Outdoors," has advice on protecting kids from sun, insects, poisonous plants, and other hazards of nature.)

What to Take on a Hike

Even parents of infants can go hiking—babies in back carriers are a familiar site on hiking trails these days. For kids who are good walkers, investing in sturdy shoes or child-size hiking boots can make their hiking days more comfortable. Dress your child in layers to accommodate changes in temperature, and don't forget the sunscreen.

One mistake many hikers make is not carrying sufficient water. With a child along, you may not be going that far, but summer sun could still cause dehydration. Take water bottles for each family member, some snack foods, and a small first-aid kit.

Also, take a map and a compass. In case your child gets tired, you'll want to know the shortest route back to the trail head where you started.

Caution your children not to drink stream water.

Gone Fishing

A few simple precautions can prevent you hooking people instead of fish. When carrying the rod, keep the hook secured to the hook keeper on the rod or cover the sharp barb on the end with a cork. Teach your child to not fish in the same area with swimmers and to keep some distance between herself and other people fishing.

If the hook becomes impaled in your child's skin, don't pull it out unless just the point has entered the skin. If the shank has entered, too, push it on through the skin so the point emerges and you can cut off the barb on the end with pliers or clippers. Then you can safely pull the hook back out the way it went in, disinfect the wound and cover with a bandage. Then consult your doctor because of the risk of infection.

Never remove a fish hook that has entered your child's face or eye. Instead, seek medical help immediately.

Gadget Guide

Cellular phones may be a nice convenience, but they shouldn't be relied on for summoning help on a hike. For one thing, you may not be in an area that can pick up your phone signal. Also, if you haven't been tracing your steps on a map, you can't tell rescuers where you are! This is one time when old-fashioned gadgets—compasses and maps—work better.

Weather Wisdom

Check a weather forecast before going on a hike to get an idea of how much clothing to take. Skip the hike if the forecast calls for storms. Lightning strikes the tallest objects in the area, so if thunder and lightening develop unexpectedly while you're hiking, move from higher to lower ground and don't stand near tall trees or on hills. If you are in a forest, seek shelter under low growth, saplings or smaller trees.

If an electrical storm threatens while you're in your tent, it's safer to wait it out in your vehicle, especially if your tent has metal poles. If you are boating or swimming, get out of the water immediately.

Avoiding Animal Bites

One of the joys of a camping vacation is seeing wildlife up close. Unfortunately, many campers want to get close enough to pet animals or feed them even when signs warn visitors not to. Explain to your children that this is a dangerous practice because animals are unpredictable and may bite or kick. People-food can hurt the animals' digestive systems, too. Watch from a safe distance and don't attempt to feed them.

Safety Savvy

It's important for family members to be trained in first aid and CPR since you may not be close to medical help when you are camping. Taking a well-equipped first-aid kit on your trip is a must, too.

Safety Savvy

If you take your dog camping with you, make sure its rabies vaccination is up-to-date. Otherwise, it could get rabies from the bite of a wild animal and become a danger to your family.

Another risk is rabies. Raccoons, skunks, bats, and other creatures are prime carriers you should stay clear of. If your child is bitten, treatment to prevent rabies could be necessary unless the animal can be captured and determined to be healthy, an unlikely possibility in the wild.

Avoiding Carbon Monoxide Poisoning

Carbon monoxide (CO), a colorless, odorless gas, kills approximately 30 campers each year and sends hundreds more to the hospital. The source of this gas is generally a portable camping heater, lantern, or stove that has been brought inside a tent, camper, or vehicle with poor ventilation. Usually, the victims are sleeping when they are overcome.

Sometimes rain causes campers to pull their charcoal grills inside the shelter of their tent to finish cooking a meal. This, too, is dangerous because burning charcoal generates CO. Don't store a grill inside an enclosed area until the coals are completely cold. Until then, the coals continue to release the dangerous gas.

The Least You Need to Know

➤ If your child is too young to identify herself and her parents, stick a piece of paper with your name and the phone number of the place you're staying in her shoe or pocket.

➤ When flying, all children under 40 pounds should be restrained in a car seat secured to the plane seat.

➤ Whether you stay in a hotel or at a relative's house, check for hazards that could harm your young child.

➤ In an amusement park, tell your child that if he becomes separated from you he should seek help from a staff member wearing the park's ID badge.

➤ On camping trips, teach your child not to feed or touch wild animals and use camping equipment with care.

Chapter 23

The Great Outdoors

> **In This Chapter**
>
> ➤ Sun without sunburn
>
> ➤ Coping with rashes
>
> ➤ Banishing bug bites
>
> ➤ Animals: friends and foes
>
> ➤ Picnics with safe food

Winter or summer, the great outdoors beckons kids to explore, run, slide, hike, swim, swing, climb, and shout. Whether it's building sand castles on the beach or snowmen in the backyard, there are a million things for kids to do outside that they can't do indoors.

They'll have tons more fun if you take precautions to protect them from a few of the drawbacks of communing with nature—sunburn and bug bites, for example. In this chapter, we'll also give you tips on preventing animal bites, and on keeping food safe when you picnic or barbecue.

Skin Sense

The most important thing you can do for your child outdoors is protect her from sunburn. It's not hard, but requires diligence. Many parents are conscientious about skin protection when they take their kids to the beach or the swimming pool but neglect it

Safety Savvy

The American Academy of Dermatology estimates that 80 percent of harmful sun exposure occurs before age 18. That's because kids spend more time outdoors than adults do, especially in summer. Babies and young children can't protect themselves from sunburn, so the adults have to do it for them.

when the children are playing in the backyard or on a sports team. Sun protection is needed all the time.

We all know how painful a sunburn can be. And children are more likely to suffer because their skin is more sensitive than adults' and burns more easily.

More important is the potential long-term effect. Adults who get skin cancer typically got too much sun when they were kids. Just one or two blistering sunburns in childhood can greatly increase the risk of developing skin cancer in adulthood. If that sounds scary, we mean it to be. Skin cancer is the most common kind of cancer in the United States. Some types can be deadly.

The basic prevention steps include using sunscreen lotions, wearing hats and other protective clothing, and limiting exposure time. Avoiding the hours when the sun's rays are strongest, 10 A.M. to 4 P.M., is a good idea, but not always practical.

Special Issues for Babies

Until babies are 6 months old, pediatricians usually don't recommend using sunscreens because the risks of these chemicals on infants are not known. Covering up an infant and keeping her out of direct sun for the first six months are much preferred.

Keep your baby in the shade of a tree, under an umbrella, or in a stroller with a canopy. Even on cloudy days, harmful ultraviolet (UV) rays can cause sunburn. If you're on sand, water, snow, or concrete, be especially careful because UV rays can bounce back from these surfaces.

When you're outdoors, dress your baby in light, loose-fitting clothing that covers his body. Clothes with a tighter weave offer more protection. You can check this by holding the garment up to the light and noticing how much passes through. Always have him wear a hat with a brim because that will shade his face and also protect the ears.

A young child can get a sunburn while riding in the car. Juvenile products stores carry a variety of sunshades for car windows. Using one not only protects your child from the sun's rays and shades out some of the hot sun, but also increases the likelihood of him napping comfortably, making your car ride a lot more pleasant.

Tales from the Safety Zone

The strong sun in Australia has caused such an alarming rate of skin cancer that the country mounted a national health campaign urging citizens to take steps to avoid sunburn. Its slogan is "Slip, Slop, Slap"—slip on a shirt, slop on sunscreen, and slap on a hat. You might want to teach this funny little slogan to your kids.

The Skinny on Sunscreens

Once your baby is past the 6-month mark, you can start using sunscreen. You'll want a broad-spectrum, waterproof lotion with an SPF of at least 15. If your child is fair-skinned or has freckles, an SPF of 30 is better because it offers more (although not twice as much) protection. Broad-spectrum means the sunscreen works on ultraviolet A (UV-A) and ultraviolet B (UV-B) rays. The shorter UV-B rays are what cause sunburn on the skin's surface. UV-A rays penetrate to deeper skin layers, causing skin to age. Both types contribute to skin cancer.

You don't need to buy a special "for kids" brand unless your child is sensitive to regular brands and needs a hypoallergenic formula.

It's best to apply sunscreen a half-hour before your children go outside, so it has time to be absorbed. Make sure it covers all exposed areas, including hands, feet, and the tops of the ears. Be careful around the eyes, avoiding the eyelids. The American Academy of Pediatrics (AAP) recommends that, if your baby rubs sunscreen in her eyes, you wipe the hands and eyes with a damp cloth. If the sunscreen burns her eyes, the AAP suggests switching to a sunblock with titanium dioxide or zinc oxide.

Don't worry if your baby sticks her hand in her mouth after you've rubbed in the sunscreen. It won't hurt her, but, as with any over-the-counter medication, you should keep the bottle out of the reach of young children.

The biggest mistake people make with sunscreen is not using enough. It should be reapplied every two hours. Don't wait until your little one starts to look red, because sunburn may not appear until hours after the fact. If your child has been swimming, dry her off and then reapply the lotion. Put a roomy T-shirt or cover-up on her when she's not in the water. Kids who burn easily should wear a shirt even in the water.

Make sure other people who care for your child, such as baby-sitters or grandparents, also know the importance of sun protection. Keep them adequately supplied with sunscreen to put on your child.

Soothing a Sunburn

If a baby under age 1 gets a sunburn, you should call your pediatrician immediately because this can be an emergency. For a child older than age 1, call the pediatrician if there is blistering, pain, or fever.

Remedies for kids with sunburns include soaking in cool water and drinking lots of liquids to replace lost fluids. Don't use medicated lotions on your baby unless your doctor okays it. Older children can be treated with hydrocortisone cream and children's pain reliever. Don't let your child go out in the sun again until the burn has healed.

Weathering the Weather

When it's really hot or really cold outside, help your kids avoid the ill effects that little bodies can suffer in extreme weather.

In the Good Old Summertime

Playing in the sun can lead to dehydration, so make sure your children drink plenty of fluids. Don't wait until they ask for drinks because, if they're hard at play, they might not notice they're thirsty.

The best drink is water, because it doesn't contain calories and it won't spoil your child's appetite the way sugary drinks can. Milk is good, too, because it not only quenches thirst but provides calcium and vitamins as well. Fruit juice is fine, but should be offered more sparingly because of its high sugar content. Fruits such as oranges and watermelons also replenish fluids. Ice pops are a great way to quench kids' thirst. Make them yourself with water and fruit juice or buy the 100 percent juice pops.

Protecting Little Eyes

If you can convince your children to wear them, child-size sunglasses help protect their eyes from UV rays. The latest versions are soft and flexible for a comfortable fit, and some have adjustable headbands to keep them on kids as young as 6 months.

Baby, It's Cold Outside

Your mother probably told you to bundle up when you went outside in winter so you wouldn't catch cold. You probably caught colds anyway because they are caused by viruses, not by plunging temperatures. The real reason children should dress warmly is to prevent frostbite or hypothermia. This is especially important when the kids will be outside for prolonged periods, such as an afternoon spent skiing or sledding.

Frostbite

Kids are much more likely to get frost "nip" than frostbite. You recognize frost nip by the bright red skin color. Bring the child in where it's warm so the skin can warm up and return to normal. Remove wet clothes and have a warm drink. Drinking fluids helps improve circulation.

Frostbite is far more serious because the tissue—typically fingers, toes, or other extremities—has actually frozen. It will look pale, grayish yellow or waxy and will feel hard to the touch. Blisters may develop. Call your doctor immediately if you suspect frostbite. Put the affected areas into warm—not hot—water, but don't rub the skin.

Hypothermia

Hypothermia occurs when the body's core temperature drops below normal. It can be a life-threatening condition. Symptoms may include uncontrollable shivering, clumsy movement, slurred speech, and bluish skin or lips.

Treat mild cases by bringing your child inside, removing her wet clothes, and wrapping her in warm blankets. If the symptoms are more severe, seek immediate medical attention.

Watch Out!

It's easy to forget about using sunscreen in the winter, especially when so little skin is exposed. The part that is exposed, however, usually the face and neck, is just as vulnerable to sunburn in winter months as in summer. Skiers have to be especially cautious, because UV rays are stronger at higher elevations where the air is clearer and because the snow reflects the sun.

Safety Savvy

Snowy weather calls for waterproof gloves and boots, plus hats and scarves to keep heads and ears warm. If your kids will be playing on playground equipment in the winter, buy gloves and boots that have gripping surfaces to minimize the risk of falls. If ice has formed on the surfaces of playground equipment, don't let your kids play on it.

Watch Out!

Hypothermia isn't just a winter weather threat. A child who swims in cold ocean or pool water and sits around in a wet swimsuit in a cool breeze can suffer from the condition, too. If that happens, change him into dry clothes and wrap him in towels.

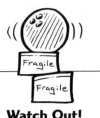

Watch Out!

Sand on the beach or in sandboxes at school and community playgrounds can contain bacteria, pinworms, and other nasty things. If your child has any cuts or scrapes, bandage them before letting her play in the sand. Wash her hands when she's finished.

Skin That Goes Itch

Children can get rashes at any time of year, but some are more common in summer when kids are outdoors more, wearing less clothing, and exposing skin to plants, bugs, and other rash producers.

Usually, baby's first summer produces a case of prickly heat, little red bumps that form where babies perspire most, such as the folds in their necks. Try to keep your baby cool and dry. Cotton is better than synthetic fibers, and wearing only a diaper indoors is cooler still. Read on for more summer rash prevention tips.

Swimmers Beware

Chlorine from the swimming pool irritates some children's skin. So can microscopic organisms in fresh water (which may lead to "swimmer's itch") or in ocean water (which can cause "sea bather's eruption"). Bumps form in the areas covered by the swim suit. These rashes usually heal in a week or two. Your doctor may recommend hydrocortisone cream to relieve itching. The best prevention measure is having your child rinse off between dips and take a bath when he gets home.

Marine life is fascinating but also potentially harmful. The best way to avoid being stung is to stay away from harmful sea creatures. Teach your kids to look but not touch. Stings from jellyfish are painful but seldom dangerous. If your child is stung, wipe the affected area with alcohol to neutralize the venom. Applying an ice pack helps if there's a lot of swelling. If your child has symptoms indicating a severe allergic reaction, such as difficulty breathing, seek medical attention immediately.

Poisonous Plants

Poison ivy, oak, and sumac all contain resin that causes red blisters when it touches skin. Your child doesn't have to actually touch a plant to get a rash. The resin can be carried on your dog's fur or on clothing that has brushed against the leaves.

Not all of these plants grow in all parts of the country. Teach your child to recognize those he's likely to encounter. If he comes in contact with one, washing can help remove the resin. A rash can be treated with hydrocortisone cream. Severe cases should be seen by your pediatrician.

Banishing Bug Bites

When the kids go out to play, so do mosquitoes, bees, wasps, ticks, black flies, and all manner of other tiny critters. If your child is playing in an area that's buggy, apply an insect repellent with no more than 10 percent of the chemical DEET to exposed skin. If the repellent you use is an aerosol, spray it on your palms and then spread it on your child, rather than spray him directly, to minimize what he might inhale or get in his eyes.

Safety Savvy

Bug repellent with DEET can make sunscreen less effective; if you use them simultaneously, get a sunscreen with a higher SPF. Or, you can try the combination sunscreen-bug repellents now on the market.

Follow the instructions on the container carefully, use it sparingly, and consult your pediatrician before applying bug repellent to an infant. Wash it off your child when she comes inside for the day.

Long-sleeve shirts and long pants are good protection against bugs, too, but kids may object to wearing them when playing in hot summer weather. Whatever kids wear, light-colored clothing is better. Bugs can't see it as well and therefore aren't as attracted to it as to clothing in dark colors.

For itchy bites, such as those from mosquitoes, an anti-itch lotion provides relief.

Lyme Disease

Lyme disease is a bacterial infection transmitted to humans primarily through deer tick bites. One sign of Lyme disease is a rash that looks like a red bulls-eye. Other symptoms are flu-like and include fever, headache, and fatigue. Even though you've probably heard scary things about the disease's potential effects if left untreated, it can be cured easily with antibiotics when caught early.

Kids are most likely to be bitten while playing in wooded areas or long grass. Bug repellent with DEET provides some protection, as does clothing. It's also a good idea to check your kids when they get home from playing in areas that might harbor deer ticks. Because they can be as small as a pin head, a magnifying glass helps. Pay extra attention to the scalp. Then have your child shower and dry off with a rough textured towel in case you missed any.

In only a tiny fraction of cases does a tick bite result in Lyme disease. The Centers for Disease Control and Prevention says ticks are most likely to transmit the infection after being attached to the skin for at least two days, so prompt removal is a good prevention method.

If you find a tick attached to your child, apply mineral or olive oil and leave it there for 30 minutes. This will close the tick's breathing pores and loosen or detach it. Complete the removal by using tweezers to grasp it near its head and pull with slow, steady force. Make sure you get all the parts. After removal, wash the area with soap and water and apply an antibacterial cream.

Although a vaccine administered in shots is now available to prevent Lyme disease, it has not yet been approved for children. The Food and Drug Administration allows its use only in people older than 15. The vaccine is not 100 percent effective, so people who are immunized still are advised to take precautions in tick-infested areas.

Summer Stingers

Picnics attract bees, yellow jackets, and other stinging insects, especially when sweet foods and liquids are on the menu. These critters also go for fragrance from soap or perfume. They get aggressive when they feel harassed, so teach your child not to swat at them.

Safety Savvy

Sometimes a bee flies into a can of soda or bottle of juice and gets trapped when a child puts his mouth over the opening. The angry bee stings the child's lips in order to escape. If you pour the liquid into a wide-mouth cup, your child can check for bees before drinking, thus avoiding a nasty surprise.

If your child gets stung, try to remove the stinger by gently scraping it with your fingernail. Then wash the area and apply ice or cold compresses to relieve the pain. If you can't see the stinger, go ahead with the washing and compresses.

A few children are allergic to certain insect stings. If you notice symptoms, seek medical treatment immediately. Some of the symptoms are swelling in areas of the body other than the sting site (such as eyes, lips, or tongue), difficulty breathing, bluish skin color, hives, and nausea.

Once you discover your child is allergic, you'll probably be advised to carry a drug with you at all times that will counter the affects of future stings. Since stings can be life-threatening to an allergic child, make sure everyone who cares for her has access to the medication and knows how to administer it.

Avoiding Dog Bites

Dogs may be man's best friend, but they're not always friendly to children.

Whether it's your own or a stranger's pet, your child should be taught how to approach a dog or deal with one that appears threatening. It's best if kids avoid dogs they don't know and remember not to chase, tease, or pull the tail of a dog they do know.

The Humane Society of the United States offers these additional tips for children:

➤ Ask permission before petting someone else's dog (or cat). If the owner says it's okay, let the dog smell the back of your hand before you touch him.

➤ If a dog approaches you, stand still and quiet with your hands at your sides so you don't appear threatening. Avoid eye contact.

➤ Don't run if a dog tries to chase you. His instinct is to chase and catch someone or something. If you stop, he'll likely sniff you and leave you alone.

➤ Don't pet or approach a dog or cat while it's eating, sleeping, chewing on a toy, or guarding something. Dogs are especially protective of their owners, owners' children, and property such as houses and yards.

➤ Don't approach an injured animal. Instead, tell an adult.

Safety Savvy

You can prevent your own dog from biting a child—yours or someone else's—by training and socializing it to be comfortable around people, having it spayed or neutered, and keeping it on a leash or in a fenced yard when it's not inside your house. For more information, check out the Humane Society Web site at www.nodogbites.org.

Wild animals also are a threat to children. See Chapter 22, "Travels with My Children," for more on creatures that might be encountered in the wild.

Tales from the Safety Zone

An estimated 4.7 million Americans are bitten by dogs each year, and most of them are children. More than half the children over age 12 report that they have been bitten by dogs. More bites happen in summer, when kids and dogs spend more time outdoors.

If Someone Gets Bitten

If a dog bites your child (or anyone, for that matter), immediately wash the wound well with soap and water and contact your doctor. Also, report the incident to the local animal control agency, especially if the dog's a stray, so it can be captured and observed for 10 days to determine whether it's healthy or if your child will need shots to prevent rabies.

Watch Out!

Keep your children away from grills or outdoor cooking fires at all times. Barbecue tools should be off limits, too.

Food Safety

Summer wouldn't be complete without picnics and barbecues. But be careful: Federal government studies show that cases of food-borne illness rise in summer for two reasons. First, bacteria grow faster in the warm summer months, especially when humidity is high. Second, more people are cooking and eating outdoors where refrigerators and sinks aren't available.

Most adults have healthy immune systems that protect them from getting sick from contaminated food. Young children are more vulnerable to food-borne bacteria, because of their immature immune systems.

There are some simple steps to keep your food safe in summer. The most important safety measure is washing your hands with hot, soapy water before handling food and after using the bathroom, changing diapers, or handling pets. If you're eating away from home, use disposable wipes or antibacterial gels and dry your hands with paper towels.

Gadget Guide

"Instant read" thermometers are designed to be inserted in fast-cooking foods such as hamburgers to test for doneness. These are not the same as meat and poultry thermometers that stay in the food throughout the cooking process.

Prevent Cross-Contamination

Cross-contamination during preparation, grilling, and serving food is another prime cause of food-borne illness.

When you pack your cooler, wrap raw meats or poultry securely so the juices won't come in contact with other foods. Wash plates, utensils, and cutting boards that held raw meat or fish before using them again.

Don't Undercook

Foods should be heated long enough and at a high enough temperature to kill harmful bacteria. Meat and poultry cooked on a grill often brown fast on the outside but may be undercooked inside. Check them with a thermometer.

Cook meat and poultry completely at the picnic site. Partial cooking of foods ahead of time allows bacteria to survive and multiply to the point that subsequent cooking can't destroy them.

Here are the U.S. Department of Agriculture's (USDA) recommended temperatures for some meats, expressed in degrees Fahrenheit:

➤ Cook hamburger and other ground meats to an internal temperature of 160°F and ground poultry to 165°F. You cannot determine if the meat is safe simply by the color.

➤ Cook steaks and roasts that have been tenderized, boned, rolled, etc., to 160°F for well-done. Whole steaks and roasts may be cooked to 145°F for medium rare.

➤ Whole poultry should be cooked to 180°F. Breast meat should be cooked to 170°F.

Refrigerate Promptly

Luncheon meats, cooked meats, chicken, fish, potato or pasta salads, and other perishables should be kept in an insulated cooler with several inches of ice or ice packs. Replenish the ice when it starts to melt. Don't put food out until your family is ready to eat it.

Try to pack beverages in one cooler and perishable foods in another cooler, because the beverage cooler probably will be opened frequently. If possible, keep the cooler on the seat of the car instead of in the hot trunk, and put it in the shade when you unpack the car.

Handling Leftovers

Stow leftovers back in the cooler as soon as you finish eating. Food left out of refrigeration for more than two hours may not be safe to eat. At 90°F or above, food left out over one hour can spoil. If in doubt, throw it out!

Safety Savvy

For additional food safety information, call the toll-free USDA Meat and Poultry Hotline at 800-535-4555. It is staffed by home economists, registered dietitians, and food technologists weekdays year round from 10 A.M. to 4 P.M. Eastern time. An extensive selection of food safety recordings can be heard 24 hours a day using a touch-tone phone. Or visit the Web site www.USDA.gov for more information.

The Least You Need to Know

➤ All children older than six months should wear sunscreen whenever they play outside.

➤ Cover up an infant and keep her out of direct sun until she's old enough to wear sunscreen.

➤ When playing in the heat, kids should drink plenty of liquids to avoid becoming dehydrated.

➤ Winter weather calls for protective clothing and occasional indoor rest breaks to prevent hypothermia and frostbite.

➤ To avoid dog bites, tell your kids not to tease or chase dogs and to stand still and remain quiet if a strange dog approaches them.

➤ To reduce the risk of food-borne illness, wash hands before touching foods, keep perishables cold, and cook meat thoroughly.

➤ Keep your children away from grills or outdoor cooking fires at all times.

Down on the Farm

For people who live in big cities, life in the country evokes images of children spending carefree days in fresh air and sunshine far from the dangers of urban life. While this can be true, there is another side that might surprise urban dwellers: children who live in rural areas are at significantly greater risk of fatal injury than those who live in big towns and cities.

Agriculture is especially hazardous because it's a business where children both live and play on the work site. Tractors and other farm machinery can be dangerous to children. Livestock can bite and kick. Children who grow up in rural areas are more likely to drown because of the large number of open bodies of water they can encounter while unsupervised. They have high rates of injury in traffic collisions, especially because of the common rural practice of allowing kids to ride in the beds of pick-up trucks. Horseback riding can result in falls that cause serious head injuries.

Gadget Guide

When buying a riding helmet, check that it meets the American Society for Testing and Materials (ASTM) standards and is certified by the Safety Equipment Institute (SEI). Make sure it fits well. Insist that your child fasten the strap before getting on the horse and not unfasten it until dismounting.

When city dwellers move to rural areas, they're probably unfamiliar with the injury risks their children face. Estimates are that one-third to one-half of nonfatal childhood agricultural injuries occur to children who don't live on farms. Whether your children live on a farm or ranch or just visit them, they need to know how to avoid getting hurt.

Horses

Does your family photo album have a picture of Junior's first pony ride? If so, is his face happy—or is it in tears? More than a few preschoolers cry when they realize they are sitting high off the ground on a large, unpredictable beast. Kids who take up horseback riding when they're a little older would be well-advised to keep in mind that unpredictability. Even the gentlest animal can be spooked and act up. That's why equestrian organizations and physicians strongly urge kids to wear helmets when they ride.

The idea of trading a cowboy hat for a helmet is one many children resist, but the evidence is overwhelming that helmets can prevent large numbers of serious—sometimes fatal—head injuries. Remind your little rider that ballplayers, car racers, and astronauts all wear helmets.

More Horse Safety Tips

When picking a horse for your child, choose one that is quiet, gentle, and small enough so that when your child mounts, her feet reach at least halfway down the horse's sides.

The National Children's Center for Rural and Agricultural Health and Safety offers these additional tips for riders:

➤ When using stirrups, wear boots or shoes that have heels and that completely cover the ankles.

➤ Inspect the saddle and all other equipment, checking for wear or stretching. Make sure all equipment is securely fastened.

➤ Never tie yourself to the horse. Don't wrap the lead rope or reins around your hand or waist. Never strap yourself or someone else to the saddle.

Safety When You're Not Riding

While most equestrian injuries requiring hospitalization are due to falls from horses, up to one fifth of head injuries occur when a child is caring for the horse—feeding, leading, or grooming it.

For tips on handling horses and other animals, see the "Animals" section, later in this chapter.

Farm Children at Play

If you live on a working farm you know that supervising preschoolers and carrying out farm chores at the same time is tough. Finding child care is difficult, too, because the farm's work schedule doesn't fit neatly into a day care center's hours, and facilities can be few and far between in rural areas. Creative and flexible families can find solutions, however.

Watch Out!

Never ride double with your child. She should begin riding only when she has the muscle strength and balance to ride by herself and only when she's old enough to understand and follow the directions of a knowledgeable instructor.

Child-Care Options

If there are no relatives nearby, you may need to hire a child-care provider during peak seasons. You could also try setting up a baby-sitting cooperative with other families so parents can take turns watching several children at once.

If there's a day care center in your area, it might be persuaded to offer flexible hours that fit with the times you and other nearby families are busiest on the farm.

Play Areas

Supervising young children is easier if you can keep the work areas off limits. A fenced yard with play equipment is the easiest way to do that. (See Chapter 14, "Life's a Playground," for tips on creating a safe play area.)

Farm Ponds

About one fourth of farm deaths of children are drownings. As kids get older and venture beyond their play-yard, they must be taught never to go into a body of water without supervision.

Safety Savvy

Fertilizer, animal waste, pesticide run-off, and other substances can contaminate a farm pond. If you allow swimming in your pond, have the water tested annually by a certified laboratory.

Watch Out!

Wood planks often are used to cap abandoned wells, but they aren't adequate because the wood can rot. At the least, an old well should have a heavy, solid covering that children can't remove. A safer alternative is filling it in.

If you have a pond on your farm, it's best to fence it and post "No Trespassing" signs. If you want to use the pond for swimming, put up a rescue post near the edge of the water—a sturdy pole securely fixed in the ground. Hang four things on it:

➤ A nylon rope with a buoy on the end that you can throw across the width of the pond

➤ A strong, lightweight pole (such as one made from aluminum) that a swimmer can grasp to be pulled out if necessary

➤ A sign with the phone number of your rescue squad

➤ A chart with instructions on first aid for drowning victims

For more information on preventing drowning, see Chapter 15, "On the Waterfront."

Children at Work on Farms and Ranches

One of this country's traditions is having children help with the work on family farms and ranches. Safety advocates who work on rural childhood injury prevention try to help parents maintain this tradition—which often is an economic necessity—while making sure the kids don't tackle jobs for which they aren't developmentally ready.

What's Safe and What's Not?

Each year, more than 100 children die and approximately 100,000 more are seriously hurt in incidents involving tractors, farm machinery, livestock, and falls. Many injuries could be prevented if parents had better information about what's safe and what isn't when involving children in the family business.

How Old Is Old Enough?

It's difficult for a farm family to decide when a child is old enough to take on a particular farm task safely. Many injuries occur when a child's physical or cognitive development isn't adequate for the job.

The North American Guidelines for Children's Agricultural Tasks (NAGCAT) is a tool for parents to use as they make these decisions. The guidelines analyze 62 agricultural jobs. They include a checklist to help parents assess their child's readiness for each job based on the mental, physical, and psychosocial skills needed to perform it. The guidelines also point out the key hazards for each job, the recommended level of adult supervision, and steps necessary to do the job safely.

Issued in June 1999, the guidelines were developed over a three-year period by experts in child development, industrial hygiene, ergonomics, and other relevant fields. Farm families in both the United States and Canada were consulted as the guidelines were prepared.

Safety Savvy

The National Children's Center for Rural and Agricultural Health and Safety, part of the Children's Safety Network, provides technical assistance to professionals and collaborates with groups promoting child safety on farms. For more information, call 888-924-SAFE (888-924-7233) or visit www.marshmed.org/nfmc/children. A leading grassroots organization helping parents, Farm Safety 4 Just Kids, has fact sheets on farm safety topics. Call 800-423-5437 or visit www.fs4jk.org.

Tales from the Safety Zone

Marilyn Adams, a leading farm safety advocate, speaks from the heart when counseling families about injury-prevention measures. Her 11-year-old son, Keith, was killed in a farm machinery incident. In 1987, a year after Keith's death, Adams founded Farm Safety 4 Just Kids as a way to work through her grief by helping prevent such profound loss for other families. Her illustrated book, *Rhythm of the Seasons: A Journey Beyond Loss*, recounts her son's life and death and the ways that she and her family coped. This brief but moving volume would comfort any family struggling with the loss of a child. It can be ordered from Farm Safety 4 Just Kids; see the previous Safety Savvy sidebar.

Safety Savvy

Parents can view an abbreviated version of the guidelines for each job at www.nagcat.com, or order the full text of guidelines by calling 1-800-382-8473 or visiting www.gemplers.com.

Watch Out!

Small children should be kept away from areas where a tractor is in operation because the driver may not be able to see them.

Tractors and Young Children Don't Mix

Tractors are a major cause of deaths and injuries to children on farms. Children should never be passengers on a tractor. The driver has a seat belt and a rollover protection structure (required on tractors made since 1976). However, the tractor isn't designed to hold passengers, and any who ride along can block the driver's vision or access to the controls. Children can fall from the tractor.

The no-passenger rule also applies to all-terrain vehicles, riding lawn mowers, and other motorized equipment. Never allow your child to ride in the bed of a pick-up truck; have him sit inside, properly restrained in a seat.

Chemical Hazards

Farms typically use hazardous chemicals. Keep them locked away, in their original containers. Discard empty containers and utensils where young children can't get to them. Keep kids and their toys away from areas where you are applying chemicals, and keep the number of the poison control center by your telephone in case of an emergency. See Chapter 7, "You Put *What* in Your Mouth?: Poison Prevention," for more information.

Away from the Grains

Children can become trapped and suffocate in large quantities of grain. Kids should never ride on grain wagons or go into grain storage areas. Keep them away from areas where grain is being loaded or unloaded.

Animals

One of the first chores a child might be assigned on a farm is feeding and caring for animals. All animals, even those that appear friendly, should be treated with respect. Loud sounds or unfamiliar settings or people can be frightening to them.

A child who visits a farm may not be aware of the safest way to approach a large animal. Tell him to move slowly and speak calmly. He should avoid the hind legs and approach the animal at the shoulder. Children should not approach animals who have newborns. When working with animals in close quarters, discuss an escape route for children in case the animal becomes unruly.

To avoid foot injuries, children who care for livestock should wear steel-toed shoes.

Falls

The hay loft is a favorite place for farm children to play, but it's also a place where many have gotten hurt from falls. Children are also drawn to other high structures on farms. Preschoolers should be kept away from ladders and high places. School-age children can be taught to safely climb a ladder but only to reach areas where there are no hazards. Grain bins and silos should be off limits.

Have your child wear boots or shoes with slip-resistant soles—free of mud or manure—if he is going to climb on ladders, wagons, or other farm equipment.

Safety Savvy

Animal care and some other farm chores must be done no matter what the weather. If your child works outside for long periods of time, learn how to prevent and treat hypothermia in winter and dehydration in summer. See Chapter 23, "The Great Outdoors," for details.

Emergency Response

One reason the number of injury deaths is higher in rural areas is that trauma care facilities often are far away from the scene of the injury and treatment is delayed. That's why it's critical that farm families prepare in advance for emergencies.

Since the first few minutes can be crucial in treating an injured child, you and other adults and teens working on the farm should learn first aid and CPR. (See Chapter 27, "First Aid to the Rescue!") Post emergency numbers beside every telephone.

If children are working in remote locations on the farm, know where they are and have them check in with you at specified intervals.

Gadget Guide

Cell phones can be invaluable in an emergency on a ranch or farm. Use them to keep in touch with family members and to summon medical help if needed.

The Least You Need to Know

➤ Teach your children never to go into a farm pond without adult supervision.

➤ The North American Guidelines for Children's Agricultural Tasks can help parents decide when a child is ready for specific farm chores.

➤ Please, no passengers on tractors, riding lawn mowers, or other motorized vehicles!

➤ Children should ride in a passenger seat, not in the bed of a pickup truck.

➤ All adults and teens on farms should learn first aid and CPR and know how to summon help in an emergency.

Chapter 25

It's My Body: Personal Safety

In This Chapter

➤ The role of self-esteem in self-defense

➤ Dealing with unwelcome touching

➤ Street smarts

➤ Handling bullies

➤ Safety on the Internet

As you've seen, most of the topics in this book deal with unintentional injuries to children, but intentional injuries hurt kids, too. The threats range from schoolyard bullies to sexual predators.

These are the injuries that could happen when you're not around to protect your child, and that's why you have to teach your child to protect himself. Start the education process when he's very young and continue through adolescence.

Imparting these lessons can be a tough balancing act. On the one hand, you don't want to scare your children so much that they're afraid of anyone they don't know. On the other, you have to make them aware that even someone they know can behave in a way that makes them uncomfortable or might even cause them serious harm.

One way to approach this is to help your child develop a strong sense of self-esteem. A child who is insecure may be reluctant to speak up in defense of herself or may be afraid to act in her own interests for fear others won't like her. She may not have the inner strength to challenge an adult who bothers her, or she may blame herself for being the cause. The child who believes in her own self-worth and her right to protect her own body will not only be in a better position to handle threats, but will be less likely to be victimized in the first place.

Much of this chapter deals with helping children stay safe when they're away from home. See also Chapter 5, "What Was That Noise?: Kids Home Alone," for safety tips for kids who are home alone.

Early Lessons

Human touch—hugs, kisses, stroking—are a basic part of healthy lives. Such warm and intimate relationships between young children and parents are essential for healthy development. That's why it's tricky to explain to a young child that some kinds of touching are wrong.

Teach your child to say "no" firmly if anyone tries to touch her in a way that is uncomfortable or frightening. The parts of her body that her swimsuit covers are especially off-limits. Tell her to inform you or a trusted grown-up if she experiences any unwanted touching.

Instead of telling your children to avoid strangers, talk about situations to avoid. Young children don't have a clear concept of what a stranger is. They might think someone who appears unattractive or threatening is a stranger but not someone who is attractive and kind or friendly. The "avoid strangers" message overlooks the more likely possibility that they might be harmed by someone they know.

Tales from the Safety Zone

A television crew went to a park to find out how well kids have gotten the message about not talking to strangers. The pretty anchorwoman approached individual children, explaining that she had lost her puppy and needed help finding it. Nearly all the children readily agreed to accompany her, even into bushes. The parents and caregivers of the children who were interviewed afterward expressed shock at how easily the kids were fooled.

Check-In

Another early lesson to impart to your child is the importance of keeping adults informed of her whereabouts. When your little one goes outside to play in the back yard, for instance, she should let you or her caregiver know first. Acquiring this habit early will make it more likely that she'll remember, when she's older, to keep you informed about where she's going, when, with whom, and when she'll be back.

Teach your child never to get into someone else's car, even someone he knows, without checking with you first.

Don't put your child's name in a visible spot such as on the outside of a backpack or baseball cap. A stranger can use this information to trick your child into thinking she's dealing with someone who knows her: an acquaintance of your family, for instance.

I'm Lost!

Probably every parent has had that moment of terror, often in a store, when a child wanders out of sight. Almost all are located eventually, but not before a few embarrassed folks are summoned on the public address system.

Teach your child not to wander around looking for you but to go to a clerk wearing a store badge and ask for help. As your child gets older, pick a landmark, such as a clock tower, information booth, or fountain in the middle of a shopping mall, as a central place to meet in case the family gets separated.

Tales from the Safety Zone

Wal-Mart has a procedure called Code Adam that is used when a parent reports losing a child. Employees go immediately to exterior doors until the child is found. This prevents the possibility that a stranger could sneak out with the child. The program is named for kidnap victim Adam Walsh, whose father founded the National Center for Missing and Exploited Children.

When It's Not a Stranger

It's hard for kids to believe they can be abused by adults whom they know and like. Relatives, teachers, coaches, ministers, or family friends are people children look up to, and rightly so in most cases, but children should understand that they have a right not to be touched or treated in a way that makes them uncomfortable.

Usually, touching by friends and relatives is an innocent gesture of affection, but if your child is uncomfortable with the tickling from a sibling, the arm punches from a buddy, or hugs from an uncle, for example, she can learn to say so in a polite but firm way. Otherwise, the person will assume the behavior is okay.

Warn your child to be especially wary if a person asks her to keep some activity between them a secret or threatens to harm her if she tells. Reassure your child that it's okay for her to lie that she'll keep the secret if that stops the unwanted behavior, but afterward she must tell you or another trusted adult. Help her understand that telling is the only way she can protect herself from the unwanted behavior in the future. Work at open communication with her at all times, so she knows she can come to you and won't be blamed or made to feel guilty.

If your child comes to you, listen carefully. Too often, parents fail to believe their children when the complaint involves someone the family knows. It's up to you to protect her when she's unable to protect herself.

Life on the Street

Here are some of the basic messages to teach your child once he starts venturing out on his own by foot or on a bicycle:

➤ Stay in areas with other people around. Don't take short cuts through alleys, deserted parking lots, or vacant lots.

➤ It's better to be with a friend or a group of friends than to travel alone.

➤ Stay alert to your surroundings. Notice who is walking near you, particularly at your side or behind you. Be aware of places you could go to get help from an adult if need be.

➤ Avoid going into a public restroom alone. If you must, take the stall nearest the door and exit promptly when you're finished.

➤ Never talk to strangers. Adults don't need to ask for help or directions from children. Don't take things from them, either. Keep a distance of two arm lengths between you and strangers so you are out of grabbing reach.

➤ Don't walk or ride your bike near parked cars.

➤ Possessions can be replaced, but you can't be. If a bully threatens you on the way home from school, for example, be ready to drop your backpack or books if you have to run away.

➤ Listen to your gut. If your instincts tell you something feels wrong, don't wait to find out if your fears are justified. Leave fast and go to a safe area that has adults around who can help.

Scenes from the Mall

Today's Main Street is the shopping mall, with its stores, movie theaters, restaurants, and arcades. It's a magnet for kids. Unfortunately, it also attracts assailants.

Tales from the Safety Zone

Parents have jammed Internet sites to find out if any of their neighbors is a convicted sex offender. When North Carolina set up its site, there were 340,000 visitors in the first month. Contacts were so numerous on Virginia's site, the state police had to get new equipment to double the capacity. Many states have statutes, patterned after New Jersey's "Megan's Law," requiring that registries of violent sex offenders and their addresses be made public. The lists typically are available by mail, sometimes for a fee. Several states have made the information easier to obtain by posting it on the Internet despite protests from those who see this as an invasion of offenders' privacy.

When you determine that your child is mature enough to go to the mall without you, require her to be in the company of friends rather than going there alone. Drop kids off and pick them up in a well-lighted and populated area; a spot near the mall doors is much safer than in the parking lot. Give your child small bills and remind her not to flash her money around. Make sure she has coins for a phone call if she wants you to pick her up early.

Remind her that if her instincts tell her someone might pose a threat, she should speak to a security guard or store clerk. Better to be safe than sorry!

The People on the Bus

Kids in urban areas often use public buses or even subways to go to and from school. If your child feels he's ready to start riding public transportation, go with him the first time or two to make sure he's familiar with the stops and has safe places to wait.

Tell him to sit as close to the driver as possible and to pay attention so he doesn't miss his stop and end up someplace unfamiliar. Make sure he has coins to phone you if he misses the bus or train and will be late.

Talk to him about how to protect himself if someone bothers him, such as telling the person to stop in a voice loud enough to alert other passengers.

Don't Look Like a Victim

Kids may not realize they can avoid trouble just by the way they walk. Imagine a thief is sizing up people on the street to choose his next victim. Is he more likely to prey on someone who's staring down at her feet, who doesn't look directly at others,

or who doesn't look likely to put up a fight? Or is he going to choose someone who walks confidently and whose body language says she's alert and observing the people and the scene around her?

Avoid Distractions

A child is more vulnerable if she's listening to a personal tape player through headphones or reading something while she walks. These distractions make it unlikely that she'll notice someone coming from behind.

Forget Miss Manners!

Kids want to be helpful; they don't want to appear impolite. They've probably seen their parents answer a question from a stranger or give directions. Children might encounter a homeless person asking for coins or a street vendor looking to make a sale.

Teach your child to say "no" (and sound as if she means it) while looking directly at the person and then moving on. She shouldn't apologize or worry about hurting someone's feelings. If she doesn't want to do this, she can walk briskly on without responding at all.

The same advice applies to encounters with strangers in places other than the street. If your youngster is taking an elevator, for example, when the door opens she should look at who's inside before entering; if she feels uncomfortable, she can wait for the next one. If she's worried about someone who gets on after her, she can push the button to get out at the next floor.

Anytime your child is in public and feels her safety is threatened, her best defense is to yell for help. Assailants understandably prefer not to attract attention.

Handling Bullies

Every schoolyard has a few bullies. (Adults have to deal with bullies sometimes, too, so lessons learned in childhood about handling them will be useful for a lifetime.)

Explain to your child that bullies are cowards. That's why they tend to pick on kids who are smaller and weaker; they know they probably can best them. Encourage your child to come to you when he's sorting out schoolyard problems even if he doesn't want you to intervene, because you may be able to offer a creative solution.

One defense against being picked on is to gather allies. Bullies are less likely to pick on kids who are with their friends.

Another is to remember the adage "Sticks and stones may break my bones but words can never hurt me." Bullies sometimes hurl insults to get a rise out of their victims. If the child won't take the bait, the bully will likely lose interest. Teach your child to ignore the bully or agree with him rather than escalating the situation by hurling an insult back.

Continually remind your child that he has a right to feel safe. Even if a bully has threatened to harm him if he tells, your child should report the offender to you or to a teacher.

Tales from the Safety Zone

Take a look the next time you pass your fire department, local businesses, hospitals, libraries, and other facilities. Is there a sign on display with the words "Safe Place"? This program, now in more than 300 communities, started in 1983 as an outreach effort by the YMCA in Louisville, Kentucky, to give young people in crisis, such as victims of abuse, a safe way to get professional help. Sometimes the kids they help are simply lost and need directions or are locked out of their homes. This is also a good place for kids to turn if they feel threatened by a stranger. If you have a program in your town, take your child to visit your neighborhood Safe Place so he will be familiar with them if he ever needs help.

Safe Place logo.
(Used with permission)

In Case Your Child Is Missing

If your child is supposed to be at home but is missing, make a thorough search of any places he could be hiding or could have crawled into and fallen asleep or become trapped. Check with neighbors and friends quickly and then call the police. Give them a complete description; especially include the clothes your child was wearing.

Safety Savvy

Your child may be more receptive to personal safety information if it comes from sources other than lectures from you. One example is *The Safe Zone: A Kid's Guide to Personal Safety* (Morrow Junior Books, 1998), recommended for ages 9 and up. It's full of situations a child might find herself in and suggestions for how to handle them. Ask your librarian or bookstore clerk for this title or other books or videotapes appropriate for your child's age.

Gadget Guide

Ask your local police department to fingerprint your child. Sometimes the police provide this service at school fairs and other gatherings where young children are found, but you also can go to the police station to have it done. The police won't keep the record on file, so put it in a safe place at home.

If your child is away from home and is missing, such as in a store, notify the manager and ask for immediate help.

Working with the Authorities

In the event that you have to summon police to find your lost child, it's helpful if you've prepared ahead of time.

Have a complete, written description of your child, including glasses, braces, birthmarks, and other distinguishing features. Take photos of your child every six months, and keep the most recent handy. Head-and-shoulder shots are best. Recent videotapes are also helpful.

After reporting your missing child to the police, call the hotline of the National Center for Missing and Exploited Children (NCMEC), 800-THE-LOST (800-843-5678). This 24-hour, toll-free number is operated in conjunction with the U.S. Department of Justice and has helped in the recovery of thousands of lost children. The NCMEC has access to the FBI's National Crime Information Center Missing Person Files and can make sure data about your child is disseminated to law enforcement officers nationwide.

Safety in Cyberspace

The Internet can be a wonderful tool and toy for kids. They can get help with homework, play games, or chat with children around the world.

Unfortunately, they also can be exposed to pornography, violent material, and hate messages. The biggest danger is that kids will communicate unknowingly with child predators who can lure them into dangerous situations. This is not a reason to prevent your children from enjoying the riches the Internet has to offer, but it does mean that you have to arm them with the knowledge of how to protect themselves from harm. It means you have to keep an eye on where your little Web surfer is surfing.

You don't want to act like a spy, but you do want to know how he's spending his time on the Internet. Try this tactic:

Since kids often are more adept at computer use than their parents, they love to play teacher to the grown-up. Ask your child to show you some of the tricks he's learned about using the Internet. Let him take you on a visit to his favorite chat rooms or Web sites. Check in periodically under the guise of perfecting your own skills.

Online Safety Rules

Teach your kids these safe-surfing rules:

➤ Don't give out personal information without your parent's permission, including your full name, address, phone number, name of your school, or anything that would reveal your actual identity. Don't provide information about your family or friends, either.

➤ Don't meet in person someone you met on-line unless your parents agree that it's okay and they or another adult can accompany you.

➤ Don't respond to messages or comments in chat rooms that make you feel uncomfortable or threatened. If you respond, it just invites more of the same. Instead, tell your parents or a trusted adult.

Set limits on the amount of time your kids may spend online and what areas on the Internet are appropriate for them to enter. Get their agreement to abide by the rules and to ask permission before venturing into other areas.

Safety Savvy

One of the most effective strategies for keeping your child safe on the Internet is to place your computer in the family room or kitchen rather than in the child's bedroom. He'll be less tempted to access inappropriate material if he knows another family member could walk by at any moment.

Watch Out!

It's harder to control your children's Internet use outside the home. Libraries are struggling with how to restrict the Internet sites children can access on library computers while still providing full access for adults. Some are installing filters or requiring parents to provide written permission for children to use library Internet services. Ask about your library's policy and also that of your child's school.

Chat Rooms

Chat rooms enable live conversations with a group of other people. Some have private areas where two or more friends can engage in a private chat. Some have moderators who lead discussions, and others have monitors who will kick someone out for inappropriate language or subject matter.

Safety Savvy

If you or your child receives information online that you think is illegal or threatening to you or others, contact the National Center for Missing and Exploited Children's 24-hour, toll-free child pornography tip line. Operated in cooperation with the U.S. Customs Service and the Postal Inspection Service, the CyberTipline may be reached at 800-843-5678 or on the Web at www.missingkids.org.

Chat rooms probably are the most dangerous aspect of the Web for kids. This is the place where strangers make friends. Child predators may enter these sites, strike up conversations with young people, and, in rare cases, lure them into face-to-face meetings.

Explain to your kids that just because a chat room participant identifies herself as a 13-year-old girl doesn't mean she *is* a 13-year-old. She might actually be a 35-year-old with harmful intentions. A chat room that's for kids only doesn't necessarily have only kids in it.

Handling Junk E-Mail

Many commercial enterprises send unsolicited e-mail—sometimes called "spam"—to sell their products or services. Some of these businesses may operate sexually explicit web sites and send messages that lure potential customers—and in some cases, kids—to a sample of a site. Return addresses can be deliberately misleading, so a message that looks innocent may not be. If you receive objectionable material through e-mail, contact your Internet service provider so it can investigate its origin.

Safety Savvy

To avoid harassment, girls especially should pick gender-neutral names to use as their identifiers in chat rooms.

Web Site Safety

Some kids set up their own Web sites, or home pages, through their schools or their home Internet providers. If your child wants to try it, caution her not to put her address, phone number, or photo on the site.

When visiting Web sites, kids sometimes encounter an offer to enter a contest or receive a promotional item. These usually require them to enter information about themselves. Typically, this data is used for marketing products. Tell your kids to check with you before providing any data to a Web site.

Filtering Software

If you feel you need help setting Internet limits for your child, look into software that screens out unwanted content. Some such child-friendly Internet software allows you to pre-select the sites you want your children to be able to access, and keep your kids from entering chat rooms. No system is foolproof, however. For this reason, it's important to establish clear guidelines about what your child can and cannot do when using the Internet.

Many Internet providers make these types of controls available for free with their service. Check your provider to see what it offers.

Safety Savvy

"Kids and Company: Together for Safety" is the title of a personal-safety curriculum for grades K–8 that was developed by the National Center for Missing and Exploited Children. Endorsed by such leading groups as the National Education Association and the National Association of Secondary School Principals, the program can be used in both schools and community groups. For more information, call 800-892-7430.

The Least You Need to Know

➤ Children should be taught to say "no" and then to tell you if they experience unwelcome touching or requests for it.

➤ Talk about situations to avoid rather than "strangers."

➤ Require your children to keep you or a caregiver informed about their whereabouts at all times.

➤ Kids with a strong sense of self-esteem will be better equipped to protect themselves from bullies and others who may wish them harm.

➤ Set rules for your child's Internet use and stay involved so you know the rules are being followed.

Part 6
Coping with the Unexpected

No matter how careful you and your child are, mishaps are bound to happen. That's when the Boy Scout motto, "Be prepared," pays off. If both you and those who care for your kids learn first aid, your child's life might be saved someday. You'll also have to make judgments about whether an injury can be handled at home or needs immediate medical attention. In this section, we'll help you sort out these questions and tell you what to do in an emergency until the ambulance arrives.

Nannies Need to Know

In the minds of our kids, the definition of a good baby-sitter is someone who is fun to play with, gives them their favorite snacks, and lets them do things their parents don't.

Adults, on the other hand, look first for someone who is responsible and who genuinely likes kids. These are very important traits, to be sure, but whether you're hiring a full-time child-care provider or just an occasional baby-sitter, the most important qualification for the job is the ability to keep your child from getting hurt.

As the parent, you've got to be a partner with your caregiver when it comes to child safety.

Just what does this mean? It means making your home safe and providing the caregiver with important information she'll need if an emergency arises. If she hasn't been trained in first aid or hasn't had a refresher lately, you might offer to pay or at least share the cost of a course. It's a wise investment.

Picking the Right Caregiver

Good nannies are hard to find. If you're seeking a full-time child-care provider, plan on spending considerable time locating and screening candidates.

Seeking Applicants

To find qualified candidates, ask friends, neighbors, colleagues, ministers, and pediatricians. Visit your neighborhood playground to meet others' nannies and ask if they have friends who are looking for new positions. Put signs up in nearby churches, grocery stores, and libraries. Call your local community college about recent child-development graduates.

You also can advertise in the newspaper, but be warned: You'll probably get lots of phone calls! Be specific in all your advertising about exactly what you are looking for. That should narrow the pool a bit, although you'll probably still get calls from people who don't meet your criteria.

The Interview

It's best if both parents participate in the interviews, because one of you may pick up on something the other misses. Prepare a list of questions to ask all the candidates so you can compare their answers.

Sample Interview Questions for Nannies

Why are you looking for a new job?

Please provide the names, addresses, and phone numbers of previous employers.

What ages of children did you care for in your previous jobs?

What level of education have you completed?

Do you have a driver's license?

Do you smoke?

What do you enjoy about working with children?

What kinds of activities will you engage in with our child?

How do you handle discipline?

Have you had a first-aid course and if so, how recently?

How would you handle ...? (Fill in situations the caregiver might encounter such as potty training, sibling conflict, or a medical emergency.)

To test the applicants' safety knowledge, ask some open-ended questions about how they would handle a specific emergency situation such as a house fire. Ask the candidate's attitudes about discipline. If you have an infant, ask if the candidate puts babies to sleep on their backs. (This is the safest position for sleeping babies and helps prevent sudden infant death syndrome.)

When you advertised, you should have noted that you only wanted a non-smoker, but some applicants may have overlooked or ignored the requirement. Secondhand smoke can have harmful health effects on children. During the interview, ask the candidate if she smokes, and don't hire her if she does even if she says she won't do it in your child's presence. You don't want her out on the porch lighting up and leaving your child unsupervised.

Reference Checks

Check several references for your final candidate even if not all of them employed her in a child-care capacity. You want to know how reliable she is and the level of child-care experience she's had, particularly with your child's age group. Ask if she ever had to deal with an emergency situation and how well she handled it. Ask about her approach to discipline.

If she drove the children in her previous position, ask about how safe a driver she is and whether, to the best of the reference's knowledge, she always used child safety restraints. Then compare the answers she gave to what her references say.

Watch Out!

Ask how the candidate was disciplined as a child. If she says, for instance, her parents spanked her, and she believes it's an appropriate discipline technique, look for another candidate. No one should hit your child, for discipline or any other reason.

A Clean Bill of Health

Day care center workers are typically required to have medical checks to assure that they don't have communicable diseases such as tuberculosis. That should be one of your requirements, too. Before you finalize your decision, ask your candidate if she has had a recent physical exam and if not, offer to pay for one. Also, get her permission to request a report from her doctor.

Background Checks

If your nanny will be driving your child, it's a good idea to find out whether the candidate has a clean driving record. With her permission, you may be able to do this through your local traffic court. Don't think it excessive to want to check for a criminal record and credit history, too; you won't be the first parents to have done this.

Because state procedures and charges for these background checks vary, it may be easier to hire a firm that specializes in this service. If you use a firm, it should check all the places the candidate has lived, not just the current state of residence. To find a firm, look for "Investigators" in the Yellow Pages.

The Job Description

Some parents think they can hire a full-time nanny and get a house-cleaner, too. That may work if your children are older and in school part of the day. Young children need a lot of supervision, and that should be the priority. You know yourself that you can't keep a spotless house, cook a nice meal, and keep track of a toddler at the same time. Set realistic expectations and communicate to your nanny that minding the kids is her primary responsibility.

A Trial Run

Before making your final hiring decision, invite your nanny candidate to care for your children for at least a couple of days, with pay, while you are at home. This gives you an opportunity to help your children adjust to the new nanny as well as to observe how she handles her duties. A weekend may be preferable if it means both parents can be there.

After the trial run, you should feel a lot more comfortable about the candidate you've selected. Trust your gut instincts. If you have nagging doubts about her ability, it's better to keep looking than to hire someone you're not really enthusiastic about.

Using a Nanny Agency

If you can feel a headache coming on and the muscles in your neck are getting tense right about now, relax; there's relief in sight. No, not a couple of aspirin (although that might help, too!), but a nanny agency, also called a placement service. For a fee, it will do all the recruiting and the initial candidate screening for you.

Agencies differ a lot—and so do parents' experiences in using them. You have to go into this process with the understanding that it's the agency's job to find qualified candidates, but that ultimately it's up to you to make the hiring decision.

It's wise to interview more than one agency, then check references before you settle on your final choice. Don't just look in the phone book and go with the one that charges the least.

What should you ask an agency? Start with these questions:

➤ How long have you been in business?

➤ What are your fees?

➤ What is your refund or replacement policy?

➤ Do you conduct follow-up evaluations of the nanny's performance and/or mediate disputes?

➤ Do you train candidates in first aid? In any other skills?

➤ Are your candidates bonded, and do you perform background checks?

This last question is very important. Understand that being bonded just means that you're protected against theft, but only if the nanny is convicted. If the agency performs background checks, find out exactly how extensive the check is.

Any reputable agency will check nanny candidates' references, but you should do it, too, once you've made your final choice. The agency will have asked general questions about the candidate's employment history including promptness and reliability, but you need to know more.

Safety Savvy

To find agencies in your area that subscribe to the standards and ethics code of the Alliance of Professional Nanny Agencies, call 800-551-2762.

Sharing a Nanny

Some parents reduce the considerable expense of a full-time nanny by sharing with another family. With this arrangement, you not only have to find a nanny you like but also a family with whom you and your child are compatible.

A key question is whether the kids will be cared for in only one family's home or if you will alternate. If the kids will sometimes be at the other family's house, you need to make sure that family is as conscientious as you in eliminating safety hazards in its home and yard. (You may want to share this book with them, or at least review with them the room-by-room checklist in the front of the book.)

Both families should participate in interviewing candidates. Talk ahead of time about the questions you want to ask applicants, including their safety knowledge. Agree that if the final candidate has not had first-aid training recently, you'll send her and split the cost.

If the other parents seem less concerned about safety than you are, you may want to look for another family to share with. Otherwise, you'll always be worried that their home isn't safe or, because they don't insist on it, the caregiver isn't taking all the precautions you think she should.

Watch Out!

In some communities, a home where two or more unrelated children are cared for may be considered a day care home and require a license. Check out your legal obligations and also talk to your insurance company about whether your liability coverage is adequate if the other family's child is injured at your house.

Hiring an Au Pair

The case of a British au pair convicted of causing the death of an 8-month-old Massachusetts baby in her care left a lot of parents worrying about whether the au pair program is a good way to get a child-care provider. Well, as in most everything else, there are pros and cons. Some American families have loved their au pair experience, others regretted it.

One thing we can say with certainty, though, is that those families that were most pleased with their au pair understood what the program is about and didn't rely totally on an agency to choose an au pair for them.

A Child-Care Worker or Exchange Student?

Before pursuing the au pair option, you've got to understand the background of this federally sanctioned program. The U.S. government issues visas for one year so that young people from overseas can take classes and learn about American culture, in exchange for performing 45 hours of child care a week for their host family. Eight government-approved au pair agencies administer the program, and they must follow federal regulations.

Au pairs are between the ages of 18 and 25. They must speak English (although some are much less proficient than others!). They must have a doctor's certificate attesting to good health and up-to-date immunizations. They also must have some child care experience. Au pairs who will be caring for children younger than 2 must have at least 200 hours of prior experience caring for children that young. The agencies also are required to provide training, including first aid and CPR.

Safety Savvy

Before signing up with an au pair agency, ask for references and talk to other families, particularly those in your community who have used that agency. The large agencies operate nationwide but have local representatives who oversee the program. Ask the families about the screening process and the effectiveness of the agency's ongoing support to au pairs after placement.

Au pairs must take six hours of academic courses during the year, and host families are required to pay up to $500 of the cost. Some au pairs never enroll in classes and some families ignore the work limit, because enforcement of the rules is spotty. The result can be overworked au pairs who resent their situation and the families they live with.

When the one-year visa is up, the au pair must return home and families have to go through the selection process again.

Screening Au Pair Candidates

The agency gathers information about your family and provides you with information about potential candidates, including biographies and photos, but you should screen the candidates, too. Phone interviews can be helpful. Also, calling a couple of references, even though that involves extra international phone charges, should give you a more complete picture of the candidate than the agency provides.

Drivers Wanted

Many au pairs have driver's licenses. If you want your au pair to drive your children, check the license bureau in your community to see what the requirements are. Before letting her chauffeur your kids, ride with her yourself in various conditions, such as heavy traffic and rain, to see that she is careful behind the wheel and can operate your car. Finally, make sure she knows how to use your child safety seat and get her to promise that she will always buckle up your child and herself.

Orientation

When your nanny or au pair starts work, allow ample time to familiarize her with your house. At a minimum, she needs to know how to lock and unlock the doors and windows, operate the appliances, and find the fuse box, the first-aid kit, and a flashlight. She also should be briefed on your fire evacuation plan.

It's important that she knows how to get in touch with you at all times and how to summon emergency help. Fill in the "Information for Your Baby-Sitter" form or adapt it for your family's particular situation. Then photocopy it and leave it by the telephone with your "Consent for Medical Care and Medical Information" form. Point out its location to each sitter. Be sure to keep it up-to-date. If you have phones on more than one floor of your house, it's a good idea to put the list by each one so the sitter can get to it quickly, no matter where she is.

If there is a medical emergency, your caregiver will need a signed permission form authorizing her to approve treatment in case you can't get to the hospital right away. Otherwise, your child's medical treatment could be delayed while the doctors try to track you down.

Fill in the following "Consent for Medical Care and Medical Information" form, attach a photocopy of your medical insurance card, and put it in an envelope by the phone where your caregiver can find it easily, near the "Information for Your Baby-Sitter" form. If your caregiver will be taking your child away from home, she should carry it with her. In an emergency, she can give this form to medical personnel who want evidence of your permission before they treat your child. Ask your pediatrician if medical personnel and institutions in your area require information not on this form.

Safety Savvy

Even your parents need to have a signed medical permission form when they're caring for their grandchild. The child's stepparent does, too. Make additional copies of this form to fill in whenever you leave your kids with someone other than their regular baby–sitter.

Information for Your Baby-Sitter

For ambulance, fire, or police: Dial 911 (or other numbers you choose to insert here).

For additional information, see the "Consent for Medical Care and Medical Information" form.

Our Address: _____

Our Home Phone Number: _____

Mother's Name: _____

Phone at Work: _____

Cellular Phone: _____ Pager: _____

Father's Name: _____

Phone at Work: _____

Cellular Phone: _____ Pager: _____

Emergency contacts in case parents can't be reached:

_____

Neighbor's Name: _____

Home Phone: _____

Phone at Work: _____

Cellular Phone: _____ Pager: _____

Family Friend's Name: _____

Home Phone: _____

Phone at Work: _____

Cellular Phone: _____ Pager: _____

Relative's Name: _____

Home Phone: _____

Phone at Work: _____

Cellular Phone: _____ Pager: _____

Pediatrician's Name: _____

Address: _____

Daytime Phone: _____

Night/Weekend/Holiday Phone: _____

Poison-Control Center Phone Number: _____

Nearest Hospital's Phone: _____

Address: _____

Directions: _____

_____

Other Important Information (such as child's fears, disabilities, etc.):

_____

_____

_____

(Reprinted with permission of Peterson's, a division of International Thomson Publishing Inc. From The Working Parents Help Book, *by Susan Crites Price and Tom Price, © 1996.)*

Consent for Medical Care and Medical Information

Permission

In our absence during _____ (dates and time period),
_____ (name of caregiver) is authorized to present our
children, _____ (name of children), for emergency medical
attention, including diagnostic procedures, surgical and medical treatment and blood transfusions
by qualified medical personnel as they in their professional judgment determine to be necessary.
We acknowledge that we are responsible for reasonable charges in connection with this care.

_____
(Parent's signature)

_____
(Parent's signature)

Date: _____

_____
(Witness' signature)

Date: _____

Medical Information

Our Address: _____

Our Home Phone Number: _____

Mother's Name: _____

Phone at Work: _____

Cellular Phone: _____ Pager: _____

Father's Name: _____

Phone at Work: _____

Cellular Phone: _____ Pager: _____

Pediatrician's Name: _____

Address: _____

Daytime phone: _____

Night/Weekend/Holiday Phone: _____

Dentist's Name: _____

Address: _____

Daytime phone: _____

Night/Weekend/Holiday Phone: _____

Opthalmologist's Name: _____

Address: _____

Daytime Phone: _____

Night/Weekend/Holiday Phone: _____

Insurance Company Name: _____

Group Number: _____

Family ID Number: _____

Child's ID Number (child's name): _____

Child's ID Number (child's name): _____

Child's Name: _____

Birth Date: _____

Allergies (to drugs, insect bites, etc.): _____

_____

Medications Child Is Taking: _____

Dose: _____

Frequency: _____

Dose: _____

Frequency: _____

Dietary Restrictions: _____

_____

Date of Last Tetanus Booster: _____

History of Serious Illness or Injury (include specialists your child sees):

_____

_____

Illness/Injury: _____ Date: _____

Doctor's Name: _____

Phone: _____

Illness/Injury: _____ Date: _____

Doctor's Name: _____

Phone: _____

Other Important Information (such as child's fears, disabilities, etc.):

_____

_____

_____

Child's Name: _____

Birth Date: _____

Allergies (to drugs, insect bites, etc.): _____

_____

Medications Child Is Taking: _____

Dose: _____

Frequency: _____

Dose: _____

Frequency: _____

Dietary Restrictions: _____

_____

Date of Last Tetanus Booster: _____

History of Serious Illness or Injury (include specialists your child sees):

_____

_____

Illness/Injury: _____ Date: _____

Doctor's Name: _____

Phone: _____

Illness/Injury: _____ Date: _____

Doctor's Name: _____

Phone: _____

Other Important Information (such as child's fears, disabilities, etc.):

_____

_____

_____

(Reprinted with permission of Peterson's, a division of International Thomson Publishing Inc. From The Working Parents Help Book, *by Susan Crites Price and Tom Price, © 1996.)*

Candid Camera?

As careful as parents have been to screen and train the nannies they hire, many still worry about what goes on when the caregiver is alone with their child. Alarmed by "hidden camera" stories on news shows about nannies who neglect or mistreat their young charges, some parents have been drawn to companies that offer surveillance systems for home use.

But is spying on your caregiver a good idea? We think not.

First, there's the question of trust. You could lose a good caregiver if she discovers she's been taped and doesn't want to work for employers who are so distrusting. Videotaping also has limitations. It isn't practical to set up cameras in every room or outside, so you won't have a complete picture of a day in the life of your child anyway.

There may be legal issues, too. Secret taping could be illegal in your state. It also could make you vulnerable to a civil suit if she finds out.

There are other ways of assessing her performance. When you employ a new nanny, you might ask your neighbors to let you know if they see anything questionable. Try to drop in at home unexpectedly once in a while, perhaps on your lunch hour. Most important, communicate with her frequently while you build a relationship based on trust. Give her opportunities to raise concerns she might have about the job requirements. Ask her enough questions so you know how she and your child spend the day. If your child is old enough to talk, listen for comments that give you a sense of how the nanny is performing.

See Chapter 25, "It's My Body: Personal Safety," for more information on preventing caregiver child abuse.

Safety Savvy

If your local college has teacher training programs or a department of early childhood education, those are good places to look for students who are headed for careers working with children. You might even be able to obtain faculty recommendations on their best students.

Watch Out!

Make sure anyone caring for your child understands that in case of fire, he should gather the kids and leave immediately by the nearest exit, going to a neighbor's to call the fire department. Make sure he's familiar with all the escape routes from your house.

The Occasional Baby–Sitter

So far in this chapter we've talked about hiring and supervising a full-time caregiver, but sometimes you need an occasional sitter for an evening or weekend. For this, many parents turn to the neighborhood teenager, preferably someone they know. If you don't know the sitter, it should be someone recommended by your friends who have used the teenager's services. The sitter should be at least 13 or 14 and very responsible.

Many hospitals and community organizations offer courses for young teens who want to be baby-sitters. If your sitter hasn't had such a course, you might offer to pay for her to attend. The course usually doesn't cost much and it might pay off handsomely if your sitter learns a life-saving skill, such as giving aid to a choking child.

Where Do You Find Them?

Nearby colleges often provide a good source of baby-sitters. Some give parents lists of available students or have bulletin boards where you can post requests. But these baby-sitters likely haven't been screened by the college. Don't just hire one sight unseen. Meet the candidate, interview her and check references. If you think your kids will be spooked by being left with a sitter they don't know, arrange for them to meet her ahead of time.

Getting to Know You

The first time you use a sitter, ask the person to arrive early, so you have time to orient him or her to your house. A quick walk-through should include the locations of your first-aid kit, flashlight, and important phone numbers—including where you can be reached.

Make sure the sitter knows how to lock and unlock the doors and windows and operate the microwave, VCR, and any other appliances she might be called upon to use.

Give the sitter any special instructions verbally before you leave, focusing especially on safety issues. You can also leave a written list if you wish, but don't rely only on this. The sitter may not take the time to read a note, or might just take a quick glance. If you go through important safety information point by point, you can watch the sitter's reactions and be assured she understands it all.

The more routine details—the children's bedtime, approved snacks, favorite activities, house rules— might be better if written out ahead of time for the sitter's review after you've left. Otherwise, there may be too much information for her to remember.

Make Expectations Clear

Teen sitters should be reminded not to let anyone in the house who hasn't been pre-approved. Decide whether you're comfortable having the sitter invite a friend to join her while she baby-sits. This might be okay if you know the other person, too. But make it clear you don't want the sitter distracted so she fails to attend the children.

If she is sitting for you during the day, let her know whether it's okay to take the children into the yard to play and whether she has permission to take them somewhere else, such as the park or the ice cream shop. Make sure the kids understand the rules, too. Reassure yourself of the sitter's driving ability before agreeing to let her chauffeur the children somewhere.

Baby-Sitting Co-Ops

Perhaps the safest sitters of all are other parents you already know. This comfort factor—and the benefit of saving money—can make baby-sitting co-ops mighty attractive.

Safety Savvy

Some parents expect their sitters not only to watch the kids but to clean up the toys, wash the dinner dishes, or perform other household chores. Tidying up should not be done at the expense of constant supervision of very young children. Tell your sitters to skip the chores unless they have time to do them after your child has gone to sleep.

Safety Savvy

Instead of starting your own co-op, find out if one already exists in your area. Try calling your neighborhood school to reach one of the parent association officers. These folks are usually plugged into the parent grapevine and can tell you who to contact.

Here's how they work: Several families in the same general neighborhood agree to be in a pool of potential sitters. Most co-ops have some sort of scrip—paper money representing time—that parents use as currency to pay each other for a few hours of child care.

Typically, one person volunteers to be in charge of matches, a job that can rotate every month or two. The matcher takes calls from parents needing sitters and then phones others on the list until he finds someone who is available. The more you sit, the more scrip you earn so you can "hire" more sitters yourself.

The Least You Need to Know

➤ Carefully check references of any nanny, au pair, or other caregiver you hire.

➤ Trust your instincts; don't hire someone with whom you don't feel comfortable.

➤ If your nanny or au pair hasn't had first-aid training, pay for her to get it.

➤ Make sure she knows how to summon emergency help and how to reach you in an emergency.

➤ Leave contact information and a signed medical permission form with anyone caring for your child.

➤ Familiarize all your sitters with your fire evacuation plan.

Chapter 27

First Aid to the Rescue!

In This Chapter

➤ Good reasons for taking first-aid courses

➤ Stocking your first-aid cabinet

➤ Help for choking children

➤ What to do for some common childhood injuries

➤ Preparing ahead for a trip to the hospital, and coping when you get there

Even if you take every reasonable precaution to keep your children safe, it's almost inevitable that you'll experience a few emergencies during their growing-up years.

Not all emergencies need to become stressful or serious ones—if you're prepared to handle them. Something as simple as prompt treatment of a cut can head off a dangerous infection. Knowing how to administer cardiopulmonary resuscitation (CPR) can mean life or death to a drowning child.

Often the challenge is to determine whether the injury is something you can handle on your own or if your child should be seen by a doctor. In this chapter, we provide you with some basic first-aid tips along with information about handling serious emergencies. This should not be construed as medical advice; you should always contact your doctor if you have any doubt about how to handle an injury.

Note: In Chapter 26, "Nannies Need to Know," there's a checklist of information you can post by your telephone to be used in case of emergencies.

Get Thee to a Class!

The most important thing you can do to prepare for an emergency is to take a first-aid course. Not just any course. If you're a new parent, you need to learn the techniques for performing CPR on an infant, for example, because the procedure is different from CPR for older children and adults. The proper method of rescuing a child who is choking also varies according to age.

Learning first aid will give you more confidence as a parent and will likely keep you from panicking in an emergency. It also will help you keep things in perspective. A seizure or convulsion in a feverish toddler is frightening to behold, but if you know what's happening, and that it typically is not dangerous, you'll be better prepared to deal with it (see "Seizures," later in this chapter for what to do in such situations).

Anyone who cares for your child—including baby-sitters and grandparents—should be trained in first aid. You can find out about courses offered in your community by calling the American Red Cross, the American Heart Association, your local hospital or your health care provider. Some pediatricians' offices hold courses, too.

Stocking Up on First-Aid Supplies

At the top of the list is a good book. Check any one of a number of handy medical reference books, such as those from the American Red Cross and the American Medical Association. They provide simple advice for handling all kinds of injuries and illnesses.

Every House Should Have 'Em

Here are some first-aid items you should keep on hand:

➤ Adhesive bandages in assorted sizes

➤ Sterile gauze pads in assorted sizes

➤ Waterproof, adhesive tape

➤ Elastic bandages

➤ Butterfly bandages

➤ Antiseptic soap

➤ Cotton balls and swabs

➤ Topical antibiotic cream

➤ Antihistamine (for allergic reactions)

➤ Tweezers

➤ Sterile eye wash and an eye cup

➤ Rubbing alcohol

➤ Ice pack

➤ Scissors

➤ Syrup of ipecac (to induce vomiting, but only if you are told to by your poison center or doctor)

➤ Hydrocortisone cream for rashes and itching

➤ Thermometer

➤ Medicines such as pain- and fever-relievers, cough suppressants, and stomach settlers, but only as recommended by your doctor.

Restocking the Medicine Chest

Inspect your first-aid supplies and medicines periodically. Restock items as necessary and throw out anything that has passed its expiration date, looks or smells funny, or no longer has a label. Make sure all supplies are locked away from small children.

Medicines are best stored in a cool, dry place. Since bathrooms can get hot and steamy, it's better to lock medicine containers in a box or cupboard in another room or, if you must leave them in the bathroom, store them in sealable plastic bags. For more on safe medicine storage, see Chapter 7, "You Put *What* in Your Mouth?: Poison Prevention."

First-Aid Supplies on the Go

Along with the supplies you keep in your home, you should keep another first-aid kit in your car. Also put a small container of supplies in your diaper or tote bag for outings at the park or other places where your car isn't handy.

Gadget Guide

We recommend using an unbreakable, digital thermometer rather than a glass one which, if broken, can cause exposure to mercury, a toxic substance.

Safety Savvy

Find the location and phone number of the nearest 24-hour pharmacy where your doctor can call in a prescription or you can purchase first-aid supplies if there's an emergency late at night.

Watch Out!

Never use your finger to try fishing a stuck object from your child's throat; you could push the object down farther. Don't use those old remedies of slapping your child on the back or raising his arms over his head. They can do more harm than good.

Helping a Choking Child

Little kids are notorious for putting all manner of things in their mouths and for trying to swallow large bites of food without chewing.

Knowing what to do if the food gets stuck could save your child's life. As we've already said, taking a class is the best way to learn life-saving procedures. To stay fresh, review what you've learned periodically. What follows is a brief description of how to aid a choking child. It should not, however, be considered a substitute for taking a class from a qualified instructor.

Safety Savvy

The American Academy of Pediatrics has a chart showing basic first aid on one side and instructions for administering CPR and assisting a choking child on the other. You can get the chart by sending a check for $2.95 to the AAP, Attention: Publications, P.O. Box 747, Elk Grove Village, IL 60007-0747.

If your child is able to cough or make other noises, the object hasn't covered the windpipe and you should let him try to cough it up. If the object is stuck but your child can breathe, call an ambulance. If he can't cough or breathe or make a sound, have someone call 911 while you immediately start first aid.

The Heimlich Maneuver

Sometimes called abdominal thrust, the Heimlich maneuver can be used on children over age 3. Get behind your child in a squatting or kneeling position so you can wrap your arms around his middle. Form a fist and place the thumb side between his tummy button and the lower end of his breast bone. Grabbing the fist with your other hand, give him quick thrusts inward and upward forcefully enough that the object pops out. Keep trying if it doesn't work the first time.

If he becomes unconscious, lay him on his back on the floor, tilt his head back a little, close his nose and give him two breaths. If his chest doesn't rise, that means the object is still blocking the airway. While straddling his thighs, put the heels of your hand, one on top of the other, on his abdomen, and administer five thrusts. Look in his mouth to see if the object has loosened. If you haven't gotten results, repeat the whole process until help arrives or your child starts breathing on his own.

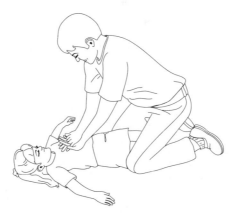

For kids between ages 1 and 3, skip the part where you stand behind the child. Begin by placing your child on his back on the floor as described above and follow the same procedure.

Helping a Choking Infant

If your baby cannot cough or make a noise, hold her face down on your forearm, using your hand to support her head, neck and chest. Her head should be lower than the rest of her body. Use the heel of your hand to give her up to five rapid, forceful blows between the shoulder blades.

If she doesn't start coughing, turn her face up on your arm with her head below her chest. Put two of your fingers along her breast bone just below her nipples and make four or five downward thrusts. Alternate back blows and chest thrusts until you can see the object in her mouth and can sweep it out with your finger.

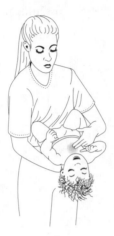

If she becomes unconscious, lay her down on her back and check to see if she's breathing. If she's not, tilt her head back, put your mouth completely over both her nose and mouth and give her two breaths. If her chest rises, that means the air is getting in. Continue the breaths every three seconds until she starts breathing on her own. If her chest doesn't rise, repeat the back blows, chest thrusts, and breaths, checking each time to see if the blows have dislodged the object. Keep this up until help comes.

Worth a Thousand Words

Even if you have had CPR and first-aid training, you might forget the routines in a crisis. It's a good idea to have an illustration with procedures for administering CPR or helping a choking victim. Keep copies in more than one part of your house, especially on the inside of a kitchen cupboard door since that's where children usually choke on food. If you have a pool, post a copy of CPR instructions near it, too.

First Aid for Some Other Common Injuries

Here are a few tips for handling other injuries you could encounter as a parent.

(See also Chapters 7 and 23 for advice on what to do in case of poison ingestion, dehydration, hypothermia, and insect bites.)

Burns

The proper treatment for a burn depends on what kind it is.

With first-degree burns, the skin is red, such as from a sunburn. Second degree describes skin that is mottled or has blisters. Both of these usually can be treated at home by immersing the area in cold (not icy) water or blotting with cold, clean compresses for a few minutes to ease the pain. Then gently blot the skin dry with a clean cloth. Aloe vera or other burn creams can help soothe the affected spot. Sunburn lotions (not sunscreens) will help ease pain from minor sunburns and promote healing. If there are blisters, apply antibiotic ointment to reduce the chance of infection. If blisters are severe, cover a large area, or are on the face, hands, or feet, call your doctor.

Watch Out!

Never treat a burn with butter, grease, or oil. They don't help, and they may cause infection.

Third-degree burns are the most serious. If the skin looks white or charred, call an ambulance immediately. Don't remove clothes stuck to the burn. Apply cold cloths or water to cool the burns. Elevate burned extremities higher than the heart if possible. Be prepared to perform CPR if necessary.

Cuts

Bleeding usually can be stopped by applying direct pressure. Press gauze or a clean cloth directly on the wound until the bleeding stops. Elevating the wound higher than the heart can help, but don't do that if there is the possibility of a broken bone. Once bleeding is controlled, apply an anti-bacterial cream and a bandage, firmly but not tightly.

Safety Savvy

Direct pressure works for a nose bleed, too. With his head leaned slightly forward, pinch the lower end of your child's nostrils together for about five minutes. If the bleeding hasn't stopped, pack the nostril with gauze and pinch closed for another 10 minutes. Call the doctor if the bleeding continues after that.

If you can't stop the bleeding after about 10 minutes, call an ambulance or take your child to the emergency room while continuing to apply pressure to the wound. Even if you are able to stop the bleeding, your child still might need stitches if the cut appears deep, irregular, or is on the face. Stitches close the wound and help prevent scarring.

Watch Out!

Don't move your child if you suspect he has suffered a neck or spinal injury. Trained paramedics are needed in this situation. Symptoms include neck pain, tingling, or paralysis. Be prepared to administer CPR but without tilting the head back.

Safety Savvy

Nursemaid's elbow is a dislocation that commonly happens to children when they are lifted or swung by their arms. It causes immediate pain that must be remedied by a doctor who can pop the joint back into place. Never lift your child by the arms.

Broken Bones or Dislocations

Some signs of a broken bone include pain when the injured area is moved or touched, or in some cases, difficulty in moving that part of the body. The injured part might be swollen and it might move unnaturally.

Try to immobilize the area with something rigid that can be used as a temporary splint—a board, a rolled up magazine, or a stick, for example. Use cloths or bandages for padding and to attach the splint above and below the injury. Then seek medical attention.

If a broken bone is protruding from the skin, control the bleeding, and then cover the wound with a clean dressing. Don't try to clean it, and don't try to push the bone back in. Seek medical attention immediately.

Treat dislocations the same as you would a fracture by immobilizing the area. Don't try to reset the bone yourself. Get medical help.

Sprains

It's hard to tell the difference between a sprain and a break. The only way to know for sure is to have an x-ray taken. Keep the injured area immobilized and seek medical treatment.

Seizures

In some children, high fevers bring on seizures. A few children get them after a head injury. Sometimes a seizure will happen for no apparent reason. Seizures themselves don't usually cause damage, but they can be frightening to a parent. The child's body may stiffen, he may have jerky or uncontrolled movements, and he may froth at the mouth.

Don't try to restrain your child if he's having a seizure. Just keep the area clear of objects on which he could hurt himself and try to cradle his head so it doesn't get injured. When the seizure subsides, usually in a couple of minutes, turn him on his side so saliva can drain out of his mouth, and call your doctor. If your child's lips or skin start to turn blue, call an ambulance.

A Knocked-Out Tooth

If a permanent tooth is knocked out, try to hold it in its socket and make a dash for your dentist. If you can't get it back in the socket, put it in cold milk right away to take to the dentist who then may be able to re-attach it.

Just a Bump on the Head— or a Concussion?

If your child falls and gets a nasty bump on the head, you won't be able to tell by the size of the bump whether he's likely to have a concussion. (A concussion is a blow to the head that can cause bruising or swelling of brain tissue.) You have to observe how he acts. Changes in his regular behavior patterns—such as a longer than usual nap, projectile vomiting, one dilated pupil or uneven movement when walking—are signs of a possible concussion and should be reported to your doctor immediately. To treat the bump, apply an ice pack or cold cloths to minimize swelling.

Watch Out!

Don't put anything in your child's mouth. It's a myth that a person having a seizure can swallow his tongue. A foreign object, such as a pencil or tongue depressor, *could* cause further injury if it breaks.

Gadget Guide

You can buy cold packs to keep in the freezer for treating bumps and bruises, or you can purchase chemical cold packs that don't need refrigeration. If you don't have a cold pack, try using a bag of ice cubes or even frozen vegetables wrapped in a dish towel.

Safety Savvy

When you call 911, tell the dispatcher you are calling about a medical emergency involving a child. If you have to leave the phone during the call, don't hang up. The dispatcher will likely stay on the line and wait for you to report back on your child's condition.

Gadget Guide

A cordless phone can be invaluable in an emergency. Your child could get hurt in the yard or a room of the house with no phone. You can take your cordless phone to your child and call your doctor or 911 without leaving her. You can describe her condition and get instructions for what to do while medical personnel stay on the line with you.

Going to the Hospital

In small communities, there won't be a question about which hospital to take your child. There's probably only one choice. In larger cities, however, there could be several hospitals within a reasonable distance. Some may be better equipped to treat children than others. That's why it's smart to check out hospitals before you need one. Your medical insurance may also require you to go to one hospital over another except in an emergency. Ask your pediatrician or other health care provider about the hospitals in your community.

If you aren't transporting your child yourself but have called an ambulance, the paramedics usually will decide where to go depending on the seriousness of the injury. Your child might be taken to the closest place until he's stabilized, then transferred to a more advanced pediatric facility.

On the Way to the Hospital

Take the time to learn the route to your nearest hospital soon, if you don't know it already. You don't want to have to stop and check a map when you have a crying child with a large cut that needs stitches. If you do have to go, try to find a neighbor or someone else to drive you so that you can concentrate on comforting your child. (If you can't concentrate well when under stress, you'll certainly want to find someone else to drive so that you don't risk having an accident on the way to the emergency room!)

No matter what the emergency, try to remain calm (at least on the outside!) so your child won't become more alarmed than she is already. Talk in a reassuring and soothing voice. While you wait for the ambulance or drive to the hospital, try to distract your child with conversation that will take her mind off the injury as much as possible.

Have Health Information Handy

You'll need information about your health insurance, your child's allergies, medications he is taking, the date of his last tetanus shot, and your pediatrician's phone number. Keep this in your wallet so you'll always have it handy whether your child is injured at home or away from home. If you have a caregiver, make sure she has all this information in a handy place, too.

Hospitals vary as to their admission and emergency room procedures. You may be seen first by a triage nurse who determines which emergencies should be given the highest priority. That means that if you've brought your child for a fairly minor injury, you may have to wait a long time to be seen.

Safety Savvy

If your poison center has advised you to go to a hospital for treatment of poison ingestion, take the labeled container with you so the doctors will know exactly what was in the substance.

Don't hesitate to ask the staff questions. You may, for example, want to know whether you can remain with your child during treatment or whether you can have a consultation with a specialist. You may also want to phone your pediatrician from the emergency room for advice.

The Least You Need to Know

➤ You and everyone who cares for your child should have first-aid and CPR training.

➤ The procedures for handling a baby who is choking or not breathing are different from the procedures used on older children and adults. Learn both.

➤ Every home needs not only a well-stocked first-aid cabinet but a good medical reference book.

➤ Carry in your wallet the information you'll need to provide at a hospital.

More Helpful Resources

General Safety Information

The Consumer Product Safety Commission is one of the best sources for all kinds of safety information. Call 800-638-2772 or visit its Web site at www.cpsc.gov. Order publications to be faxed to you by calling 302-504-0051 from the handset of your fax machine.

Through the CPSC you can:

➤ Find out if a product has been recalled.

➤ Learn how to return a recalled product or arrange repair.

➤ Obtain information on what to look for when buying products.

➤ Report an injury caused by a product.

➤ Report a product that poses a choking hazard.

➤ Report a malfunctioning product.

➤ Phone or visit the Web site to ask to receive regular notices of product recalls.

The CPSC also has a Web site for kids ages 8 to 12 at www.cpsc.gov/kids/kids/html. The site has educational, interactive, and fun activities about safety issues kids encounter every day.

The National SAFE KIDS Campaign is one of the leading groups working to prevent injuries to children. SAFE KIDS coalitions are active in every state, the District of Columbia, and Puerto Rico. To find out if there is a coalition near you, call 202-662-0600 or check the Web site at www.safekids.org, which also contains lots of injury-prevention information.

The American Academy of Pediatrics (AAP) is an important source of injury prevention information for both doctors and parents. Your pediatrician may have AAP brochures to give you. You also can get information from the organization's Web site, www.aap.org. The book *The American Academy of Pediatrics Guide to Your Child's Symptoms* is full of illustrated charts about handling injury and illness. It can be found in stores or ordered online or by calling 800-433-9016. The academy sells a chart displaying basic first-aid information on one side and instructions for administering CPR and assisting a choking child on the other. You can get the chart by mailing a check for $2.95 to the American Academy of Pediatrics, Attention: Publications, P.O. Box 747, Elk Grove Village, IL 60007-0747.

Animal Safety

For information on raising a dog that will not bite children—yours or someone else's—check out the Humane Society Web site at www.nodogbites.org.

Camps

Camps accredited by the American Camping Association are listed at the Web site www.acacamps.org. A printed copy can be found in many libraries or purchased for $19.95 by calling 800-428-2267.

Child Care

For guidance on what child-care centers should be doing to protect children's health and safety, check the guidelines of the National Resource Center for Health and Safety in Child Care. They appear under the title "Stepping Stones" at http://nrc.uschsc.edu.

A sign of a qualified child-care center is accreditation from the National Association for the Education of Young Children, the nation's largest organization for early childhood professionals. You can get a list of accredited centers in your area by calling 800-424-2460, extension 601, or by visiting the Web site at www.nayec.org.

To identify licensed day care providers in your area, contact the nearest child-care resource and referral agency. You can get the agency's phone number from the National Association of Child Care Resource and Referral Agencies at 800-424-2246 or at www.naccrra.net.

To locate agencies in your area that subscribe to the standards and ethics of the Alliance of Professional Nanny Agencies, call 800-551-2762.

Get a safety checklist for parents and child-care providers by sending a postcard to Child Care Safety Checklist, CPSC, Washington, D.C. 20207, or by visiting www.cpsc.org.

Child Safety Seats

For a free video and brochure on child passenger safety, call the National SAFE KIDS Campaign at 800-441-1888.

If you purchase a used child's car seat, make sure it hasn't been recalled by checking with the National Highway Transportation Safety Administration at 800-424-9393 or www.nhtsa.dot.gov.

Experts teach parents proper installation and use of their child safety seat in a program sponsored by General Motors and the National SAFE KIDS Campaign. For a list of scheduled instruction sessions, visit www.safekids.org.

The National Highway Transportation Safety Administration publishes a list by zip code of trained car seat checkers at www.nhtsa.dot.gov.

Cycling

The Consumer Product Safety Commission provides bike helmet information for parents—and activities for kids—at www.bikehelmet.org. Information also is available at 800-638-2772.

Get a brochure on safety and BMX competition by phoning the National Bicycle League at 800-886-BMX1 (800-886-2691) or by visiting www.NBL.org.

Fire Safety

Get a free packet on fire safety by calling the National Fire Protection Association (NFPA) at 617-984-7826. Obtain information about NFPA's safety curriculums for schools by calling 617-984-7285. More information is available on its family safety Web site, www.sparky.org, and its organizational Web site, www.nfpa.org.

Food Safety

Questions about food safety are answered by home economists, registered dietitians, and food technologists weekdays from 10 A.M. to 4 P.M. Eastern time on the U.S. Agriculture Department's Meat and Poultry Hotline, 800-535-4555. Recorded information is accessible 24 hours a day at that phone number. Information also is offered at its Web site, www.USDA.gov.

In-Line Skating

To find a certified instructor to teach your child in-line skating or roller hockey, call the International Inline Skating Association at 910-762-7004 or visit the Web site at www.iisa.org.

Roller hockey information—including rules, instructors, and leagues—is available from USA Hockey at 800-566-3288 or on the Web at www.usahockey.com.

Personal Safety

The National Center for Missing and Exploited Children provides a wide range of services that address the problems of children who run away or are preyed upon. If your child is missing, you should tell your local police department, then call the missing children's hotline at 800-THE-LOST (800-843-5678), which is operated in conjunction with the U.S. Justice Department.

If you or your child encounters illegal or threatening information on the Internet, phone the child pornography tip line at 800-843-5678 or visit the CyberTipline Web site at www.missingkids.org. The service is provided in cooperation with the U.S. Customs Service and the Postal Inspection Service.

Phone 800-892-7430 for information about the personal-safety curriculum for schools and community groups, "Kids and Company: Together for Safety."

Playgrounds

Request the "Handbook for Public Playground Safety" from the Consumer Product Safety Commission by calling 800-638-2772.

Other sources of information include:

The American Academy of Orthopaedic Surgeons at 800-824-BONE (800-824-2663) or www.AAOS.org.

The National Recreation and Park Association, at 703-858-0784 or www.nrpa.org.

The National Program for Playground Safety, at 800-554-PLAY (800-554-7529) or www.uni.edu/playground.

Rural Safety

Information about keeping kids safe on the farm is provided by:

The National Children's Center for Rural and Agricultural Health and Safety, at 888-924-SAFE (888-924-7233) or www.marshmed.org/nfmc/children.

Farm Safety 4 Just Kids, at 800-423-5437 or www.fs4jk.org.

The North American Guidelines for Children's Agricultural Tasks include checklists for assessing whether a child is ready to perform specific farm jobs. An abbreviated version for each job can be viewed on the Internet at www.nagcat.com. The full text can be ordered by calling 800-382-8473 or visiting www.gemplers.com.

Schools

Tips on keeping your school safe are offered by:

The National Parent-Teacher Association, at 800-307-4782 or www.PTA.org.

The U.S. Department of Education, at 800-USA-LEARN (800-872-5327) or www.ed.gov.

The National School Safety Center, at 805-373-9977 or www.nssc1.org.

The Center to Prevent Handgun Violence has created a program for schools called "Straight Talk About Risks" that teaches children of all ages how to avoid becoming a victim and how to manage conflicts without resorting to violence. You can learn about the program by phoning 202-289-7319 or visiting www.handguncontrol.org.

The U.S. Environmental Protection Agency, in cooperation with the National Education Association and other school-related groups, has developed an "Indoor Air Quality Tools for Schools Action Kit." It's free to schools. Individuals can purchase it for $22 and obtain other information by calling 800-438-4318. Most of the kit can be downloaded from www.epa.gov/iaq.

Shopping

The Juvenile Products Manufacturers Association, which represents 95 percent of its industry, sponsors a voluntary certification program to help parents identify and select safe products. Look for the JPMA seal on products and check the list of certified products at www.JPMA.org.

Kids in Danger is a nonprofit organization that educates parents about recalls. Its Web site is www.kidsindanger.org.

A helpful book is *Guide to Baby Products,* by Sandy Jones with Werner Freitag and the Editors of Consumer Reports Books.

If you have trouble finding child-safety products in stores, you can order them from catalog companies that specialize in these items. Among them are Perfectly Safe, at 800-837-5437, and Safe Beginnings, at 800-598-8911.

Sports

For information about hockey safety equipment, call USA Hockey at 800-566-3288 or visit its Web site at www.usahockey.com.

Soccer information can be obtained from the U.S. Youth Soccer Organization at 800-4-SOCCER (800-476-2237) or www.youthsoccer.org.

To learn about swimming courses for children and CPR/first-aid courses for adults, contact your local Red Cross chapter or visit www.crossnet.org.

Get detailed guidelines for constructing barriers around pools from the Consumer Product Safety Commission at 800-638-2772 or www.CPSC.gov.

The Children's Safety Network offers information about safe use of all-terrain vehicles, personal water craft, and snowmobiles. Call 888-924-SAFE (888-924-7233) or visit www.marshmed.org/nfmc/children/.

Travel

If your child has a medical problem—such as a breathing difficulty or the need to wear a cast—that necessitates a special car seat, you may be able to obtain a loaner by checking with your pediatrician, the nearest children's hospital, or the National Easter Seal Society (800-221-6827). For information about flying safely, call the Federal Aviation Administration's consumer hotline at 800-FAA-Sure (800-322-7873) or visit www.faa.gov.

For Americans traveling abroad, the U.S. Department of State's Bureau of Consular Affairs issues travel advisories about individual countries that include information about needed immunizations and security or health concerns. The department also produces a publication with detailed advice for traveling safely, which can be useful for Americans traveling domestically as well as overseas. The information is available at the State Department Web site at http://travel.state.gov, or by phoning 202-647-5225. You can request a fax to be sent to you by dialing 202-647-3000 from your fax machine.

The Centers for Disease Control and Prevention has health information for international travelers on its Web site, www.CDC.gov/travel.

Index